500
LOW-CARB
RECIPES

500

LOW-CARB
RECIPES

Dana Carpender

APPLE

Published in the UK in 2003 by
Apple Press
Sheridan House
112-116A Western Road
Hove
East Sussex BN3 1DD
UK

ISBN 1-84092-431-4

10 9 8 7 6 5 4 3 2 1

Design: Leslie Haimes
Cover design by DW Design
Cover photography by Bobbie Bush, www.bobbiebush.com

Printed in Finland

Because of the slight risk of salmonella, recipes containing raw or partially cooked eggs should not be served to the very young, the ill or elderly, or to pregnant women.

To my husband, Eric Schmitz,
who has unfailingly helped me,
supported me and believed in me.
I couldn't have done it without you.
I love you with all my heart.

And to the readers of my Internet newsletter,
Lowcarbezine! You have taught me how
much enthusiasm, humour, intelligence,
caring and love can come through
a fibre-optic cable. You have also taught me my job.
This book is for you, and for low-carbers everywhere.

CONTENTS

Welcome to Low-Carbohydrate Variety!

What's the hardest thing about your low-carb diet? And what's the most common reason that people abandon their low-carb way of eating and all the health benefits and weight loss that come with it?

Boredom. People just plain get bored. After a few weeks of scrambled eggs and bacon for breakfast, a hamburger with no bun for lunch and a steak – no baked potato – for dinner, day after day, people get fed up and quit. They just can't face a life of food monotony. Sound familiar?

If you've been getting bored with your low-carb diet, this is the book for you. You'll find dozens of exciting ways to vary a hamburger, a steak, pork chops, chicken and even fish. You'll find a wide variety of side dishes and salads. You'll find snacks and party foods that you can eat without feeling like you're depriving yourself. You'll even find recipes for bread – really, truly bread – not to mention muffins, waffles, pancakes and muesli. In short, this book has recipes for all sorts of things you never dreamed you could have on a low-carb diet.

Did I come up with these recipes for you? Heavens, no! I came up with these recipes for me.

Who am I? I'm a person who, through circumstances that surely could have happened to anyone, has spent the past several years writing about low-carbohydrate dieting. In fact, I spent so much time answering questions for the curious that I finally wrote a book, *How I Gave Up My Low Fat Diet and Lost Forty Pounds!* To supplement the book, I started an e-zine – an Internet newsletter – for low-carb dieters, called Lowcarbezine! So for the past few years, through the wonders of the Internet, I've been writing and developing recipes for a growing audience of low-carb dieters around the world.

I've always loved to cook and I've always been good at it. My friends long ago dubbed me 'The God of Food'. So when low-fat, high-carb mania hit in the 1980s, I learned how to make a killer low-fat fettuccine Alfredo, curried chicken and mixed grain pilau, black beans and rice, blue corn pancakes, low-fat cheesecake, you name it.

And I got fat. Really fat. And sick. And tired. Thank heavens, in 1995 I got smart and tried going low carb instead. Within two days my energy levels skyrocketed and my clothes were looser. It was overwhelmingly clear that this was the way my body wanted to be fed and that this was the way of eating that would make me well. I had set my foot upon a path from which there was no turning back; I was low carb for life.

The only thing that nearly derailed me was a terrible sense of Kitchen Disorientation. I had to discard the vast majority of my recipes when I dropped the grains, beans, potatoes and sugar from my diet. For the very first time in my life, I'd walk into my kitchen and have no idea what to cook – and I had always known what to cook and how to put together a menu. It really was pretty scary and it certainly was depressing. But I set out to become as good a low-carb cook as I had been a low-fat cook.

Seven years later, my mission has been accomplished and then some! What you hold in your hands is the end result of years and years of trial and error, of learning what works and what doesn't, of experimenting to find out which substitutes are nice and which are just plain miserable.

This is not, for the most part, a gourmet cookbook, which means that the recipes you find here are recipes you'll actually use. You'll find a lot of fairly simple recipes and a few more complex ones for special occasions. There's lots of family fare here – pork chops and meatloaf, burgers and chicken. You'll find lots of meals you can make on the cooker top in a simple frying pan and plenty of salads you can make ahead and keep in the refrigerator, ready to be pulled out and served when you dash in the door at a quarter-to-dinnertime. You'll find many one-dish meals that are protein and vegetables combined, from main dish salads to thick, hearty soups to casseroles. You'll also find ethnic flavours from around the world right alongside comfort foods you'll have a hard time believing are low carb!

Why Is There Such a Wide Range of Carb Counts in the Recipes in This Book?

If carbs are your problem, then they're going to be your problem tomorrow and next week and next year and when you're old and grey. If you hope to keep your weight off, you cannot think in terms of going on a low-carb diet, losing your weight and then going off your diet – you'll gain back every ounce, just as sure as you're born. You'll also go back to blood-sugar swings, energy crashes and nagging, insatiable hunger, not to mention all the health risks of hyperinsulinaemia. In short, my friend, you are in this for life.

So if you are to have any hope of doing this forever – and at this writing, I've been doing this for going on seven years – you are going to need to enjoy what you eat. You're going to need variety, flavour, colour and interest. You're going to need festive dishes, easy dishes and comfort foods – a whole world of things to eat. You need a cuisine.

Because of this, I have included everything from very low-carb dishes, suitable for people in the early, very low-carb 'induction' stage of their diet, to 'splurge' dishes which would probably make most of us gain weight if we ate them every day but which still have far fewer carbs than their 'normal' counterparts.

There's another reason for the range of carb counts: carbohydrate intolerance comes in degrees and different people can tolerate different daily carbohydrate intakes. Some of you, no doubt, need to stay in that 20-grams-a-day-or-less range, while others – lucky souls – can have as much as 90 or 100 grams a day and stay slim.

This cookbook is meant to serve you all.

Only you can know, through trial and error, how many grams of carbs you can eat in a day and still lose weight. It is up to you to pick and choose among the recipes in this book while keeping an eye on the carbohydrate counts provided. That way, you can put together menus that will please your palate and your family while staying below that critical carb level.

However, I do have this to say: always, always, always the heart and soul of your low-carbohydrate diet should be meat, fish, poultry, eggs, healthy fats and low-carb vegetables. This book will teach you a mind-boggling number of ways to combine these things and you should try them all. Don't just find one or two recipes that you like and make them over and over. Try at least one new recipe every week; that way, within a few months you'll have a whole new repertoire of familiar low-carb favourites!

You will, as I just mentioned, find recipes in this book for what are best considered low-carb treats. Do not take the presence of a recipe in this book to mean that it is something that you can eat every day, in unlimited quantities and still lose weight. I can tell you from experience that even low-carb treats, if eaten frequently, will put weight on you. Recipes for breads, cookies, muffins, cakes and the like are here to give you a satisfying, varied diet that you can live with for life, but they should not become the new staples of your diet. Do not try to make your low-carbohydrate diet resemble your former diet. That's the diet that got you in trouble in the first place, remember?

One other thought: it is entirely possible to have a bad reaction to a food that has nothing to do with its carbohydrate count. Gluten, a protein from wheat that is essential for baking low-carb bread, causes bad reactions in a fair number of people. Soya products are problematic for many folks, as are nuts. Whey protein, used extensively in these recipes, contains lactose, which some people cannot tolerate. And surely you've heard of people who react badly to artificial sweeteners of one kind or another. I've also heard from diabetics who get bad blood-sugar levels from eating even small quantities of onions or tomatoes.

Yet all of these foods are just fine for many, many low-carb dieters and there is no way I can know which foods may cause a problem for which people. All I can tell you is to pay attention to your body. If you add a new food to your diet and you gain weight (and you're pretty certain it's not tied to something else, like your menstrual cycle or a new medication), or you find yourself unreasonably hungry, tired or 'off', despite having stayed within your body's carbohydrate tolerance, you may want to consider avoiding that food. One man's meat is another man's poison and all that.

What's a 'Usable Carb Count'?

You may or may not be aware of the concept of the usable carb count, sometimes called the 'effective carb count'; some low-carb books utilise this principle, while others do not. If you're not familiar with the concept, here it is in a nutshell:

Fibre is a carbohydrate and is, at least in American nutritional breakdowns, included in the total carbohydrate count. However, fibre is a form of carbohydrate made of molecules so big that you can neither digest nor absorb them. Therefore fibre, despite being a carbohydrate, will not push up your blood sugar and will not cause an insulin release. Even better, by slowing the absorption of the starches and sugars that occur with it, fibre actually lessens their bad influence. This is very likely the reason that high-fibre diets appear to be so much better for you than some others.

For these reasons many (if not most) low-carb dieters now subtract the grams of fibre in a food from the total grams of carbohydrate to determine the number of grams of carbohydrate that are actually a problem. These are the 'usable' carbs, or the 'effective carb count'. These non-fibre grams of carbohydrate are what we count and limit. Not only does this approach allow us a much wider variety of foods and especially lots more vegetables, but it actually encourages us to add fibre to things such as baked goods.

I am very much a fan of this approach and therefore I give the usable carbohydrate count for these recipes. However, you will also find the breakdown of the total carb count and the fibre count.

Using This Book

I can't really tell you how to plan your menus. I don't know if you live alone or have a family, if you have hours to cook or are pressed for time every evening, or what foods are your favourites. I can, however, give you a few pointers on what you'll find here that may make your meal planning easier.

There are a lot of one-dish meals in this book – main dish salads, pan-fry suppers that include meat and vegetables, and hearty soups that are a full meal in a bowl. I include these because they're some of my favourite foods and to my mind, they're about the simplest way to eat. I also think they lend a far greater variety to low-carb cuisine than is possible if you're trying to divide up your carbohydrate allowance for a given meal among three or four different dishes. If you have a carb-eating family, you can appease them by serving something on the side, such as wholewheat pittas split in half and toasted, along with garlic butter, brown rice, a baked potato or some noodles.

When you're serving these one-dish meals, remember that most of your carbohydrate allowance for the meal is included in that main dish. Unless you can tolerate more carbohydrates than I can, you probably don't want to serve a dish with lots of vegetables in it with even more vegetables on the side. Remember, it's the total usable carb count you have to keep an eye on. Complement simple meat dishes, such as roasted chicken, grilled steak or pan-fried chops, with the more carbohydrate-rich vegetable side dishes.

There's one other thing I hope this book teaches you to do and that's to break out of your old ways of looking at food. There's no law insisting that you eat eggs only for breakfast, have tuna salad for lunch every day and serve some sort of meat and two side dishes for dinner. Short on both time and money? Serve eggs for dinner a couple of nights a week; they're fast, cheap and unbelievably nutritious. Having a family video night or game night? Skip dinner and make two or three healthy snack foods to nibble on. Can't face another fried egg at breakfast? Throw a chop or a hamburger on the electric tabletop grill while you're in the shower and you've got a fast and easy breakfast. Sick of salads for lunch? Take a protein-rich dip in a snap-top container and some cut-up vegetables to work with you.

Helpful General Hints

🍴 **If you're not losing weight, go back to counting every carb**. Remember that snacks and beverages count, even if they're made from recipes in this book. A 6-gram muffin may be a lot better for you and your waistline than a convenience store muffin, but it's still 6 grams and it counts! Likewise, don't lie to yourself about portion sizes. If you make your cookies really big, so that you only get two dozen instead of four dozen from a recipe, the carb count per cookie doubles and don't you forget it.

🍴 **Beware of hidden carbohydrates**. It's important to know that food processors are sometimes allowed to put '0 grams of carbohydrate' on the label if a food has less than 0.5 grams per serving and 'less than 1 gram of carbohydrate' if a food has between 0.5 grams and 0.9 grams. Even some diet soft drinks contain trace amounts of carbohydrates! These amounts aren't much, but they do add up if you eat enough of them. So if you're having trouble losing, count foods that say '0 grams' as 0.5 grams and foods that say 'less than 1 gram' as 1 gram.

🍴 **Remember that some foods you may be thinking of as carb-free actually contain at least traces of carbohydrates**. Eggs contain about 0.5 gram apiece, prawns have 1 gram per 100-gram portion, natural cheeses have about 1 gram per 30 g and double cream has about 0.5 gram per tablespoon. And coffee has more than 1 gram in a 300-ml mug before you add cream and sweetener. (Tea, on the other hand, is carb-free.) If you're having trouble losing weight, get a food counter book and use it, even for foods you're sure you already know the carb counts of.

How Are the Carbohydrate Counts in These Recipes Calculated?

Most of these carbohydrate counts have been calculated using MasterCook software. This very useful program allows you to enter the ingredients of a recipe and the number of servings it makes, and it then spits out the nutritional breakdown for each serving. MasterCook does not include every low-carb speciality product, so these were looked up in food count books or on the product labels and added in by hand. Some figures were also derived from Corinne T. Netzer's *The Complete Book of Food Counts* and *The NutriBase Complete Book of Food Counts*. I have also used the USDA's Nutrient Database, a hugely useful online reference.

The carb counts for these recipes are as accurate as we can make them. However, they are not and cannot be, 100 per cent accurate. MasterCook gets its nutritional information from the USDA Nutrient Database and my experience is that the USDA's figures for carbohydrate content tend to run a bit higher than the food count books. This means that the carbohydrate counts in this book are, if anything, a tad high, which beats being too low!

Furthermore, every stick of celery, every onion, every head of broccoli is going to have a slightly different level of carbohydrates in it, because it grew in a specific patch of soil, in specific weather and with a particular kind of fertiliser. You may use a different brand of vanilla-flavoured whey protein powder than I do. You may be a little more or a little less generous with how many bits of chopped green pepper you fit into a measuring jug.

Don't fret about it. These counts are, as the old joke goes, close enough for government work. You can count on them as a guide to the carbohydrate content in your diet. And do you really want to get obsessed with getting every tenth of a gram written down?

In this spirit, you'll find that many of these recipes call for '1 large stick of celery', 'half a green pepper', or 'a clove of garlic'. This is how most of us cook, after all. These things do not come in standardised sizes, so they're analysed for the average. Again: don't fret! If you're really worried, use what seems to you a smallish stalk of celery, or green pepper or clove of garlic, and you can count on your cumulative carb count being a hair lower than what is listed in the recipe.

Low-Carb Speciality Foods

When I went low carb in 1995, it was a radical concept. Low-fat, high-carb diets were practically scriptural and while there were loads and loads of low-fat speciality foods in every supermarket, from low-calorie dinners to low-fat cakes and biscuits, there were virtually no low-carb speciality foods to be found, anywhere. As a result, eating a low-carbohydrate diet back then virtually forced me to eat real, unprocessed foods. Meat, poultry, fish, vegetables, low-sugar fruits, nuts and seeds, cheese and butter were pretty much the whole of the diet.

Another drawback is that low-carb speciality foods tend to be extremely expensive. Don't mistake what I'm saying – these products are not, in general, a rip-off. Low-carb products are more expensive to make, partly because they call for more expensive ingredients and partly because they are made in smaller quantities by smaller companies than are other processed foods. These are, after all, speciality foods and you're going to pay speciality prices for them. But I'd hate for you to start basing your diet on speciality products, decide that a low-carb diet is too expensive and go back to eating junk. Use these products wisely to add a little variety, as an occasional treat, or to fight off cravings, but not as a major part of your diet.

What a difference a few years can make! As more and more people have discovered low-carbohydrate eating, boatloads of low-carb speciality products have hit the market in many parts of the world, especially the USA – some good, some bad, some indifferent, pretty much like products in every other category.

I see this proliferation of low-carb speciality products as a double-edged sword. On the one hand, anything that helps carbohydrate-intolerant people remain happily on their diets is a good thing. On the other hand, most of these speciality products are highly processed foods and they do not equal genuine foodstuffs in nutritional value. I fear that too many people are eating these things as staples of their diet, displacing the real foods that should be the bedrock of any healthy low-carb diet.

In the United Kingdom, low-carb speciality products can be a bit more difficult to locate at the grocer's, but a good selection may be found through mail order on the Internet. I find the following Web sites to be particularly good, but I encourage you to keep searching so that you can make comparisons. All of the following will ship to the UK.

- www.carblife.com

- www.davincifinefoods.co.uk

- www.gnc.co.uk

- www.low-carb.com

- www.lowcarbdieters.com

- www.lowcarbmegastore.com

- www.netrition.com

- www.sugarfreeuk.com

- www.sugarlite.co.uk

Here's a taste of the variety of low-carb speciality products which you should be able to find:

- **Breads and bagels.** These are often quite good, but keep an eye on the portion size listed on the label. I've seen low-carb bagels with a label claiming only 4 grams per serving, but discovered that a serving was only a third of a bagel!

- **Tortillas.** Useful not only for eating with fajitas and burritos and for making quesadillas, but also in place of Chinese mu shu pancakes. Be aware that low-carb tortillas, while tasty, are not identical to either flour or corn tortillas in either flavour or texture.

- **Jams, jellies and condiments.** These do contain the carbohydrates from whatever fruit or vegetable was used to make them, but not added sugars. Generally very good in quality.

- **Pastas.** I have yet to find a brand of low-carb pasta that has really impressed me, but some of them are not too bad. I find that the texture of the pastas is not right, so they cook up either too soft or too chewy. Still, the stuff sells like low-carb hotcakes, so somebody must really like it. If you are having a hard time going without pasta, these products are worth a try.

- **Cold cereals.** I've tried two low-carb cold cereals. One is quite similar to Rice Krispies in texture and flavour, and available in a chocolate flavour as well. The other is very much like Grape Nuts. They're both quite good if you're fond of the cereals they imitate. Both of these 'cereals' are made from soya, which some people think is a lifesaving wonder food but others – including me – aren't sure is safe in large quantities. It's a moot point for me, since I just don't miss Rice Krispies or Grape Nuts enough to bother with these cereals. However, if you do miss cold cereal, these substitutes are quite good, as well as low in carbohydrates and high in protein.

- **Protein chips (or crisps).** These are all right, but not so wonderful that I've bothered to buy them often. These most closely resemble the 'usual' tortilla chips, but the texture is noticeably different. If you're mad for a bag of crisps, these are worth a try. But for me, I'd rather have pumpkin seeds.

- **Protein meal replacement shakes**. Mostly quite good and certainly useful if you can't face cooked food first thing in the morning. They're available in a wide range of flavours.

- **Protein bars**. These range from pretty good to absolutely wretched, sometimes within the same brand. Be aware that there is a lot of controversy about low-carb protein bars. Virtually all of them contain glycerine, to make them moist and chewy. The controversy is over whether or not glycerine acts like a carbohydrate in some ways in the body. Many people find that these bars knock them out of ketosis, while others don't have a problem. So I'll say it again: Pay attention to your body!

- **Cookies, biscuits and brownies**. These are getting better every day. I've had low-carb brownies that were superb and some very nice oatmeal cookies, as well. See 'About Polyols'.

- **Muffins**. Some of these are quite good, others are not so brilliant and often the same brand varies widely depending on which flavour you choose. You'll just have to try them and see which you like.

- **Other sweet low-carb baked goods**. I've tried commercially made low-carb cheesecake and cakes. The cheesecake was pretty good, but I can make better for far less money. I didn't like the cakes at all because I found them overwhelmingly sweet. But I know that they sell quite well, so somebody must like them.

- **Chocolate bars and other chocolate sweets**. These are generally superb. The best of the low-carb chocolate sweets are indistinguishable from their sugar-laden counterparts. You can get low-carb chocolate in both milk and dark. I haven't had a really bad sugar-free chocolate yet. See 'About Polyols'.

- **Other sugar-free sweets**. You can, if you look, find sugar-free boiled sweets, marshmallows, jelly beans and all manner of things. Again, the quality of these tends to be excellent. See 'About Polyols'.

About Polyols

Polyols, also known as sugar alcohols, are widely used in sugar-free sweets, cookies, biscuits, and so on. There are a variety of polyols and their names all end with 'ol' – lactitol, maltitol, mannitol, sorbitol, xylitol and the like. Polyols are, indeed, carbohydrates, but they are carbohydrates that are made up of molecules that are too big for humans to digest or absorb easily. As a result, polyols don't create much, if any, rise in blood sugar, nor do they create much of an insulin release.

Polyols are used in commercial sugar-free sweets because, unlike Splenda and other artificial sweeteners, they will give all of the textures that can be achieved with sugar. Polyols can be used to make crunchy toffee, chewy jelly beans, slick hard boiled sweets, chewy brownies and creamy chocolate, just as sugar can. Yet they are far, far easier on your carbohydrate metabolism – and on your teeth as well.

However, there are one or two problems with polyols. First of all, there is some feeling that different people have different abilities to digest and absorb these very long chain carbohydrates, which means that for some people, polyols may cause more of a derangement of blood sugar than they do for others. Once again, my only advice is to pay attention to your body.

The other problem with polyols is one that is inherent in all indigestible, unabsorbable carbohydrates: they can cause wind and diarrhoea. Unabsorbed carbs ferment in your gut, creating intestinal wind as a result. It's exactly the same thing that happens when people eat beans. I find that even half of a low-carb chocolate bar is enough to cause me social embarrassment several hours later. And I know of a case where eating too many low-carb sweets before bed caused the hapless consumer 45 minutes of serious gut-cramping intestinal distress at 4 a.m.

Don't think, by the way, that you can get around these effects of polyol consumption by taking a wind-relief product from the chemist's shop. This may work, but by making the carbohydrates digestible and absorbable. This means that any low-carb advantage is gone. I know people who have gained weight this way.

What we have here, then, is a sweetener that enforces moderation. Personally, I think this is a wonderful thing.

How much you can eat in the way of polyol-sweetened products without getting into digestive trouble will vary with each food's polyol content. So I would recommend you shouldn't eat sugar-free sweets at all if you have an important meeting or a hot date a few hours later, or if you'll be getting on an aeroplane. (Altitude can make wind swell very uncomfortably in your gut.) If you can afford some gaseousness, for lack of a better word, I'd stick to no more than one chocolate bar or three or four caramels in a day.

Where to Find Low-Carbohydrate Speciality Products

The availability of low-carbohydrate speciality products varies a great deal. Most retail outlets in the United Kingdom, including the main supermarkets, do not sell complete ranges of low-carb items for the shopper to notice instantly on the shelf, and it's necessary to check labels on individual products, as some will indicate whether they are low-carb. Health food shops are good places to look, but many are caught up in low-fat, wholegrain mania and therefore don't subscribe to low-carb thinking. Some carry things like fibre crackers and protein powder, but refuse to carry anything artificially sweetened because they pride themselves on carrying 'natural' products only. Still, you'll want to find a good health food shop to use as a source of many ingredients called for in this book, especially those for low-carb baking, so you may as well look in any health food shops in your area and see what you can find.

Little speciality groceries often carry low carbohydrate products as a way to attract new and repeat business. In my town in the USA, Sahara Mart, a store that has long specialised in Middle Eastern foods, has become the best source for low-carb speciality products, as well.

If you can't find a local source for such things as sugar-free chocolate, low-carb pasta, brownies or whatever else you want, your best bet is to go online. Hit your favourite search engine and search for 'low-carbohydrate products', 'sugar-free sweets', or whatever it is you're looking for. There are increasing numbers of low-carb 'e-tailers' out there; find the ones with the products and prices you want. If you don't care to use your credit card online, enquire about other ways to pay.

On the Importance of Reading Labels

Do yourself a favour and get in the habit of reading the label on every food product, and I do mean every food product, that has one. I have learned from long, hard, repetitive experience that food manufacturers can, will and do put sugar, syrup, cornflour and other nutritionally empty, carb-laden garbage into every conceivable food product. I have found sugar in everything from salsa to tinned clams, for heaven's sake! (Who it was who thought that the clams needed sugaring, I'd love to know.) You will shave untold thousands of grams of carbs off your intake in the course of a year by simply looking for the product that has no added junk.

There are also a good many classes of food products out there to which sugar is virtually always added; the cured meats come to mind. There is almost always sugar in sausage, ham, bacon, hot dogs, liver sausage and the like. You will look in vain for sugarless varieties of these products, which is one good reason why you should primarily eat fresh meats instead. However, you will find that there is quite a range of carb counts among cured meats, because some manufacturers add more sugar than others do. I have seen ham that has 1 gram of carbohydrate per serving and I have seen ham that has 6 grams of carbohydrate per serving – that's a 600 per cent difference! Likewise, I've seen hot dogs that have 1 gram of carbohydrate apiece and I've seen hot dogs that have 5 grams of carbohydrate apiece.

If you're in a position where you can't read the labels (for instance, at the deli counter at the grocer's shop), ask questions. The counter staff will be glad to read the labels on the ham and salami for you and they might be able to tell you what goes into the various items they make themselves. You'll want to ask at the meat counter, too, if you're buying something they've mixed up themselves, such as Italian sausage or marinated meats. I've found that if I simply state that I have a medical condition that requires me to be very careful about my diet – and I don't come at the busiest hour of the week – people are generally very nice about this sort of thing.

In short, you need to become a food sleuth. After all, you're paying your hard-earned money for this stuff and it is quite literally going to become a part of you. Pay at least as much attention as you would if you were buying a car or a computer.

CHAPTER ONE

Ingredients You Need To Know About

This is by no means an exhaustive rundown of every single ingredient used in this book; these are just the ones I thought you might have questions about. I've grouped them by use and within those groupings they're alphabetised, so if you have a question about something used in a recipe, flip back here and read up on whatever you're curious about.

Eggs

There are a few recipes in this book in which raw or undercooked egg is present in the finished product (for example, mayonnaise). Raw or undercooked eggs have in the past been implicated in some cases of salmonella poisoning, and therefore need to be used with caution. I would therefore advise that these are not given to young children, pregnant women, elderly people, or any other person who is not in the very best of health.

One useful thing to know about eggs: While you'll want very fresh eggs for frying and poaching, eggs that are at least several days old are better for hard-boiling. They're less likely to stick to their shells in that maddening way we've all encountered. So if you like hard-boiled eggs (and they're certainly one of the most convenient low-carb foods), buy a couple of extra cartons of eggs and let them sit in the refrigerator for at least three or four days before you hard-boil them.

Fats and Oils

Bland Oils

Sometimes you want a bland oil in a recipe, something that adds little or no flavour of its own. In that case, I recommend peanut, sunflower or canola (rapeseed) oil. These are the oils I mean when I simply specify 'oil' in a recipe. Avoid highly polyunsaturated oils such as safflower; they deteriorate quickly both from heat and from contact with oxygen and they've been associated with an increased risk of cancer.

Butter

When a recipe says 'use butter,' will you? My opinion of margarine is that it's nasty stuff, full of hydrogenated oils, trans fats and artificial everything, and that it's terrible for you. So use the real thing. If real butter strains your budget, watch for special offers and stock up; butter freezes beautifully.

Coconut Oil

Coconut oil makes an excellent substitute for hydrogenated vegetable shortening, which you should shun. You may find coconut oil at health food shops, or possibly in Asian food stores. One large local grocer's shop carries it in the 'ethnic foods' section, with Indian foods. My health food shop keeps coconut oil with the cosmetics. They're still convinced that saturated fats are terrible for you, so they don't put it with the foods, but it is sometimes used for making hair dressings and soaps. Coconut oil is solid at room temperature, except in the summer, but it melts at body temperature. Surprisingly, it has no coconut flavour or aroma; you can use it for sautéing or in baking without adding any unwanted flavour to your recipes.

Olive Oil

It surely will come as no surprise to you that olive oil is a healthy fat, but you may not know that there are various kinds. Extra-virgin olive oil is the first pressing. It is deep green, with a full, fruity flavour and it makes all the difference in salad dressings. However, it's expensive and also too strongly flavoured for some uses. I keep a bottle of extra-virgin olive oil on hand, but use it exclusively for salads.

For sautéing and other general uses, buy whatever cheaper, milder-flavoured type of olive oil is available at your supermarket or grocer's shop.

Be aware that if you refrigerate olive oil it will become solid. This is no problem, as it will be fine once it warms up again. If you need it quickly, you can run the bottle under warm water.

Flour Substitutes

As you are no doubt aware, flour is out, for the most part, in low-carb cooking. Flour serves a few different purposes in cooking, from making up the bulk of most baked goods and creating stretchiness in bread dough to thickening sauces and casseroles. In low-carb cooking, we use different ingredients for these various purposes. Here's a rundown of flour substitutes you'll want to have on hand for low-carb cooking and baking:

Brans

Because fibre is a carbohydrate that we neither digest nor absorb, brans of one kind or another are very useful for bulking up low-carb baked goods. I use different kinds in different recipes. You'll want to have at least wheat bran and oat bran on hand; both of these are widely available. If you can also find rice bran, it's worth picking up, especially if you have high cholesterol. Of all the kinds of bran tested, rice bran was most powerful for lowering high blood cholesterol.

Ground Almonds and Hazelnuts

Finely ground almonds and hazelnuts are wonderful for replacing some or all of the flour in many recipes, especially cakes and cookies. If you can purchase almond meal and hazelnut meal locally, these should work fine in the recipes in this book. If you can't, simply grind nuts in your food processor, using the S-blade. The nuts are not the texture of flour when ground, but more the consistency of coarsely ground cornmeal. Whenever a recipe in this book calls for ground almonds or hazelnuts, this is what I use.

It's good to know that these nuts actually expand a little during grinding. This surprised me because I thought they'd compress a bit.

Guar and Xanthan Gums

These sound just dreadful, don't they? But they're in lots of your favourite processed foods, so how bad can they be? If you're wondering what they are, anyway, here's the answer: they're forms of water-soluble fibre, extracted and purified. Guar and xanthan are both flavourless white powders; their value to us is as low-carb thickeners. Technically speaking, these are carbs, but they're all fibre, nothing but, so don't worry about using them.

You'll find guar or xanthan used in tiny little quantities in a lot of these recipes. Don't go dramatically increasing the quantity of guar or xanthan to get a thicker product, because in large quantities they make things gummy and the texture is not terribly pleasant. But in these tiny quantities they add 'oomph' to sauces and soups without using flour. You can always leave the guar or xanthan out if you can't find it; you'll just get a somewhat thinner result.

You'll notice that I always tell you to put the guar or xanthan through the blender with whatever liquid it is that you're using. This is because it is very difficult simply to whisk guar into a sauce and not get little gummy lumps in your finished sauce or soup, and the blender is the best way to combine your ingredients thoroughly.

If you don't own or don't want to use a blender, there is one possible alternative: put your guar or xanthan in a salt shaker and sprinkle it, bit by bit, over your sauce, stirring madly all the while with a whisk. The problem here, of course, is there's no way to know exactly how much you're using, so you'll just have to stop when your dish reaches the degree of thickness you like. Still, this can be a useful trick.

Your health food shop may well be able to order guar or xanthan for you (I slightly prefer xanthan, myself) if they don't have them on hand. You can also find suppliers online. Keep either one in a jar with a tight lid and it will never go bad. I bought 500 g of guar about 15 years ago and it's still going strong!

Low-Carbohydrate Bake Mix

There are several brands of low-carbohydrate bake mix on the market. These are generally a combination of some form of powdery protein and fibre, such as soys, whey and sometimes oats, plus baking powder and sometimes salt. These mixes are the low-carb world's equivalent of the average cake mix, although low-carb mixes differ in that they do not have shortening added. You will need to add butter, oil or some other form of fat when using them to make pancakes, waffles, biscuits and such. I mostly use low-carb bake mix in lesser quantities, for 'flouring' chicken before baking or frying, or in place of the flour used as a thickener in a casserole. If you can't find low-carbohydrate bake mix locally, search online.

Oat Flour

One or two recipes in this book call for oat flour. Because of its high-fibre content, oat flour has a lower usable carb count than most other flours. Even so, it must be used in very small quantities. Oat flour is available at health food shops. In a pinch, you can grind up oatmeal in your blender or food processor.

Psyllium Husks

This is another fibre product. Because psyllium has little flavour of its own, it makes a useful high-fibre 'filler' in some low-carb bread recipes. Look for plain psyllium husks at your health food shop. Mine carries them in bulk, quite cheaply, but if yours doesn't, look for them among the laxatives and 'colon health' products. (A brand called 'Colon Cleanse' is widely available.)

Rice Protein Powder

For savoury recipes such as entrées, you need a protein powder that isn't sweet and preferably one that has no flavour at all. There are a number of these available and some are blander than others. I tried several kinds and I've found that rice protein powder is the one I like best.

Rolled Oats

Also known as old-fashioned oatmeal – you know, oat grains that have been squashed flat. These are available in every grocer's shop's shop and supermarket in the Western Hemisphere. Do not substitute instant or quick-cooking oatmeal.

Soya Powder, Soya Flour and Soy Protein Isolate

Some of my recipes call for soya powder. None call for soya flour, although one or two of the recipes from other people do. If you use soya flour in a recipe that calls for soya powder, you won't get the results I got. You also won't get the right results with soya protein powder, also known as soya protein isolate. What is the difference? Soya protein isolate is, as the name suggests, a protein that has been extracted from soya beans and concentrated into a protein powder. Soya flour is made from raw soya beans that have simply been ground up into flour and it has a strong bean flavour. Soya powder, also known as soya milk powder, is made from whole soya beans, like soya flour, but the beans are cooked before they're ground up. For some reason I don't pretend to understand, this gets rid of the strong flavour and makes soya powder taste quite mild. If your local health food shop doesn't stock soya powder or soya milk powder, they can no doubt order it for you.

You should be aware that despite the tremendous marketing build-up soya has enjoyed over the years, there are some problems emerging. Soya is known to interfere with thyroid function, which is the last thing you need if you're trying to lose weight. It also can interfere with mineral absorption. It is also less certain, but still possible, that regular consumption of soya causes brain deterioration in middle-aged and older folks, and genital defects in boy babies born to mothers with soya-heavy diets. For these reasons, while I do not shun soya entirely, I use other options when possible.

Vital Wheat Gluten

Gluten is a grain protein. It's the gluten in flour that makes bread dough stretchy so that it will trap the gas released by the yeast, letting your bread rise. We are not, of course, going to use the usual plain flour, with its high carbohydrate content. Fortunately, it is possible to buy concentrated wheat gluten. This high-protein, low-starch flour is absolutely essential to making low-carbohydrate yeast breads.

Buying vital wheat gluten can be a problem, however, because the nomenclature is not standardised. Some packagers call this 'vital wheat gluten' or 'pure gluten flour', while others simply call it 'wheat gluten'. Still others call it 'high-gluten flour'. This is a real poser, since the same name is frequently used for regular flour that has had extra gluten added to it; that product is something you definitely do not want.

To make sure you're getting the right product, you'll simply have to read the label. The product you want, regardless of what the packager calls it, will have between 75 and 80 per cent protein, or about 24 grams in 30 g. It will also have a very low carbohydrate count, somewhere in the neighbourhood of 6 grams of carbohydrate in that same 30 g.

More and more grocer's shops are beginning to carry this line of products. If your grocer's shop doesn't yet, you might request them.

Wheat Germ

The germ is the part of the wheat kernel that would have become the plant if the grain had sprouted. It is the most nutritious, highest-protein part of the wheat kernel and is much lower in carbohydrates than the starchy part that becomes white flour. A few recipes in this book call for raw wheat germ, which is available at health food shops. Raw wheat germ should be refrigerated, as it goes rancid pretty easily. If your health food shop doesn't keep the raw wheat germ in the refrigerator, I'd look for another health food shop.

Whey Protein Powder

Whey is the liquid part of milk. If you've ever seen yoghurt that has separated, the clearish liquid on top is the whey. Whey protein is of extremely good quality and the protein powder made from it is tops in both flavour and nutritional value. For use in any sweet recipe, the vanilla-flavoured whey protein powder is best and it's readily available in health food shops. (Yes, this is the kind generally sold for making shakes with.) Keep in mind that protein powders vary in their carbohydrate counts and look for the one with the least carbohydrate. Also beware of sugar-sweetened protein powders, which can be higher in carbs.

Natural whey protein powder is just like vanilla-flavoured whey protein powder, except that it has not been flavoured or sweetened. Its flavour is bland, so it is used in recipes where a sweet flavour is not desirable. Natural whey protein powder is called for in some of the recipes that others have donated to this book; I generally use rice protein powder when a bland protein powder is called for.

Liquids

Beer

One or two recipes in this book call for beer. One of the lowest-carbohydrate beers I've been able to find is Miller Lite, at 3.5 grams per can. This is good to use in cooking and what I recommend you drink, if you're a beer fan. Look around to see if you can find any other brands so low in carbs. It's good to have choices.

Stocks

Cans or cartons of chicken and beef stocks are very handy items to keep around, and it's certainly quicker to make dinner with these than it would be if you had to make your own from scratch. However, the quality of most of the tinned stock you'll find at your local grocer's shop is appallingly bad. The chicken stock has all sorts of chemicals in it and often sugar, as well. The 'beef' stock is worse, frequently containing no beef whatsoever. I refuse to use these products and you should, too.

However, there are a few tinned and cartoned stocks worth buying, so look around. Decent packaged stock won't cost you a whole lot more than the stuff that is made of salt and chemicals. If you watch for special offers, you can often get it as cheaply as the bad stuff, so you can put some spares in your store cupboard.

One last note: You may also find tinned vegetable stock, particularly at health food shops. This is tasty, but it runs much higher in carbohydrates than the chicken and beef stocks. I'd avoid it.

Vinegar

Various recipes in this book call for wine vinegar, cider vinegar, sherry vinegar, rice vinegar, tarragon vinegar, white vinegar, balsamic vinegar and even raspberry vinegar, for which you'll find a recipe. If you've always thought that vinegar was just vinegar, think again! Each of these vinegars has a distinct flavour all its own and if you substitute one for the other, you'll change the whole character of the recipe. Add just one splash of cider vinegar to your Asian Chicken Salad and you've traded your Chinese accent for an American twang. Vinegar is such a great way to give bright flavours to foods while adding very few carbs that I keep all of these varieties on hand. This is easy to do, because vinegar keeps for a very long time.

As with everything else, read the labels on your vinegar. I've seen cider vinegar that has 0 grams of carbohydrate per 30 ml and I've seen cider vinegar that has 4 grams of carbohydrate per 30 ml – a huge difference. Beware, also, of apple cider-flavoured vinegar, which is white vinegar with artificial flavours added. I bought this once by mistake. (You'd think someone who constantly reminds others to read labels would be beyond such errors, wouldn't you?)

Wine

There are several recipes in this cookbook calling for either dry red or dry white wine. I find the inexpensive wines in a carton very convenient to keep on hand for cooking. The simple reason for this is that they don't go bad because the contents are never exposed to air. These are not fabulous vintage wines, but they're fine for our modest purposes and they certainly are handy. I generally have both Burgundy and Chablis wine-in-a-box on hand. Be wary of any wine with 'added flavours.' Too often, one of those flavours will be sugar. Buy wine with a recognisable name, such as Burgundy, Rhine, Chablis, Cabernet and the like, rather than stuff like 'Chillable Red', and you'll get better results.

Nuts, Seeds and Nut Butters

Nuts and Seeds

Low in carbohydrates and high in healthy fats, protein and minerals, nuts and seeds are great foods for us. Not only are they delicious for snacking or for adding crunch to salads and stir-fries, but when ground, they can replace some of the flour in low-carb baked goods. In particular, you'll find quite a few recipes in this book calling for ground almonds, ground hazelnuts and ground sunflower seeds. Since these ingredients can be pricey, you'll want to shop around. In particular, health food shops often carry nuts and seeds in bulk at better prices than you'll find at the grocer's shop. I have also found that speciality ethnic groceries often have good prices on nuts. I get my best deal on almonds at my wonderful Middle Eastern grocery, Sahara Mart.

By the way, along with pumpkin and sunflower seeds, you can buy sesame seeds in bulk at supermarkets or health food shops for a fraction of what they'll cost you in a little shaker jar at the grocer's shop. Buy them 'unhulled' and you'll get both more fibre and more calcium. You can also get unsweetened coconut flakes at the same outlets.

Flax seed comes from the same plant that gives us the fabric linen and it is turning out to be one of the most nutritious seeds there is. Along with good-quality protein, flax seeds have tons of soluble, cholesterol-reducing fibre and are a rich source of EPAs, the same fats that make fish so heart-healthy.

Most of the recipes in this book that use flax seed call for it to be ground up into a coarse meal. You can buy pre-ground flax seed meal but I much prefer to grind my own. The simple reason for this is that the fats in flax seeds are very stable so long as the seeds are whole, but they go rancid pretty quickly after the seed coat is broken.

Grinding flax seed is very easy if you have a food processor. Simply put the seeds in your food processor with the S-blade in place, turn on the machine and forget about it for about 5 minutes. (Yes, it takes that long!) You can then add your flax seed meal to whatever it is you're cooking.

If you don't have a food processor, you'll just have to buy flax seed meal pre-ground. If you do, keep it in an airtight container, refrigerate or freeze it, and use it up as quickly as you can.

Nut Butters

The only peanut butter called for in this cookbook is 'natural' peanut butter, the kind made from ground, roasted peanuts, peanut oil, salt, and nothing else. Most supermarkets now carry natural peanut butter; it's the stuff with the layer of oil on top. The oil in standard peanut butter has been hydrogenated to keep it from separating out (that's what gives big name-brand peanut butters that extremely smooth, plastic consistency) and it's hard to think of anything worse for you than hydrogenated vegetable oil. Except for sugar, of course, which is also added to standard peanut butter. Stick to the natural stuff.

Health food shops carry not only natural peanut butter, but also almond butter, sunflower butter and sesame butter, generally called 'tahini'. All of these are useful for low-carbers. Keep all natural nut butters in the refrigerator unless you're going to eat them up within a week or two.

Seasonings

Stock Concentrates

Stock concentrate comes in cubes, crystals or liquids. It is generally full of salt and chemicals and it doesn't taste notably like the animal it supposedly came from. It definitely does not make a suitable substitute for good-quality stock if you're making a pot of soup. However, these products can be useful for adding a little kick of flavour here and there, more as seasonings than as soups, and for this I keep them on hand. I generally use chicken stock crystals, because I find them easier to use than cubes. I also keep liquid beef stock concentrate on hand. I chose this because, unlike the cubes or crystals, it actually has a bit of beef in it. Choose Bovril!

Fresh Ginger

Many recipes in this book call for fresh ginger, sometimes called root ginger or gingerroot. Fresh ginger is an essential ingredient in Asian cooking, and dried, ground ginger is not a substitute. Fortunately, fresh ginger freezes beautifully; just drop your whole ginger root (called a 'hand' of ginger) into a freezer bag and toss it in the freezer. When the time comes to use it, pull it out, peel enough of the end for your immediate purposes and grate it. (It will grate just fine while still frozen.) Throw the remaining root back in the bag and toss it back in the freezer.

Ground fresh ginger root in oil is available in jars. I like freshly grated ginger better, but the jarred version will also work in these recipes.

Garlic

Garlic is a borderline vegetable. It's fairly high in carbohydrates, but it's very, very good for you. Surely you've heard all about garlic's nutritional prowess by now. Garlic also, of course, is an essential flavouring ingredient in many recipes. However, remember that there is an estimated 1 gram of carbohydrate per clove and go easy.

I only use fresh garlic, except in the occasional recipe that calls for a sprinkle-on seasoning blend. Nothing else tastes like the real thing. To my taste buds, even the jarred, chopped garlic in oil doesn't taste like fresh garlic. And we won't even talk about garlic powder. You may use jarred garlic if you like; 1/2 teaspoon should equal about 1 clove of fresh garlic. If you choose to use powdered garlic, well, I can't stop you, but I'm afraid I can't promise the recipes will taste the same, either. So 1/4 teaspoon of garlic powder is roughly equivalent to 1 clove of fresh garlic.

By the way, the easiest way to crush a clove or two of garlic is to put the flat side of a big knife on top of it and smash it with your fist. Pick out the papery skin, which will now be easy, chop your garlic a bit more and toss it into your dish. Keep in mind that the distinctive garlic aroma and flavour only develops after the cell walls are broken (that's why a pile of fresh garlic bulbs in the grocer's shop doesn't reek), so the more finely you crush or mince your garlic, the more flavour it will release.

Sweetenings

Black Treacle

What on earth is treacle doing in a low-carb cookbook? It's practically all carbohydrate, after all. Well, yes, but I've found that combining Splenda (see below) with a very small amount of treacle gives a good brown-sugar flavour to all sorts of recipes.

Why not use some of the artificial brown sugar-flavoured sweeteners out there? Because I've tried them and I haven't tasted even one I would be willing to buy again!

Splenda

Splenda is the latest artificial sweetener to hit the market and it blows all of the competition clear out of the water! Feed non-dieting friends and family Splenda-sweetened desserts and they will never know that you haven't used sugar. It tastes that good.

Splenda has some other advantages. The table sweetener has been bulked so that it measures just like sugar, spoon-for-spoon, gram for gram. This makes adapting recipes much easier. Also, Splenda stands up to heat, unlike aspartame, which means you can use it for baked goods and other things that are heated for a while.

However, Splenda is not completely carb-free. Because of the malto-dextrin used to bulk it, Splenda has about 0.5 gram of carbohydrate per teaspoon, or about 1/8 of the carbohydrates of sugar. So count half a gram per teaspoon, 1 1/2 grams per tablespoon and 24 grams per 100 g approx.

Vegetables

Carrots

Because carrots have a higher glycaemic index than many vegetables, a lot of low-carbers have started avoiding them with great zeal. But while carrots do have a fairly high blood sugar impact, you'd have to eat heaps of them to get the quantity that is used to test with. So don't worry when you see a carrot used here and there in these recipes, okay? I've kept the quantities small, just enough to add flavour, colour and a few vitamins, but certainly not enough to spoil your diet.

Frozen Vegetables

You'll notice that many of these recipes call for frozen vegetables, particularly broccoli, green beans and cauliflower. I use these because I find them very convenient and I think that the quality is quite good. If you like, you may certainly substitute fresh vegetables in any recipe. You will need to adjust the cooking time and if the recipe calls for the vegetable to be used thawed, but not cooked, you'll need to 'blanch' your vegetables by boiling them for just three to five minutes.

It's important to know that frozen vegetables are not immortal, no matter how good your freezer is. Don't buy more than you can use up in four to six weeks, even if they're on special offer. You'll end up throwing them away.

Onions

Onions are borderline vegetables. They're certainly higher in carbohydrates than, say, lettuce or cucumbers. However, they're loaded with valuable phytochemicals, so they're very healthy and of course they add an unmatched flavour to all sorts of foods. Therefore I use onions a lot, but I try to use the smallest quantity that will give the desired flavour. Indeed, one of the most common things I do to cut carb counts on 'borrowed' recipes is to cut back on the amount of onion used. If you have serious diabetes, you'll want to watch your quantities of onions pretty carefully and maybe even cut back further on the amounts I've given.

If you're not an accomplished cook, you need to know that different types of onions are good for different things. There are mild onions, which are best used raw, and there are stronger onions, which are what you want if you're going to be cooking them. My favourite mild onions are sweet red onions, these are widely available and you'll see I've used them quite a lot in the recipes here. Spring onions also are mild and are best eaten raw, or quickly cooked in stir-fries. To me, spring onions have their own flavour and I generally don't substitute for them, but your kitchen won't blow up or anything if you use another sort of sweet onion in their place.

When a recipe simply says 'onion', what I'm talking about is good old yellow globe onions, the ones you can buy lots of at a time in net sacks. You'll be doing yourself a favour if you pick a sack with smallish onions in it so that when a recipe calls for just a small amount, you won't be left with half an onion. For the record, when I say 'small onion', I mean one about 4 cm in diameter, or about 30 g. A medium onion would be about 5 cm in diameter and would yield between about 50 and 75 g. A large onion would be 6 or 7 cm across and would yield about 100 g. Personally, I'm not so obsessive about exact carb counts that I bother to measure every scrap of onion I put in a dish; I think in terms of small, medium and large onions, instead. If you prefer to be more exact, that's up to you.

Tomatoes and Tomato Products

Tomatoes are another borderline vegetable, but like onions they are so nutritious, so flavourful and so versatile that I'm reluctant to leave them out of low-carb cuisine entirely. After all, lycopene, the pigment that makes tomatoes red, has been shown to be a potent cancer-fighter and who wants to miss out on something like that?

You'll notice that I call for tinned tomatoes in a fair number of recipes, even in some where fresh tomatoes might do. This is because fresh tomatoes aren't very good for much of the year, while tinned tomatoes are all packed at the height of ripeness. I'd rather have a good tinned tomato in my sauce or soup than a mediocre fresh one. Since tinned tomatoes are generally used with all the liquid that's in the tin, the nutritional content doesn't suffer the way it does with most tinned vegetables.

I also use plain tinned tomato sauce, tinned pizza sauce, tinned pasta sauce and jarred salsa. When choosing these products, you need to be aware that tomatoes, for some reason, inspire food packers to flights of sugar-fancy. They add sugar, syrup and other carb-laden sweeteners to all sorts of tomato products, so it is very important that you read the labels on all tomato-based products to find the ones with no added sugar. And keep on reading them, even after you know what's in them. The good, cheap brand of salsa I used for quite a while showed up one day with 'New, Improved!' on the label. Can you guess how they'd improved it? Right – they'd added sugar. So I found a new brand.

Yeast

All of the bread recipes in this book were developed using plain old active dry yeast, not 'bread machine yeast' and certainly not 'rapid-rise' yeast. Indeed, one of my testers had some spectacular failures using rapid-rise yeast in her bread machine with one of my recipes, but the recipe worked brilliantly for another tester who used 'ordinary' yeast.

The best place to buy yeast is at a good health food shop, where yeast is generally available in bulk for a tiny fraction of what it would cost you in little packets at the grocer's shop. Yeast should be stored in a refrigerator at the health food shop – and at home.

One last note: don't buy more yeast than you're likely to use up in, say, four to six weeks. It will eventually die on you and you'll end up with dough that won't rise. When you're using expensive ingredients, as we do, this is almost more than a body can bear.

Yoghurt and Buttermilk

Yoghurt and buttermilk both fall into the category of 'cultured milks' – milk that has deliberately had certain bacteria added to it and then been kept warm until the bacteria grow. It is these bacteria that give yoghurt and buttermilk their characteristic thick textures and tangy flavours.

If you look at the label of either of these cultured milk products, you'll see that the nutrition label claims 12 grams of carbohydrate per 225 ml (and, by the way, 8 grams of protein). This is the same carbohydrate count as the milk these products are made from. For this reason, many low-carbers avoid yoghurt and buttermilk.

However, in *GO-Diet*, Dr Goldberg and Dr O'Mara explain that in actuality, most of the lactose (milk sugar) in the milk is converted into lactic acid by the bacteria. This is what gives these foods their sour taste. The labels say '12 grams carbohydrate' largely, they say, because carbohydrate count is determined by 'difference'. What this means is that the calorie count is determined first. Then the protein and fat fractions are measured and the number of calories they contribute is calculated. Any calories left over are assumed to come from carbohydrate.

However, Goldberg and O'Mara say, this is inaccurate in the cases of yoghurt and buttermilk and they say we should count just 4 grams of carbohydrate per 225 ml for these cultured milks. Accordingly, I have added them back to my diet and I have had no trouble with them, meaning no weight gain and no triggering of 'blood sugar hunger'. I really enjoy yoghurt as a snack! Based on this, the carb counts in this book are calculated using that 4-grams-of-carbohydrates-per-225 ml figure.

Keep in mind that these numbers only apply to plain yoghurt. The sweetened kind is always higher in carbohydrate. If you like fruit-flavoured yoghurt, flavour it yourself. You'll find a recipe for making your own plain yoghurt, easy as pie, in the Eggs and Dairy chapter, but any purchased plain yoghurt is fine.

CHAPTER TWO

Hors D'oeuvres, Snacks and Party Nibbles

Unlike most snack and party foods, the recipes in this chapter are actually nutritious and filling. This means two things: one, that if you serve one or two of these items before dinner, you may want to cut back a bit on quantities at the meal itself, and two, that you can actually use many of these recipes as light meals in themselves. This is a particularly nice idea for family TV movie night – just put out a big tray of cut-up vegetables and dip, some chicken wings and a bowl of nut mix, and call it supper.

꩜ Wonderful Wings

These are utterly, totally addictive! They are a bit messy and time-consuming to make, but worth every minute. Your friends will love them, too, and you'll wish you'd made more of them. They also taste great the next day.

2 kg chicken wings

150 g grated Parmesan cheese

2 Tbsp dried parsley

1 Tbsp dried oregano

2 tsp paprika

1 tsp salt

1/2 tsp freshly ground black pepper

100 g butter

🍓 Not sure what to do with those wingtips? Freeze them for soup – they make great broth.

1. Preheat the oven to 180°C/Gas Mark 4. Cut the wings into drumsticks, saving the pointy tips.

2. Combine the Parmesan cheese and the parsley, oregano, paprika, salt and pepper in a bowl.

3. Line a shallow baking tin with foil (do not omit this step, or you'll still be scrubbing the tin a week later).

4. Melt the butter in a shallow bowl or pan. Dip each drumstick in butter, roll in the cheese and seasoning mixture and arrange in the foil-lined tin.

5. Bake for 1 hour (and kick yourself for not having made a double recipe!).

Yield: About 50 pieces, each with only a trace of carbohydrate, a trace of fibre and 4 grams of protein.

☌ Chinese Peanut Wings

If you love Chinese barbecued spare ribs, try making these.

> 75 ml soy sauce
>
> 3 Tbsp Splenda
>
> 3 Tbsp natural peanut butter
>
> 2 Tbsp dry sherry
>
> 1 Tbsp oil
>
> 1 Tbsp cider vinegar
>
> 2 tsp Chinese Five Spice powder
>
> 1/4 tsp chilli flakes (or more, if you want them hotter)
>
> 1 clove garlic, crushed
>
> 12 whole chicken wings, cut into 24 joints

1. Put the soy sauce, Splenda, peanut butter, sherry, oil, vinegar, spice powder, chilli flakes and garlic in a blender or food processor and blend well.

2. Arrange the wings in a large baking tin and pour the blended sauce over them, then turn them over to coat on all sides. Leave to marinate for half an hour to an hour.

3. Meanwhile preheat the oven to 170°C/Gas Mark 3. At the end of the marinating time, bake the wings for an hour, turning every 20 minutes during baking.

4. When they are done, put them on a serving platter and scrape the sauce from the tin back into the blender or food processor. Blend again for just a moment to make it smooth and serve with the wings.

Yield: 24 pieces, each with 1 gram of carbohydrate, a trace of fibre and 5 grams of protein.

⌒ Hot Wings

If you want to simplify this recipe, use purchased Buffalo Wing sauce instead of the mixture of dry spices. Most wing sauces don't have any sugar in them and are quite low in carbs.

>   1 tsp cayenne pepper
>   2 tsp dried oregano
>   1 tsp curry powder
>   2 tsp paprika
>   2 tsp dried thyme
>   1 kg chicken wings, jointed

1. Preheat the oven to 190°C/Gas Mark 5.
2. Combine the pepper, oregano, curry, paprika and thyme well in a bowl.
3. Arrange the wings in a shallow baking tin and sprinkle the mixture evenly over them, turning to coat both sides. Roast for 45 to 50 minutes, or until crisp.
4. Serve with the traditional accompaniments of ranch or blue cheese dressing and celery sticks, if desired.

Yield: About 24 pieces, each with a trace of carbohydrate, a trace of fibre and 4 grams of protein.

↻ Paprika Wings

20 chicken wing joints
3 Tbsp olive oil
2 cloves garlic, crushed
Salt
Freshly ground black pepper
Paprika

1. Preheat the oven to 180°C/Gas Mark 4.
2. Arrange the wings in a baking dish so that they are not touching. Combine the oil and garlic and spoon the mixture over the wings. Make sure you get a little of the crushed garlic on each piece.
3. Sprinkle the wings with salt and pepper to taste and then with enough paprika to make them reddish all over.
4. Roast for 15 to 20 minutes, then turn them over and sprinkle the other side with salt, pepper and paprika.
5. Roast for another 45 minutes to 1 hour, turning every 15 to 20 minutes.

Yield: 20 pieces, each with a trace of carbohydrate, a trace of fibre and 4 grams of protein.

Stuffed Eggs

Don't save these recipes for parties: if you're a low-carb eater, a refrigerator full of stuffed eggs is a beautiful thing. Here are six varieties. Feel free to double or triple any of these recipes – you know they'll disappear.

◌ Classic Devilled Eggs

These are everybody's supper favourite.

> 6 hard-boiled eggs
> 5 Tbsp mayonnaise
> 2 tsp Dijon mustard
> 1/4 tsp salt
> Paprika

1. Slice the eggs in half and carefully remove the yolks into a mixing bowl.
2. Mash the yolks with a fork. Stir in the mayonnaise, mustard and salt and mix until creamy.
3. Spoon the mixture back into the hollows in the egg whites. Sprinkle with a little paprika for colour.

   Yield: 12 halves, each with a trace of carbohydrate, a trace of fibre and 3 grams of protein.

◌ Onion Eggs

> 6 hard-boiled eggs
> 5 Tbsp mayonnaise
> 1 tsp Dijon mustard
> 2 1/2 tsp very finely chopped sweet red onion
> 5 drops Tabasco
> 1/4 tsp salt

1. Slice the eggs in half and carefully remove the yolks into a mixing bowl.
2. Mash the yolks with a fork. Stir in the mayonnaise, mustard, onion, Tabasco and salt and mix until creamy.
3. Spoon the mixture back into the hollows in the egg whites.

Yield: 12 halves, each with a trace of carbohydrate, a trace of fibre and 3 grams of protein.

↻ Fish Eggs

That's eggs with fish, not eggs *from* fish. If you thought stuffed eggs couldn't go to a really smart party, these will change your mind.

> 6 hard-boiled eggs
>
> 2 Tbsp mayonnaise
>
> 2 Tbsp soured cream
>
> 50 g smoked salmon, well mashed
>
> 1 Tbsp bottled, grated horseradish
>
> 2 tsp finely chopped sweet red onion
>
> 1/8 tsp salt

1. Slice the eggs in half and carefully remove the yolks into a mixing bowl.
2. Mash the yolks with a fork. Stir in the mayonnaise, soured cream, salmon, horseradish, onion and salt and mix until creamy.
3. Spoon the mixture back into the hollows in the egg whites.

Yield: 12 halves, each with a trace of carbohydrate, a trace of fibre and 3 grams of protein.

↻ Kali's Eggs

Curried and buttery – and good!

> 6 hard-boiled eggs
>
> 1 Tbsp butter
>
> 1 tsp curry powder
>
> 1 clove garlic, crushed
>
> 1 spring onion, including the crisp part of the green shoot, finely chopped
>
> $1/4$ tsp Tabasco
>
> $1/3$ cup mayo
>
> $1/2$ tsp salt

1. Slice the eggs in half and carefully remove the yolks into a mixing bowl.
2. In a small, heavy frying pan over low heat, melt the butter. Add the curry powder and garlic and stir for 2 minutes.
3. Scrape the butter mixture into the yolks. Stir in the spring onion, Tabasco, mayo and salt and mix until creamy.
4. Spoon the mixture back into the hollows in the egg whites.

Yield: 12 halves, each with 1 gram of carbohydrate, a trace of fibre and 3 grams of protein.

↻ Hammond Eggs

Devilled ham gives these eggs a country flavour.

> 6 hard-boiled eggs
>
> 50 to 60 g devilled ham
>
> 4 tsp Dijon mustard
>
> 3 Tbsp mayonnaise
>
> $1/4$ tsp salt
>
> Paprika

1. Slice the eggs in half and carefully remove the yolks into a mixing bowl.
2. Mash the yolks with a fork. Stir in the ham, mustard, mayonnaise and salt and mix until creamy.
3. Spoon the mixture back into the hollows in the egg whites. Sprinkle with a little paprika for colour.

Yield: 12 halves, each with 1 gram of carbohydrate, a trace of fibre and 4 grams of protein.

⟲ Cajun Eggs

6 hard-boiled eggs

100 ml mayonnaise

2 tsp horseradish mustard

1 tsp Cajun Seasoning (see page 420)

1. Slice the eggs in half and carefully remove the yolks into a mixing bowl.
2. Mash the yolks with a fork. Stir in the mayonnaise and mustard and mix until creamy.
3. Add the Cajun seasoning and blend well.
4. Spoon the mixture back into the hollows in the egg whites.

Yield: 12 halves, each with 1 gram of carbohydrate, a trace of fibre and 3 grams of protein.

☽ Artichoke Parmesan Dip

Serve this party favourite with pepper strips, cucumber rounds or celery sticks.

> 400 g tinned artichoke hearts
> 250 ml mayonnaise
> 150 g grated Parmesan cheese
> 1 clove garlic, crushed
> Paprika

1. Preheat the oven to 170°C/Gas Mark 3.
2. Drain and chop the artichoke hearts, and mix with the mayonnaise, cheese and garlic, combining well.
3. Put the mixture in a small, ovenproof casserole, sprinkle a little paprika on top and bake for 45 minutes.

   Yield: 4 servings, each with 3 grams of carbohydrate and 1 gram of fibre, for a total of 2 grams of usable carbs and 10 grams of protein.

☽ Spinach Artichoke Dip

This is a great, equally delicious version of the previous recipe, but keep in mind that it does make twice as much.

> 400 g tinned artichoke hearts
> 300 g frozen chopped spinach, thawed
> 500 ml mayonnaise
> 300 g grated Parmesan cheese
> 2 cloves garlic, crushed
> Paprika

1. Drain and chop the artichoke hearts.
2. Combine the spinach, mayonnaise, cheese and garlic in a large casserole (a 1 1/2-litre dish is about right). Sprinkle with paprika.
3. Bake at 170°C/Gas Mark 3 for 50 to 60 minutes.

Yield: 8 servings, each with 4 grams of carbohydrate and 2 grams of fibre, for a total of 2 grams of usable carbs and 10 grams of protein.

 Guacamole

This is a very simple guacamole recipe, without soured cream or mayonnaise, that lets the taste of the avocados shine through.

> 4 ripe black avocados
> 2 Tbsp chopped sweet red onion
> 3 Tbsp lime juice
> 3 cloves garlic, crushed
> 1/4 tsp Tabasco
> Salt, to taste

1. Halve the avocados and scoop the flesh into a mixing bowl. Mash coarsely with a fork.
2. Mix in the onion, lime juice, garlic, Tabasco and salt, stirring to blend well and mashing to the desired consistency.

Yield: 6 generous servings, each with 11 grams of carbohydrate and 3 grams of fibre, for a total of 8 grams of usable carbs and 3 grams of protein.

🍓 This recipe contains lots of healthy fats and almost three times the potassium found in a banana.

↻ Dill Dip

This easy dip tastes wonderful with all sorts of raw vegetables; try serving it with celery, peppers, cucumber, broccoli or whatever else you have on hand.

> 500 ml sour cream
> 1/4 small onion
> 1 heaped Tbsp dry dill
> 1/2 tsp salt

1. Put the sour cream, onion, dill and salt in a food processor and process until the onion disappears. (If you don't have a food processor, chop the onion very finely and just stir everything together.)
2. You can serve this right away, but it tastes even better if you let it chill for a few hours.

Yield: 500 ml, containing 25 grams of carbohydrate and 1 gram of fibre, for a total of 24 grams of usable carbs and 16 grams of protein in the batch. (This is easily enough for 10 to 12 people, so no one's going to get more than a few grams of carbs.)

↻ Clam Dip

With some celery sticks and pepper strips for scooping, this would make a good lunch. Of course, you can serve it at parties, too, with celery, green pepper and cucumber rounds – and with crackers for the non-low-carbers.

> 500 g cream cheese, beaten to soften
> 125 ml mayonnaise
> 2 to 3 tsp Worcestershire sauce
> 1 Tbsp Dijon mustard
> 8 to 10 spring onions, including the crisp part of the green shoot, finely chopped

400 g tinned clams, drained and chopped

Salt

Freshly ground black pepper

Combine all the ingredients well and chill. A food processor or blender works well for this, or if you prefer to leave bits of clam, you could use an electric mixer.

Yield: 12 servings, each with just under 4 grams of carbohydrate, a trace of fibre and 10 grams of protein.

☺ Northwest Dip

This is *Lowcarbezine!* reader Pat Moriarty's 'all-time favourite'!

225 g cream cheese, beaten to soften

75 ml double cream

1 spring onion, thinly sliced

2 tsp freshly squeezed lemon juice

Dash of Tabasco sauce

100 g smoked salmon, chopped

1 ripe avocado, mashed

1. In a large mixing bowl, combine the cream cheese and double cream together until smooth and creamy.
2. Stir in the onion, lemon juice and Tabasco sauce. Gently fold in the smoked salmon and mashed avocado, being careful not to overmix.
3. Serve with cucumber, celery or low-carb crackers (see page 150).

Yield: 6 servings, each with 4 grams of carbohydrate and 1 gram of fibre, for a total of 3 grams of usable carbs and 7 grams of protein.

◯ Kathy's All-purpose Dip

Lowcarbezine! reader Kathy Rice has formulated this simple dip – to go with anything!

> 75 g cream cheese, beaten to soften
>
> 2 Tbsp salsa

Blend and enjoy – that's all there is to it.

Yield: 2 servings, each with 2 grams of carbohydrate and 0.5 gram of fibre, for a total of 1.5 grams of usable carbs and 3.5 grams of protein.

◯ Avocado Cheese Dip

This dip has been known to make my mother a very popular person at parties! It can also be served over steak and it makes what are possibly the most elegant omelettes on the face of the earth.

> 500 g cream cheese, beaten to soften
>
> 180 g grated white Cheddar or Monterey Jack cheese
>
> 1 ripe black avocado, peeled and stoned
>
> 1 small onion
>
> 1 clove garlic, crushed
>
> 75 to 100 g tinned green chillies, drained
> (or jalapeños, for a hotter dip)

1. Combine all the ingredients in a food processor and process until very smooth.
2. Scrape into a pretty serving bowl and place the avocado stone in the middle.

> 🍓 For some reason, placing the avocado stone in the middle keeps the dip from turning brown quite so quickly. But if you're making this a few hours ahead of time, cover it with clingfilm, making sure the film is actually touching the surface of the dip.

Yield: About 1 1/4 litres (plenty for a good-size party), with the batch containing 45 grams of carbohydrate and 9 grams of fibre, for a total of 36 grams of usable carbs and a whopping 83 grams of protein.

☌ Smoked Gouda Veggie Dip

Great with celery, peppers or any favourite raw veggie. Combine your ingredients with a mixer, not a food processor, so you have little bits of Gouda in the dip.

> 225 g cream cheese, beaten to soften
>
> 150 ml mayonnaise
>
> 120 g grated smoked Gouda
>
> 6 spring onions, including the crisp part of the green shoot, sliced
>
> 2 Tbsp grated Parmesan cheese
>
> 1/2 tsp freshly ground black pepper

1. Beat the cream cheese and mayonnaise together until creamy, scraping the sides of the bowl frequently.
2. Add the Gouda, spring onions, Parmesan and pepper and beat until well blended.
3. Chill and serve with raw vegetables.

Yield: At least 8 servings, each with 2 grams of carbohydrate, a trace of fibre and 7 grams of protein.

↷ Kim's Crab Dip

We have my sister to thank for coming up with this delicious, low-carb treat.

> 225 g cream cheese, beaten to soften
>
> 125 ml soured cream
>
> 175 g tinned crab meat, drained
>
> 1 tsp horseradish
>
> 2 Tbsp fresh chives (or 1 Tbsp dried if fresh are unavailable)
>
> 1/4 tsp dry mustard
>
> 1/8 tsp salt
>
> 1/8 tsp freshly ground black pepper

1. Beat the cheese and soured cream together at a high speed until very smooth.
2. Set the beater to a low speed and mix in the crab, horseradish, chives, mustard, salt and pepper.
3. Chill. Serve with raw vegetables.

> Yield: 12 servings, each containing 1 gram of carbohydrate, a trace of fibre and 5 grams of protein.

↷ Bacon Cheese Spread

Another recipe from Jen Eloff's *Splendid Low-Carbing*. Jen, of sweety.com, says, 'Your friends will beg you for this recipe!'

> 225 g light cream cheese, beaten to soften
>
> 125 ml mayonnaise
>
> 180 g grated Cheddar cheese
>
> 2 Tbsp chopped fresh chives or spring onions
>
> 1 tsp dried parsley
>
> 1/4 tsp garlic powder
>
> 8 rashers bacon, cooked until crisp

1. Preheat the oven to 180°C/Gas Mark 4.

2. In a food processor with the S-blade in place or in a blender, process the cream cheese and mayonnaise until smooth.

3. In a medium bowl, combine the cream cheese mixture, Cheddar, chives, parsley and garlic powder until well combined. Spread the mixture evenly on the bottom of a 23-cm glass pie plate.

4. Use a pair of kitchen scissors to cut the cooked bacon into small pieces. Garnish the top of the cheese spread with the bacon pieces and bake for 15 minutes. Serve with low-carb crackers (see page 150).

Yield: 12 servings, each with 2 grams of carbohydrate, a trace of fibre and 7 grams of protein.

☊ Dukkah

My friend Lou Anne once brought this Turkish 'dry dip' along to a picnic and I've been nagging her for the recipe ever since. Although Dukkah is traditionally eaten with bread, it also adds an exotic, fascinating flavour to simple raw vegetables.

> 50 g almonds or hazelnuts
> 30 g white sesame seeds
> 30 g coriander seeds
> 30 g cumin seeds
> Salt and freshly ground black pepper, to taste

1. Toast the nuts and seeds over high heat for 1 minute, stirring constantly.

2. Use a food processor, coffee grinder or mortar and pestle to crush the toasted mixture, then season it with salt and pepper. (Don't over-grind – you want a consistency similar to coarsely ground cornmeal.)

3. Put your Dukkah in a bowl next to a bowl of olive oil and set out cut-up raw vegetables. Dip the vegetables first into the oil, then into the Dukkah and eat.

Yield: Just over 120 g or about 10 servings, each with 4 grams of carbohydrate and 1 gram of fibre, for a total of 3 grams of usable carbs and 2 grams of protein. (Analysis does not include vegetables.)

☉ Tuna Paté

This versatile dish makes a great snack or a first course at a dinner party – or a delicious lunch with some veggies for dipping.

> 2 Tbsp butter
> 2 cloves garlic, crushed
> 1/2 medium onion, chopped
> 100 g tinned mushrooms, drained
> 1/4 tsp orange extract
> 1 Tbsp Splenda
> 225 g cream cheese, beaten to soften
> 180 g tinned tuna, drained
> 2 Tbsp fresh parsley
> Grated peel of half an orange
> 1/4 tsp salt
> 1/4 tsp freshly ground black pepper

1. In a small, heavy frying pan over medium heat, melt the butter and sauté the garlic, onion and mushrooms until the onion is limp. Add the orange extract and Splenda and stir well. Allow to cool.
2. Place the cream cheese, tuna, parsley, orange peel, salt and pepper in a food processor with the S-blade in place. Pulse to blend. Add the sautéed mixture and pulse until smooth and well blended.
3. Spoon into a serving bowl and chill. Serve with celery sticks, pepper strips, cucumber rounds (and crackers for the carb-eaters).

Yield: At least 6 servings, each with 3 grams of carbohydrate and 1 gram of fibre, for a total of 2 grams of usable carbs and 11 grams of protein.

☉ Marinated Mushrooms

The quality of the vinaigrette dressing makes all the difference here, so use the best you can make or buy.

> 225 g small fresh mushrooms
> 400 ml vinaigrette dressing (home-made or purchased)

1. Thoroughly wipe the mushrooms clean with a soft cloth.
2. Place them in a saucepan, cover with the dressing and simmer over a medium low heat for 15 minutes.
3. Chill and drain the mushrooms, saving the dressing to store any left-over mushrooms in. (You can even simmer another batch of mushrooms in it when the first batch is gone.)
4. Arrange the mushrooms on lettuce with cocktail sticks for spearing.

Yield: Depending on the size of your mushrooms, this will make about 12 to 15 servings, each with about 1 gram of carbohydrate and not enough fibre or protein to talk about.

◯ Cheese Cookies

This recipe requires a full-sized food processor, so if you only have a tiny one, cut the recipe in half.

> 225 g processed cheese slices, such as Dairylea
> 225 g mature Cheddar cheese
> 110 g butter
> 110 g soya powder
> About 70 pecan or walnut halves (optional)

1. Preheat the oven to 200°C/Gas Mark 6.
2. Cut the cheeses and butter into chunks. Put the cheeses, butter and soya powder in the food processor and pulse until the dough is well combined.
3. Mist a baking tray with spray-on cooking oil. Drop spoonfuls of dough on to the tray and, if using, press half a pecan or walnut in the top of each one.
4. Bake for 8 to 10 minutes, or until the cookies are just getting brown around the edges.

Yield: This will depend on how big you make your cookies. I make mine small and get about 70, each with 1 gram of carbohydrate, a trace of fibre and 2 grams of protein.

↷ Snaps

Similar to the Cheese Cookies, but these bite back!

> 450 g processed cheese with chillies
> 110 g butter
> 110 g soya powder

1. Preheat the oven to 200°C/Gas Mark 6.
2. Cut the cheese and butter into chunks. Put the cheese, butter and soya powder in the food processor and pulse until the dough is well combined.
3. Mist a baking tray with spray-on cooking oil. Drop spoonfuls of dough on to the tray and bake for 8 to 10 minutes, or until the cookies are just getting brown around the edges.

Yield: This will depend on how big you make your cookies. As with Cheese Cookies, I make these small and get about 70, each with 1 gram of carbohydrate, a trace of fibre and 2 grams of protein.

↷ Roasted Nuts

Of course, you can buy these in a pack at the grocery store, but they're much better – and cheaper – when you roast them, freshly shelled, at home.

> 250 g shelled nuts of your choice
> (almonds, pecans, walnuts, or a combination)
> 4 Tbsp butter, melted
> Salt

1. Preheat the oven to 150°C/Gas Mark 2.
2. Spread the nuts in a shallow roasting tin. Stir in the butter, coating all the nuts.
3. Roast for 20 to 25 minutes. Remove from the oven, and salt to taste.

Yield: 8 servings. Each serving made with almonds will have 7 grams of carbohydrate and 4 grams of fibre, for a total of 3 grams of usable carbs and 7 grams of protein. Each serving made with pecans will have 5 grams of carbohydrate and 2 grams of fibre, for a total of 3 grams of usable carbs and 2 grams of protein. Each serving made with walnuts will have 5 grams of carbohydrate and 1 gram of fibre, for a total of 4 grams of usable carbs and 4 grams of protein.

↻ Soy and Ginger Pecans

I gave away tins of these for Christmas one year and got rave reviews.

> 130 g shelled pecans
> 4 Tbsp butter, melted
> 3 Tbsp soy sauce
> 1 tsp ground ginger

1. Preheat the oven to 150ºC/Gas Mark 2.
2. Spread the pecans in a shallow roasting tin. Stir in the butter, coating all the nuts.
3. Roast for 15 minutes, then remove from the oven and stir in the soy sauce. Sprinkle the ginger evenly over the nuts and stir that in as well.
4. Roast for another 10 minutes.

Yield: 8 servings, each with 6 grams of carbohydrate and 2 grams of fibre, for a total of 4 grams of usable carbs and 3 grams of protein.

⟳ Worcestershire Nuts

I like to use this combination of nuts, but feel free to use just one or the other, or to experiment with your own proportions.

> 110 g shelled walnuts
>
> 110 g shelled pecans
>
> 4 Tbsp butter, melted
>
> 3 Tbsp Worcestershire sauce

1. Preheat the oven to 150°C/Gas Mark 2.
2. Spread the nuts in a shallow baking tin and stir in the butter, coating all the nuts.
3. Roast for 15 minutes, then remove from the oven and stir in the Worcestershire sauce.
4. Roast for another 10 minutes.

Yield: 8 servings, each with 6 grams of carbohydrate and 2 grams of fibre, for a total of 4 grams of usable carbs and 3 grams of protein.

⟳ Curried Pecans

When I first came up with this combination of seasonings, I intended to use it on chicken, but I've discovered that it's also delicious on pecans.

> 130 g shelled pecans
>
> 4 Tbsp butter, melted
>
> 1 Tbsp Chicken Seasoning (see page 419)

1. Preheat the oven to 150°C/Gas Mark 2.
2. Spread the nuts in a shallow baking tin and stir in the butter, coating all the nuts. Roast for 20 to 25 minutes.
3. Remove from the oven, sprinkle Chicken Seasoning over the nuts and stir to coat.

Yield: 8 servings, each with 5 grams of carbohydrate and 2 grams of fibre, for a total of 3 grams of usable carbs and 2 grams of protein.

↻ Dana's Snack Mix

You can buy hulled sunflower seeds and pumpkin seeds in bulk at most health food shops and you should be able to get raw cashew pieces there, too.

6 Tbsp butter

3 Tbsp Worcestershire sauce

1 1/2 tsp garlic powder

2 1/2 tsp seasoned salt

1 tsp onion powder

500 g raw, shelled sunflower seeds

500 g raw, shelled pumpkin seeds

150 g almonds

110 g pecans

110 g walnuts

110 g raw cashew pieces

1. Preheat the oven to 130°C/Gas Mark 1/2.
2. In a small pan, melt the butter and stir in the Worcestershire sauce, garlic powder, seasoned salt and onion powder.
3. In a large bowl, combine the nuts and seeds. Pour the melted butter mixture over them and mix very well.
4. Put the mixture in large roasting tin and bake for 2 hours, stirring occasionally.
5. Allow the mixture to cool and store in an airtight container.

Yield: 18 servings, each with 14 grams of carbohydrate and 5 grams of fibre, for a total of 9 grams of usable carbs and 13 grams of protein.

↻ Ranch Mix

450 g raw, shelled pumpkin seeds
450 g raw, shelled sunflower seeds
225 g dry-roasted peanuts
150 g raw almonds
110 g raw cashew pieces
2 Tbsp canola (rapeseed) oil
1 packet dry ranch salad dressing mix
1 tsp lemon pepper
1 tsp dried dill
1/2 tsp garlic powder

1. Preheat the oven to 180°C/Gas Mark 4.
2. In large mixing bowl, combine the pumpkin seeds, sunflower seeds, peanuts, almonds and cashews. Add the canola oil and stir to coat. Add the dressing mix, lemon pepper, dill and garlic powder and stir until well distributed.
3. Put the seasoned nuts in a shallow roasting tin and roast for 45 to 60 minutes, stirring occasionally, until the almonds are crispy.

Yield: 16 servings, each with 15 grams of carbohydrate and 5 grams of fibre, for a total of 10 grams of usable carbs and 16 grams of protein.

↻ Asian Punks

Pumpkin seeds are good for you – they're a great source of both magnesium and zinc. And they taste pretty good, too.

450 g raw, shelled pumpkin seeds
2 Tbsp soy sauce
1/2 tsp ground ginger
2 tsp Splenda

1. Preheat the oven to 180°C/Gas Mark 4.

2. In a mixing bowl, combine the pumpkin seeds, soy sauce, ginger and Splenda, mixing well.

3. Spread the pumpkin seeds in a shallow roasting tin and roast for about 45 minutes, or until the seeds are dry, stirring two or three times during roasting.

Yield: 4 servings, each with 13 grams of carbohydrate and 3 grams of fibre, for a total of 10 grams of usable carbs and 17 grams of protein. (These are also a wonderful source of minerals.)

ꙩ Indian Punks

You can buy curry-flavoured pumpkin seeds, but the home-made version is better-tasting and better for you.

> 450 g raw, shelled pumpkin seeds
> 4 Tbsp butter
> 2 1/2 Tbsp curry powder
> 2 cloves garlic, crushed
> Salt

1. Preheat the oven to 150°C/Gas Mark 2.

2. Melt the butter in a small frying pan over medium heat. Add the curry powder and garlic and stir for 2 to 3 minutes.

3. In a mixing bowl, add the seasoned butter to the pumpkin seeds and stir until well coated.

4. Spread the pumpkin seeds in a shallow roasting tin and roast for 30 minutes. Sprinkle lightly with salt.

Yield: 4 servings, each with 15 grams of carbohydrate and 4 grams of fibre, for a total of 11 grams of usable carbs and 18 grams of protein.

🍓 In addition to all the minerals found in the pumpkin seeds, you get the turmeric in the curry powder, which is believed to help prevent cancer.

↷ Punks on the Range

Spicy-chilli-crunchy. If you like barbecue-flavoured potato crisps, try snacking on these.

> 450 g raw, shelled pumpkin seeds
> 1 Tbsp canola (rapeseed) oil
> 1 Tbsp chilli powder
> 1 tsp salt

1. Preheat the oven to 180°C/Gas Mark 4.
2. In a mixing bowl, combine the pumpkin seeds and canola oil and stir until well coated. Add the chilli powder and salt and stir again.
3. Spread the seeds in a shallow roasting tin and roast for about 30 minutes.

> *Yield:* 4 servings, each with 13 grams of carbohydrate and 3 grams of fibre, for a total of 10 grams of usable carbs and 17 grams of protein.

↷ Barbecued Peanuts

> 1 Tbsp liquid smoke flavouring
> 1 tsp Worcestershire sauce
> Dash of Tabasco
> 125 ml water
> 180 g dry-roasted peanuts
> 3 Tbsp butter
> Garlic salt

1. Preheat the oven to 130°C/Gas Mark 1/2.
2. In a saucepan, combine the liquid smoke flavouring, Worcestershire sauce, Tabasco and water. Bring to a simmer.
3. Turn off the heat and stir in the peanuts. Let the peanuts sit in the liquid for 30 minutes, stirring occasionally.

4. Drain off the liquid and spread the peanuts in a shallow roasting tin. Bake for at least 1 hour, or until well dried. (Stir occasionally to help speed up the process.)

5. When the peanuts are thoroughly dry, melt the butter and stir it into the peanuts to coat. Sprinkle lightly with garlic salt.

Yield: 3 servings, each with 16 grams of carbohydrate and 6 grams of fibre, for a total of 10 grams of usable carbs and 17 grams of protein.

☌ Antipasto

This easy dish makes a nice light summer supper. Use some or all of the ingredients listed here, adjusting quantities as necessary. Tinned or bottled pepperoncini and pimento are recommended here.

> Wedges of cantaloupe
>
> Salami
>
> Boiled ham
>
> Pepperoncini (mildly hot salad peppers)
>
> Halved or quartered hard-boiled eggs
>
> Marinated mushrooms
>
> Black and green olives
>
> Strips of pimento
>
> Solid-pack white tuna, drizzled with olive oil
>
> Sardines
>
> Marinated tinned artichoke hearts

Simply arrange some or all of these things decoratively on a platter, put out a stack of small plates and some forks and dinner is served.

Yield: Varies with your taste and needs, but here are the basic nutritional breakdowns for the items on your antipasto platter:

Cantaloupe, 1/8 of a small melon: 4.5 grams of carbohydrate and 0.5 grams of fibre, for a total of 4 grams of usable carbs and 0.5 grams of protein.

Salami, 1 average slice: 0.5 grams of carbohydrate, a trace of fibre and 3 grams of protein

Boiled ham, 1 average slice: a trace of carbohydrate, no fibre and 3.5 grams of protein

Pepperoncini, 1 average piece: 0.5 grams of carbohydrate, a trace of fibre and no protein

Hard-boiled eggs, 1/2: 0.3 grams of carbohydrate, no fibre and 3 grams of protein

Marinated mushrooms, 1 average piece: 1 gram of carbohydrate, a trace of fibre and no protein

Black olives, 1 large: 0.5 grams of carbohydrate, a trace of fibre and no protein

Green olives, 1 large: a trace of carbohydrate, a trace of fibre and no protein

Pimento, 1 slice: a trace of carbohydrate, a trace of fibre and no protein

Tuna, 3 ounces: no carbohydrates, no fibre and 22 grams of protein

Sardines, 2 average: no carbohydrates, no fibre and 5 grams of protein (not to mention 91 milligrams of calcium)

Artichoke hearts, 2 quarters: 2 grams of carbohydrate, 1 gram of fibre and no protein

◯ Maggie's Mushrooms

Lowcarbezine! reader Maggie Cosey sends this recipe.

> 650 g large mushrooms
> 20 stuffed green olives
> 500 g cream cheese, beaten to soften
> 50 to 75 ml Worcestershire sauce

1. Preheat the oven to 180°C/Gas Mark 4.
2. Wash the mushrooms and remove their stems. Chop the olives by hand or in a food processor.

3. In a mixing bowl, combine the olives, cream cheese and Worcestershire sauce. (Be careful to add the Worcestershire sauce gradually, to taste!)

4. Spoon the mixture into the mushroom caps and place them in a roasting dish.

5. Bake for 15 to 20 minutes, or until the cream cheese is slightly browned.

Yield: About 45 mushrooms, each with 1 gram of carbohydrate, a trace of fibre and 1 gram of protein.

᠑ Simple Low-Carb Stuffed Mushrooms

Lowcarbezine! reader Kayann Kretschmar reported that her Christmas Eve guests raved about these mushrooms!

> 450 g breakfast sausage, spicy or plain
> 225 g cream cheese
> 450 g medium mushrooms

🍓 Waste not, want not: if you freeze those stems and mushroom insides, you can use them for sautéed mushrooms the next time you have steak.

1. Preheat the oven to 180°C/Gas Mark 4.

2. Clean the mushrooms. Remove their stems and use a paring knife to make the hole for stuffing larger.

3. Brown and drain the sausage and stir in the cream cheese. Spoon the mixture into the mushroom caps.

4. Bake for 20 minutes.

Yield: About 30 mushrooms, each with 1 gram of carbohydrate, a trace of fibre and 3 grams of protein.

↻ Kay's Crab-Stuffed Mushrooms

These are for my cyberpal Kay, who repeatedly begged me to come up with a low-carb recipe for crab puffs. I tried and tried, but all my attempts were relatively pathetic. So I made crab-stuffed mushrooms instead and they were a big hit.

450 g fresh mushrooms

175 g tinned flaked crab

50 g cream cheese

75 ml mayonnaise

50 g grated Parmesan cheese

10 to 12 spring onions, including the crisp part of the green shoot, finely sliced

Dash of Tabasco

1/4 tsp freshly ground black pepper

1. Preheat the oven to 170ºC/Gas Mark 3.
2. Wipe the mushrooms clean with a damp cloth and remove their stems.
3. In a good-size bowl, combine well the crab, cream cheese, mayonnaise, cheese, spring onions, Tabasco and pepper.
4. Spoon the mixture into the mushroom caps and arrange them in a large, flat roasting tin.

5. Bake for 45 minutes to 1 hour, or until the mushrooms are cooked through. Serve hot or cooled.

   Yield: 25 to 30 mushrooms, each with 1 gram of carbohydrate, a trace of fibre and 3 grams of protein.

   🍳 **Warning**: You may be tempted to economise by making these with 'crab sticks', but resist! They have a ton of carbohydrates added to them.

⟲ Vicki's Crab-Stuffed Mushrooms

Another tempter from Vicki Cash's *2002 Low Carb Success Calendar*!

> 300 g medium portobello mushrooms
> 2 high fibre rye crispbreads
> 175 g crabmeat
> 1 egg
> 2 Tbsp lemon juice
> 1 Tbsp dried dill
> 1 tsp dried onion flakes
> 80 g grated Parmesan cheese

1. Preheat the oven to 200°C/Gas Mark 6.
2. Wipe the mushrooms clean with a damp cloth, and remove their stems. Set aside 50 g of stems. Place the caps on an ungreased baking sheet.
3. Use a food processor with the S-blade attached to grind the crispbreads into coarse crumbs. Add the 50 g of mushroom stems, processing until coarsely chopped. Add the crabmeat, egg, lemon juice, dill, onion and cheese. Mix thoroughly.
4. Spoon the mixture into the mushroom caps and bake for 12 to 15 minutes, or until the top of the stuffing is slightly browned. Serve hot.

   Yield: 6 starter-size servings, each with 4.5 grams of carbohydrate and 1 gram of fibre, for a total of 3.5 grams of usable carbs and 10 grams of protein.

⟨ Two-Cheese Tuna-Stuffed Mushrooms

Of all the stuffed mushrooms I've cooked or sampled, these are my absolute favourites.

> 225 g fresh mushrooms
> 400 g tinned tuna
> 80 g grated smoked Gouda
> 2 Tbsp grated Parmesan cheese
> 3 Tbsp mayonnaise
> 1 spring onion, finely chopped

1. Preheat the oven to 180ºC/Gas Mark 4.
2. Wipe the mushrooms clean with a damp cloth and remove their stems.
3. Combine the tuna, Gouda, Parmesan, mayonnaise and onion and mix well.
4. Spoon the mixture into the mushroom caps and arrange them in a shallow roasting dish. Add just enough water to cover the bottom of the pan. Bake for 15 minutes and serve hot.

Yield: About 15 servings, each with 1 gram of carbohydrate, a trace of fibre and 4 grams of protein.

↷ Turkey-Parmesan Stuffed Mushrooms

      450 g turkey mince

      100 g grated Parmesan cheese

      125 ml mayonnaise

      1 tsp dried oregano

      1 tsp dried basil

      2 cloves garlic, crushed

      1 tsp salt

      1/4 tsp freshly ground black pepper

      650 g mushrooms

1. Preheat the oven to 180°C/Gas Mark 4.
2. Combine the turkey, Parmesan, mayonnaise, oregano, basil, garlic, salt and pepper, mixing very well.
3. Wipe the mushrooms clean with a damp cloth and remove their stems.
4. Spoon the mixture into the mushroom caps and place them in a shallow roasting dish. Add just enough water to cover the bottom of the pan. Bake for 20 minutes and serve hot.

Yield: About 45 mushrooms, each with 1 gram of carbohydrate, a trace of fibre and 3 grams of protein.

◯ Rumaki

These take a little extra effort, but I think it's worth it because my husband and I both love them.

125 ml soy sauce

75 ml dry sherry

1 clove garlic, crushed

1 slice fresh root ginger, about 5 mm thick, finely chopped

12 rashers bacon

12 chicken livers

24 tinned whole water chestnuts

1. Mix together the soy sauce, sherry, garlic and ginger to make the marinade.
2. Cut the bacon rashers and chicken livers in half.
3. Wrap each chicken liver half around a water chestnut, then wrap a half-strip of bacon around each chicken liver. Spear the whole thing with a bamboo skewer, making sure you pierce the water chestnut on the way through.
4. Submerge your speared bundles in the marinade and let them marinate for at least an hour. (You can leave them overnight, if you want to pre-pare this dish well in advance.)
5. When you're ready to eat, take the bundles out of the marinade and grill them for 5 to 7 minutes on each side, until the bacon is crisp.

Yield: Makes 24. When I analysed this recipe, it came up with 10 grams of carbohydrate per piece, but the software was assuming that you consume all of the marinade, which of course you do not. These should actually have about 3 grams of carbohydrate apiece and 1 gram of fibre, for a total of about 2 grams of usable carbs and 5 grams of protein – plus all the nutrients liver is famous for.

🍓 If you like, you may leave the water chestnuts out of these and the carb count will drop to a mere trace. And remember to soak those bamboo skewers in water before using, so they don't burn while the food is being cooked.

↻ Country-Style Paté

This is really good and, as paté goes, it's easy to make.

> 6 rashers bacon
> 2 Tbsp butter
> 80 g sliced mushrooms
> 50 g chopped onion
> 225 g chicken livers
> 1/2 tsp Worcestershire sauce
> 2 Tbsp mayonnaise
> Scant 1/2 tsp salt
> 1/4 tsp freshly ground black pepper

1. In a heavy frying pan over medium heat, fry the bacon until it just starts to get crisp. Remove the bacon and drain, reserving the grease.

2. Turn the heat down to low and melt the butter and a little bacon grease in the frying pan. Sauté the mushrooms and onion in the frying pan until they're quite limp (about 15 minutes).

3. While they're sautéing, fill a medium saucepan with water and bring it to the boil. Put the chicken livers in the water (make sure you keep stirring those sautéing vegetables) and bring the water back to the boil. Turn off the heat, cover the pan and let it sit for 15 minutes.

4. Drain the chicken livers. Put them in a food processor with the S-blade in place and pulse two or three times to grind the chicken livers. Crumble and add the bacon and the mushroom and onion mixture. Pulse to combine. Add the Worcestershire, mayonnaise, salt and pepper, and pulse again until well combined. Serve with celery sticks, pepper strips or low-carb crackers (see page 150).

Yield: 12 servings, each with 2 grams of carbohydrate, a trace of fibre and 5 grams of protein.

ꙩ Christmas Liver Paté

Lowcarbezine! reader Elizabeth Czilok sent this low-carb recipe saying she always makes it at Christmas as a special treat. Save it for Christmas if you like, but my recipe tester insists it's good any time and on nearly anything.

>225 g liverwurst
>225 g cream cheese, beaten to soften
>40 g finely chopped onion
>2 to 3 Tbsp soured cream
>1/2 tsp Worcestershire sauce
>1/4 tsp Tabasco sauce (optional)
>Pimento-stuffed olives, to garnish

1. Mix the liverwurst, half the cream cheese, the onion, soured cream, Worcestershire sauce and Tabasco sauce, combining well.
2. Form a mound of paté in the centre of a serving dish. Place the dish and paté in the freezer for about 15 minutes.
3. Frost with the remaining softened cream cheese.
4. Slice a few green olives stuffed with pimentos into rings. Arrange them on the outside of the mound as a garnish and serve with low-carb crackers (see page 150) and chunked green vegetables.

Yield: Just over 450 g of paté, or 16 servings, each with 1 gram of carbohydrate, almost no fibre and 3 grams of protein. Four stuffed olives contain about 3 grams of carbohydrate, very little fibre and no protein.

ꙩ Celery Stuffed with Blue Cheese
and Cream Cheese.

This easy low-carb crowd-pleaser came from *Lowcarbezine!* reader Jeannette Regas.

>5 or 6 large sticks of celery
>30 g crumbled blue cheese, at room temperature

225 g cream cheese, at room temperature

Double cream (optional)

Salt and freshly ground black pepper

1. Clean the celery and cut into 10-cm pieces.
2. Mix the crumbled blue cheese with the cream cheese, adding a little cream to make it smooth, if necessary. Add a little salt and pepper to taste.
3. Stuff into celery and serve.

Yield: 15 to 18 pieces, each with 1 gram of carbohydrate, a trace of fibre and 2 grams of protein.

☾ Fried Cheese

This is the sort of decadence I would never have considered in my low-fat days. If you miss cheese-flavoured snacks, you've got to try this.

50 to 75 g grated Cheddar or Monterey Jack cheese

2 or 3 Tbsp olive or canola (rapeseed) oil

1. Spray a small, heavy bottomed, nonstick frying pan with nonstick cooking spray and place over medium-high heat.
2. Add the oil and then the cheese. The cheese will melt and bubble and spread to fill the bottom of the pan.
3. Let the cheese fry until crisp and brown around the edges. Use a spatula to lift up an edge and check whether the cheese is brown all over the bottom; if it isn't, give it another minute or so.
4. When the fried cheese is nicely brown, carefully flip it and fry the other side until it, too, is brown.
5. Remove the cheese from the pan, drain and lie it flat to cool. Break into pieces – and eat!

Yield: 2 servings, each with 1 gram of carbohydrate, no fibre and 11 grams of protein.

Cheesy Bowls and Taco Shells. For a tasty, cheesy, tortilla-like bowl, follow the directions for Fried Cheese, until you get to Step 5. Then remove and drain the cheese, but drape it over the bottom of a bowl to cool. When it cools and hardens, you'll have a cheesy, edible bowl to eat a taco salad out of.

You can also make a taco shell by folding the cheese disc in half and propping it partway open. Be careful when handling it, though – hot cheese can give you a nasty burn.

⌒ Saganaki

If you've never tried the Greek cheese Kasseri, you're in for a treat. This dish is fantastically delicious and has a dramatic, fiery presentation.

> 100 g Kasseri, in a slab 1 cm thick
> 1 egg, beaten
> 2 to 3 Tbsp rice protein powder, soya powder
>   or low-carb bake mix
> Olive oil
> 1 shot brandy
> 1/4 lemon

1. Dip the slab of cheese in the beaten egg, then in the protein powder, coating it all over.
2. Heat 5 mm of olive oil in a heavy frying pan over medium heat. When the oil is hot, add the cheese. Fry until golden and crisp on both sides, turning only once. Remove from the pan and put on a fire proof plate.
3. Pour the brandy evenly over the hot cheese, strike a match and set it alight. (It is traditional to shout 'Opa!' at this moment!)
4. Squeeze the lemon over the flaming cheese, dashing the flames. Divide in half and serve.

Yield: 2 servings, each with 3 grams of carbohydrate, a trace of fibre and 17 grams of protein.

↻ Southwestern Saganaki

A yummy twist on the traditional Saganaki and a perfect starter for a fiery Mexican dinner for two.

> 100 g chilli-flavoured Monterey Jack cheese, in a slab 1 cm thick
>
> 1 egg, beaten
>
> 2 to 3 Tbsp rice protein powder, soya powder
>   or low-carb bake mix
>
> Olive oil
>
> 1 shot tequila
>
> 1/4 lime

1. Dip the slab of cheese in the beaten egg, then in the protein powder, coating it all over.

2. Heat 5 mm of olive oil in a heavy frying pan over medium heat. When the oil is hot, add the cheese.

3. Fry until golden and crisp on both sides, turning only once. Remove from the pan and put on a fire proof plate.

4. Pour the tequila evenly over the hot cheese, strike a match and set the brandy alight.

5. Squeeze the lime over the flaming cheese, putting out the fire.

Yield: 2 servings, each with 3 grams of carbohydrate, a trace of fibre and 17 grams of protein.

↻ Pickled Prawns

This recipe will feed a crowd, so make it when you have plenty of people to share with.

1 1/4 litres water
75 ml dry sherry
1/2 tsp peppercorns
1 bay leaf
6 tsp salt
1 1/4 kg raw prawns, shelled and deveined
225 ml oil
150 ml lemon juice
125 ml white vinegar
3 Tbsp mixed pickling spice
2 tsp Splenda
2 sprigs fresh dill, coarsely chopped

1. In a large saucepan over high heat, bring the water, sherry, peppercorns, bay leaf and 2 teaspoons of the salt to the boil.
2. Add the prawns and bring back to the boil. Cook 1 minute longer and drain.
3. In a large bowl, combine the oil, lemon juice, vinegar, pickling spice, Splenda, dill and the remaining 4 teaspoons of salt. Add the prawns and toss with this pickling mixture.
4. Cover the bowl and chill it and the platter you will serve the prawns on in the refrigerator overnight.
5. To serve, drain off and discard the marinade and arrange the prawns on the platter. Garnish with additional dill, if desired.

   🍓 If it's going to be a long party, it's a good idea to set the platter or bowl on a bed of crushed ice in another container, to keep the prawns cold.

Yield: This is enough for a party of a few dozen people, but the carb count will differ according to how big your prawns are, of course! For, say, 24 people, each serving will have less than 1 gram of carbohydrate, a trace of fibre and 12 grams of protein.

ꙮ Crab and Bacon Bundles

This quick, hot hors d'oeuvre will impress your guests.

> 180 g tinned crab, drained
> 1 spring onion, finely chopped
> 225 g bacon
> Duck Sauce (see page 434)

1. Flake the crab, removing any bits of shell or cartilage. Stir in the chopped spring onion and set aside.
2. Cut the bacon strips in half crossways, to make two shorter strips. Place a rounded 1/2 teaspoon or so of the crab mixture on the end of a bacon strip and roll the strip up around it, stretching the bacon slightly as you go. Pierce the bundle with a cocktail stick, to hold. Repeat until all the crab and bacon strips are used up.
3. Grill about 20 cm from the heat, turning once or twice, until the bacon is crisp – no more than 10 minutes. Serve with Duck Sauce for dipping.

Yield: About 2 dozen servings, each with only a trace of carbohydrate, a trace of fibre and 4 grams of protein. (Analysis does not include Duck Sauce.)

⟳ Low-Carb Margarita Mixer

This mixer is very good for parties! And while it's not super-low in carbs, it's considerably less sugary than the commercial stuff.

400 ml lime juice, fresh or bottled
125 ml lemon juice, fresh or bottled
180 g Splenda
500 ml water
1/2 tsp orange extract

Combine all the ingredients in a blender for 1 minute and pour into a clean bottle. Refrigerate until ready to use.

To make a margarita, combine 50 ml of tequila with 180 ml of margarita mix and either put it through the blender with lots of ice, or simply serve it on the rocks.

Yield: About 1 litre. This whole recipe has about 54 grams of carbs, so figure about 10 grams in each 180-ml serving of the mix.

CHAPTER THREE

Eggs and Dairy

Before I get to the recipes, I'd like to urge you to stop thinking of eggs solely as a breakfast food. Eggs are wildly nutritious, infinitely versatile, they cook in a flash – and they're inexpensive! If you want a fast meal at any time of day, think eggs.

Because of the slight risk of salmonella, recipes containing raw or partially cooked eggs should not be served to the very young, the ill or elderly, or to pregnant women.

Omelettes 101

There's this big mystique about omelettes, maybe because they're a part of classic French cookery. People think that omelettes are difficult and that only a good chef can get them right. But I say, no! Omelettes are easy. Believe it or not, I've been known to turn out omelettes for 20 on a propane camp stove. (This is when my friends started referring to my pop-up trailer as 'Dana's House of Omelettes.')

You can learn to do this quickly. Really – you can.

Before you begin, you'll need a good pan. What's a 'good pan'? I prefer a 20-cm (medium-sized) frying pan with a heavy bottom, sloping sides and a nonstick surface. However, what I currently have is a 20-cm frying pan with a heavy bottom, sloping sides and a formerly nonstick surface. I can still make omelettes in it, I just have to use a good shot of nonstick cooking spray. The heavy bottom and sloping sides, however, are essential.

Here's the really important thing to know about making omelettes: the word 'omelette' comes from a word meaning 'to laminate', or to build up layers. And that's exactly what you do; you let a layer of beaten egg cook, then you lift up the edges and tip the pan so the raw egg runs under the cooked part. You do this all around the edges, of course, so you build it up evenly. The point is, you don't just let the beaten egg lie there in the frying pan and wait for it to cook through. If you do, the bottom will be hopelessly overdone before the top is set.

Dana's Easy Omelette Method

1. First, have your filling ready. If you're using vegetables, you'll want to sauté them first. If you're using cheese, have it grated or sliced and ready to go. If you're making an omelette to use up left-overs – a great idea, by the way – warm them through in the microwave and have them standing by.

2. Spray your omelette pan well with nonstick cooking spray if it doesn't have a good nonstick surface and set it over medium-high heat.

3. While the frying pan's heating, break between one and three eggs into a bowl and beat them with a fork. Don't add water or milk or anything, just mix them up.

4. Test your pan to see if it's hot enough: a drop of water thrown in the pan should sizzle right away. Add a tablespoon of oil or butter, slosh it around to cover the bottom, then pour in the eggs, all at once. They should sizzle, too and immediately start to set.

5. When the bottom layer of egg is set around the edges – and this should happen quite quickly – lift the edge using a spatula and tip the pan to let the raw egg flow underneath. Do this all around the edges, until there's not enough raw egg to run.

6. Turn your cooker down to the lowest heat if you have a gas cooker. (If you cook electric, you'll have to have a 'warm' burner standing by; electric elements don't cool off fast enough for this job.) Put your filling on one half of the omelette, cover the pan with a lid and let it sit over very low heat for a minute or two – no more. Peek and see if the raw, shiny egg is gone from the top surface (although you can serve it that way if you like; that's how the French prefer their omelettes) and the cheese, if you've used it, is melted. If not, re-cover the pan and give it another minute or two.

7. When your omelette is done, slip a spatula under the half without the filling, fold it over and then lift the whole thing onto a plate. Or you can get fancy and tip the pan, letting the filling side of the omelette slide on to the plate and folding the top over as you go, but that takes some practice.

This makes a single-serving omelette. I think it's a lot easier to make several individual omelettes than one big one and omelettes are so fast to make that it's not really a problem to cook each one separately. Anyway, that way you can customise your omelettes to each individual's taste. If you're making more than two or three omelettes, just set your oven to its very lowest heat setting and keep them warm in there.

Now here are some ideas for what to put in your omelettes.

↻ Cheese Omelette

This is pretty obvious, but you can't ignore a classic!

> 1 Tbsp butter
>
> 2 eggs, beaten
>
> 50 to 75 g sliced or grated cheese (Cheddar, Monterey Jack, Gruyère – or whatever is your favourite)

Make your omelette according to Dana's Easy Omelette Method (see page 87), placing the cheese over half of the omelette when you get to step 6. Cover, turn the heat down to low and cook until the cheese is melted (2 to 3 minutes). Follow the directions to finish making the omelette.

Yield: 1 serving, with 2 grams of carbohydrate, no fibre and 32 grams of protein.

↻ Macro Cheese Omelette

My husband's favourite! With all that cheese, this is mighty filling.

> 1 Tbsp butter
>
> 2 eggs, beaten
>
> 30 to 50 g Cheddar, sliced or grated
>
> 30 to 50 g Monterey Jack, sliced or grated
>
> 1 slice processed Swiss cheese

Make your omelette according to Dana's Easy Omelette Method (see page 87), placing the cheese over half of the omelette when you get to step 6. Cover, turn the heat down to low and cook until the cheese is melted (3 to 4 minutes). Follow the directions to finish making the omelette.

Yield: 1 serving, with 3 grams of carbohydrate, no fibre and 46 grams of protein.

◯ Veggie Cheese Omelette

  Olive oil or butter

  2 eggs, beaten

  1/4 green pepper, sliced in small strips and sautéed

  1/4 medium onion, sliced and sautéed

  2 or 3 mushrooms, sliced and sautéed

  50 g sliced or grated Cheddar, Monterey Jack or Gruyère cheese

Make your omelette according to Dana's Easy Omelette Method (see page 87), placing the filling over half of the omelette when you get to step 6. Cover, turn the heat down to low and cook until the cheese is melted (3 to 4 minutes). Follow the directions to finish making the omelette.

Yield: 1 serving, with 9 grams of carbohydrate and 2 grams of fibre, for a total of 7 grams of usable carbs and 27 grams of protein.

◯ Mexican Omelette

This'll open your eyes in the morning! It's one of my favourites – I really enjoy its fiery taste.

  1 Tbsp butter

  2 eggs, beaten

  50 g chilli-flavoured Monterey Jack cheese, grated or sliced

  2 Tbsp salsa

  Tabasco sauce (optional)

Make your omelette according to Dana's Easy Omelette Method (see page 87), placing the filling over half of the omelette when you get to step 6. Cover, turn the heat down to low and cook until the cheese is melted (3 to 4 minutes). Follow the directions to finish making the omelette. Top with salsa and Tabasco sauce (if using).

Yield: 1 serving, with 5 grams of carbohydrate and 1 gram of fibre, for a total of 4 grams of usable carbs and 25 grams of protein.

↷ Taco Omelette

This is a great way to use up left-over taco filling.

> 1 Tbsp butter
>
> 2 eggs, beaten
>
> 50 g beef, turkey, or chicken taco filling, warmed.
>
> 2 Tbsp grated Cheddar cheese
>
> 2 Tbsp salsa
>
> 1 Tbsp soured cream

Make your omelette according to Dana's Easy Omelette Method Method (see page 87), placing the taco filling over half of the omelette when you get to step 6. Cover, turn the heat down to low and cook until the cheese is melted (3 to 4 minutes). Follow the directions to finish making the omelette. Sprinkle with the cheese and top with salsa and soured cream.

Yield: 1 serving, with 3 grams of carbohydrate and 1 gram of fibre, for a total of 2 grams of usable carbs and 24 grams of protein. (Analysis does not include garnishes.)

 You can, if you like, jazz up this omelette with a little diced onion, olives or whatever else you like on a taco.

↷ Denver Omelette

> 1 Tbsp butter
>
> 2 eggs
>
> 50 g diced cooked ham
>
> 1/4 green pepper, cut in small strips and sautéed
>
> 1/4 small onion, sliced and sautéed
>
> 30 g Cheddar cheese, grated or sliced

Make your omelette according to Dana's Easy Omelette Method (see page 87), placing the cheese and the sautéed ham and vegetables over half of the omelette when you get to step 6.

Cover, turn the heat down to low and cook until the cheese is melted (3 to 4 minutes). Follow the directions to finish making the omelette.

Yield: 1 serving, with 7 grams of carbohydrate and 1 gram of fibre, for a total of 6 grams of usable carbs (and you can cut that by using seriously low-carb ham) and 25 grams of protein.

ᘒ Artichoke Parmesan Omelette

This is a terrific combination.

> 1 Tbsp butter
>
> 2 eggs, beaten
>
> 1 or 2 Tbsp mayonnaise
>
> 1 tinned artichoke heart, sliced
>
> 2 Tbsp grated Parmesan cheese

Make your omelette according to Dana's Easy Omelette Method (see page 87), spreading mayonnaise over one half of the omelette and topping it with the artichoke heart and Parmesan when you get to step 6. Cover, turn the heat down to low and cook until the cheese is melted (3 to 4 minutes). Follow the directions to finish making the omelette.

Yield: 1 serving, with 11 grams of carbohydrate and 5 grams of fibre, for a total of 6 grams of usable carbs and 18 grams of protein.

↷ 'My Day to Crab' Omelette

My grandmother never got to go crabbing when the family was at the shore, because she was too busy keeping house. Finally she declared that 'it's my day to crab!' If it's your day to crab, this omelette will cheer you up.

> 50 g tinned crab meat, flaked and picked over
>   for shells and cartilage
>
> 2 spring onions, sliced, including the crisp green part
>
> 1 Tbsp butter
>
> 2 eggs, beaten
>
> 1 to 2 Tbsp mayonnaise

Mix the crab meat with the spring onions and have the mixture standing by. Make your omelette according to Dana's Easy Omelette Method (see page 87), spreading mayonnaise over half the omelette and topping it with the crab and spring onion mixture when you get to step 6. Cover, turn the heat down to low and cook until the cheese is melted (3 to 4 minutes). Follow the directions to finish making the omelette.

Yield: 1 serving, with 3 grams of carbohydrate and 1 gram of fibre, for a total of 2 grams of usable carbs and 19 grams of protein.

ᔕ Left-over Lamblette

I adore roast lamb and the left-overs are far too good to throw away! This is very hearty and would make a great quick supper.

> 100 g left-over roast lamb, cut into small chunks
>
> 1/2 small onion
>
> 2 Tbsp grated Parmesan cheese
>
> 3 Tbsp mayonnaise
>
> 1/2 tsp prepared horseradish
>
> 1 Tbsp butter
>
> 2 eggs, beaten

1. In a food processor with the S-blade in place, mince the lamb and the onion together. When you have a pretty uniform consistency, add the Parmesan, mayonnaise and horseradish, and pulse until everything's combined. Place in a microwave-safe bowl and microwave on medium for just a minute or so, to warm through.

2. Make your omelette according to Dana's Easy Omelette Method (see page 87), placing the lamb mixture evenly over half of the omelette when you get to step 6. Cover, turn the heat down to low and cook until the eggs are set (60 to 90 seconds). Follow the directions to finish making the omelette.

Yield: 1 serving, with 6 grams of carbohydrate and 1 gram of fibre, for a total of 5 grams of usable carbs and 38 grams of protein.

ᔕ California Omelette

This is so reminiscent of the breakfasts they serve down near the waterfront in San Diego!

> 1 Tbsp olive oil
>
> 2 eggs, beaten
>
> 50 g Monterey Jack cheese, grated

3 or 4 slices ripe avocado

2 Tbsp alfalfa sprouts

Make your omelette according to Dana's Easy Omelette Method
(see page 87), placing the Monterey Jack over half of the omelette
when you get to step 6. Cover, turn the heat down to low and cook
until the cheese is melted (2 to 3 minutes). Arrange the avocado and
alfalfa over the cheese and follow the directions to finish making the
omelette.

Yield: 1 serving, with 4 grams of carbohydrate and 1 gram of fibre, for
a total of 3 grams of usable carbs and 26 grams of protein (and as
much potassium as a banana!).

ꕎ New York Sunday Brunch Omelette

My husband adores this. It's unbelievably filling, by the way.

1 Tbsp butter

2 eggs, beaten

50 g cream cheese, thinly sliced

50 g flaked smoked salmon

2 spring onions, sliced

Make your omelette according to Dana's Easy Omelette Method (see
page 87), placing the cream cheese over half of the omelette when you
get to step 6. (Don't try to spread the cream cheese – it won't work!)
Top with the salmon, cover, turn the heat down to low and cook until
hot all the way through (2 to 3 minutes). Scatter the spring onions over
the salmon and follow the directions to finish making the omelette.

Yield: 1 serving, with 5 grams of carbohydrate and 1 gram of fibre, for
a total of 4 grams of usable carbs and 22 grams of protein.

↻ Omelette Cordon Bleu

Tinned asparagus is fine for this, but you may cook fresh if
you prefer, or use left-over asparagus, should you have any.

>   1 Tbsp butter
>
>   2 eggs
>
>   30 g grated Gruyère cheese
>
>   30 g cooked ham
>
>   3 asparagus spears, cooked

Make your omelette according to Dana's Easy Omelette Method (see
page 87), placing the Gruyère, ham and asparagus over half of the
omelette when you get to step 6. Cover, turn the heat down to low and
cook until the cheese is melted (2 to 3 minutes). Follow the directions
to finish making the omelette.

Yield: 1 serving, with 3 grams of carbohydrate and 1 gram of fibre, for
a total of 2 grams of usable carbs and 25 grams of protein.

↻ Liver Sausage Omelette

Believe it or not, this makes a great omelette!

>   1 Tbsp butter
>
>   2 eggs, beaten
>
>   50 g liver sausage, mashed to soften
>
>   2 or 3 slices ripe tomato

Make your omelette according to Dana's Easy Omelette Method (see
page 87), spooning the mashed liver sausage over half of the omelette
and topping with the tomato slices when you get to step 6. Cover, turn
the heat down to low and cook until heated through (2 to 3 minutes).
Follow the directions to finish making the omelette.

Yield: 1 serving, with 4 grams of carbohydrate, a trace of fibre and 19
grams of protein.

◯ Pizza Omelette

Remember that the pizza sauce is where the carbs are in this omelette and govern yourself accordingly.

> 1 Tbsp olive oil
>
> 2 eggs, beaten
>
> 50 g mozzarella cheese
>
> 2 Tbsp bottled no-sugar-added pizza sauce, warmed
>
> 1 tsp grated Parmesan cheese

Make your omelette according to Dana's Easy Omelette Method (see page 87), placing the mozzarella over half of the omelette when you get to step 6. Cover, turn the heat down to low and cook until the cheese is melted (2 to 3 minutes). Follow the directions to finish making the omelette and top with the pizza sauce and Parmesan.

Yield: 1 serving, with 6 grams of carbohydrate (and you can lower that if you use the lowest-carb pizza sauce), no fibre and 24 grams of protein.

↻ Tuna Melt Omelette

It's worth making extra tuna salad just to make this omelette. This is a great lunch.

> 1 Tbsp butter
>
> 2 eggs, beaten
>
> 30 g Swiss cheese or processed Swiss-style triangles
>
> 2 or 3 Tbsp left-over Dana's Tuna Salad (see page 374), at room temperature

Make your omelette according to Dana's Easy Omelette Method (see page 87), placing the Swiss cheese over half of the omelette when you get to step 6. Spread the tuna salad over the cheese, cover, turn the heat down to low and cook until hot all the way through (3 to 4 minutes). Follow the directions to finish making the omelette.

Yield: 1 serving. The carb count of this omelette will depend on your recipe for tuna salad. The eggs and cheese will add only 2 grams of carbohydrate, no fibre and 19 grams of protein.

↻ Fajita Omelette

Again, a great way to use up left-overs!

> 1 Tbsp olive oil
>
> 2 eggs
>
> Left-over steak or chicken fajitas, warmed
>
> 1 Tbsp soured cream

Make your omelette according to Dana's Easy Omelette Method (see page 87), placing the fajitas over half of the omelette when you get to step 6. Cover, turn the heat down to low and cook for 2 to 3 minutes. Follow the directions to finish making the omelette and top with the soured cream.

Yield: 1 serving. The carb count for this omelette will depend on your recipe for fajitas. The eggs and soured cream will add only 2 grams of carbs, no fibre and 11 grams of protein.

↻ Chilli Omelette

Beef chilli or turkey chilli, it doesn't matter – they both make a great omelette.

> 1 Tbsp olive oil
>
> 2 eggs, beaten
>
> 100 g all-meat chilli, warmed
>
> 2 Tbsp grated Cheddar cheese
>
> 1 Tbsp soured cream

Make your omelette according to Dana's Easy Omelette Method (see page 87), placing the chilli over half of the omelette when you get to step 6. Top with the Cheddar, cover, turn the heat down to low and cook until the cheese is melted (2 to 3 minutes). Follow the directions to finish making the omelette and top with the soured cream.

Yield: 1 serving, with about 6 grams of carbohydrate (depending on your chilli recipe), no fibre and 33 grams of protein.

↻ Guacomelette

Should you happen to have left-over guacamole – an unlikely circumstance, I'll admit – this is a great way to finish it up.

> 1 Tbsp oil
>
> 2 eggs, beaten
>
> 50 g Monterey Jack cheese, sliced or grated
>
> 50 ml guacamole

Make your omelette according to Dana's Easy Omelette Method (see page 87), placing the cheese over half of the omelette when you get to step 6. Spread the guacamole over the cheese, cover, turn the heat down to low and cook until the cheese is melted (3 to 4 minutes). Follow the directions to finish making the omelette.

Yield: 1 serving, with 6 grams of carbohydrate and 1 gram of fibre, for a total of 5 grams of usable carbs and 26 grams of protein (and a whopping 487 milligrams of potassium!).

◯ Avocado Cheese Dip Omelette

This is perhaps the most decadently delicious omelette I know how to make and it's certainly a good enough reason to hide some of the Avocado Cheese Dip at your next party.

> 1 Tbsp olive oil
>
> 2 eggs, beaten
>
> 100 ml Avocado Cheese Dip (see page 56)

Make your omelette according to Dana's Easy Omelette Method (see page 87), placing the Avocado Cheese Dip over half of the omelette when you get to step 6. Cover, turn the heat down to low and cook until hot all the way through (3 to 4 minutes). Follow the directions to finish making the omelette.

Yield: 6 grams of carbohydrate and 1 gram of fibre, for a total of 5 grams of usable carbs and 19 grams of protein.

Frittatas

The frittata is the Italian version of the omelette and it involves no folding! If you're still intimidated by omelettes, try a frittata.

↻ Confetti Frittata

    100 g pork sausagemeat

    30 g green pepper, diced

    30 g sweet red pepper, diced

    30 g sweet red onion, diced

    30 g grated Parmesan cheese

    1 tsp Italian seasoning

    8 eggs, beaten

1. In a large, ovenproof frying pan, start browning and crumbling the sausage over a medium heat. As some fat starts to cook out of it, add the peppers and onion to the frying pan. Cook the sausage and vegetables until there's no pink left in the sausage. Spread the mixture into an even layer in the bottom of the frying pan.

2. Beat the Parmesan cheese and Italian seasoning into the eggs and pour the mixture over the sausage and veggies in the frying pan.

3. Turn the heat down to low and cover the frying pan. (If your frying pan doesn't have a lid, use foil.) Let the frittata cook until the eggs are just about set. This will take 25 to 30 minutes, but the size of your frying pan will affect the speed of cooking, so check periodically.

4. When all but the very top of the frittata is set, slide it under the grill for about 5 minutes, or until the top is golden. Cut into wedges and serve.

Yield: 4 servings, each with 4 grams of carbohydrate and 1 gram of fibre, for a total of 3 grams of usable carbohydrates and 17 grams of protein.

◯ Fajita Frittata

This makes a good supper for a family that is taco- and burrito-oriented.

> 3 Tbsp oil
>
> 1/2 green pepper, cut into small strips
>
> 1 small onion, sliced
>
> 1 boneless, skinless chicken breast, cut into thin strips
>
> 1/2 tsp chilli powder
>
> 1/2 tsp cumin
>
> 1 tsp lime juice
>
> 1/2 tsp salt
>
> 8 eggs, beaten
>
> 180 g grated Monterey Jack
> (plain or flavoured with chillies, whichever is preferred)
>
> Salsa
>
> Soured cream

1. Heat the oil in a large, heavy, ovenproof frying pan and sauté the green pepper, onion and chicken until the chicken has turned white and is cooked through. Stir in the chilli powder, cumin, lime juice and salt.

2. Spread the fajita mixture in an even layer in the bottom of the frying pan and pour the beaten eggs over it.

3. Turn the heat down to low and cover the frying pan. (If your frying pan doesn't have a lid, use foil.) Let the frittata cook until the eggs are mostly set, but still soft on top (7 to 10 minutes).

4. Scatter the cheese evenly over the top and slide the frying pan under the grill, about 10 cm from the heat, for 2 to 3 minutes or until the eggs are set and the cheese is just turning golden.

5. Cut in wedges, top each serving with a tablespoon of salsa and a couple of teaspoons of soured cream, and serve.

Yield: 4 servings, each with 5 grams of carbohydrate and 1 gram of fibre, for a total of 4 grams of usable carbs and 36 grams of protein.

◯ Artichoke Frittata

2 Tbsp butter
400 g quartered tinned artichoke hearts, drained
1 small onion, sliced
1 clove garlic
8 eggs, beaten
50 g grated Parmesan cheese
180 g grated Gruyère cheese

1. In a large, heavy frying pan sprayed with nonstick cooking spray, melt the butter and begin sautéing the artichoke hearts, onion and garlic over a medium to low heat.

2. While sautéing, stir the eggs and Parmesan together.

3. When the onions are limp, spread the vegetables evenly over the bottom of the frying pan and pour the egg mixture over them.

4. Turn the heat down to low and cover the frying pan. (If your frying pan doesn't have a lid, use foil.) Let the frittata cook until the eggs are mostly set (7 to 10 minutes).

5. Top with the grated Gruyère and slide the frying pan under the grill, about 10 cm from the heat. Grill for 2 to 3 minutes, or until the eggs are set on top and the cheese is lightly golden. Cut into wedges and serve.

Yield: 4 servings, each with 11 grams of carbohydrate and 4 grams of fibre, for a total of 7 grams of usable carbs and 29 grams of protein.

↻ Artichoke Mushroom Frittata

Similar to the Artichoke Frittata, but adding mushrooms and leaving out the Parmesan cheese gives an entirely different flavour.

3 Tbsp butter

300 g tinned, quartered artichoke hearts, drained

100 g fresh mushrooms, sliced

1/2 small onion, sliced

8 eggs, beaten

180 g grated Gruyère cheese

1. In a heavy frying pan, melt the butter and sauté the artichoke hearts, mushrooms and onion over a medium-low heat until the mushrooms are limp.

2. Spread the vegetables evenly over the bottom of the frying pan and pour the eggs over them.

3. Turn the heat down to low and cover the frying pan. (If your frying pan doesn't have a lid, use foil.) Let the frittata cook until mostly set (7 to 10 minutes).

4. Top with the Gruyère and slide the frying pan under the grill, about 10 cm from the heat. Grill for 2 to 3 minutes, or until the eggs are set on top and the cheese is lightly golden. Cut into wedges and serve.

Yield: 4 servings, each with 7 grams of carbohydrate and 3 grams of fibre, for a total of 4 grams of usable carbs and 26 grams of protein.

☽ Chorizo Frittata

A very 'South of the Border' dish. If you like chorizo Spanish sausage, you might cook some, drain it well and keep it in a container in the freezer so you can whip up one of these omelettes at short notice.

> 1 Tbsp oil
> 1/2 green pepper, diced
> 1 small onion, sliced
> 75 g cooked, crumbled, drained chorizo
> 75 ml salsa
> 8 eggs, beaten
> 180 g grated Cheddar or Monterey Jack

1. In a large, heavy frying pan over a medium heat, heat the oil and sauté the green pepper and onion for a few minutes, until tender-crisp. Add the chorizo and the salsa, stir well and heat through.

2. Spread the mixture into an even layer on the bottom of the frying pan and pour in the eggs.

3. Turn the heat down to low and cover the frying pan. (If your frying pan doesn't have a lid, use foil.) Let the frittata cook until the eggs are mostly set (7 to 10 minutes).

4. Top with the grated cheese and slide the frying pan under the grill, about 10 cm from the heat. Grill for 2 to 3 minutes, or until the eggs are set and the cheese is melted. Cut into wedges and serve.

Yield: 4 servings, each with 8 grams of carbohydrate and 1 gram of fibre, for a total of 7 grams of usable carbs and 32 grams of protein.

Scrambles

When both omelettes and frittatas are too much trouble, just make a scramble. The ways of varying scrambled eggs are endless, so you could have them several times a week and never get bored. These have been analysed assuming a three-egg serving, but if you want a lighter meal, leave out one egg and subtract 0.5 gram of carbohydrate and 6 grams of protein from my analysis.

↻ Country Scramble

This fast-and-filling family-pleaser is a great way to use up left-over ham.

> 1 Tbsp butter
> 50 g diced cooked ham
> 30 g diced green pepper
> 2 Tbsp diced onion
> 3 eggs, beaten
> Salt and freshly ground black pepper

1. Melt the butter in a frying pan over a medium heat. Add the ham, green pepper and onion, and sauté for a few minutes, until the onion is softened.

2. Pour in the eggs and scramble until they are set. Add salt and pepper to taste, and serve.

Yield: 2 servings, each with 7 grams of carbohydrate and 1 gram of fibre, for a total of 6 grams of usable carbs and 23 grams of protein.

> 🍓 Don't look at the number of servings and assume you can't feed a hungry family with a scramble – these recipes are easy to double, as long as you have a frying pan large enough to scramble in.

◌ Curry Scramble

With a green salad, this makes a great light supper whether you're a devoted curry lover or not.

> 1 Tbsp butter
>
> 1/4 tsp curry powder
>
> 1/2 clove garlic, crushed
>
> 3 eggs
>
> 1 Tbsp double cream
>
> 3 rashers bacon, cooked until crisp

1. Melt the butter in a heavy frying pan and sauté the curry powder and garlic over a medium-low heat for a minute or two.
2. Beat the eggs and cream together, pour into the frying pan and scramble until the eggs are set. Crumble bacon over the top.

   Yield: 1 serving, with 3 grams of carbohydrate, a trace of fibre and 23 grams of protein.

◌ Piperade

Pronounced 'peep-er-ahd', this Basque peasant dish has so many vegetables in it that it's a whole meal in itself.

> 2 Tbsp bacon fat or butter
>
> 30 g diced onion
>
> 50 g diced green pepper
>
> 100 ml chopped tomato (very ripe fresh, or tinned)
>
> 3 eggs, beaten
>
> Salt and freshly ground black pepper

1. Heat the bacon fat or butter in a heavy frying pan over the lowest heat. Add the onion and sauté for 5 to 7 minutes, or until the onion is soft.
2. Add the pepper and the tomato. Stir, then cover and cook at lowest heat for 15 minutes, stirring once or twice. (You want the vegetables to be quite soft.)

3. Pour in the eggs and scramble slowly until the eggs are just set. Add salt and pepper to taste, and serve.

   Yield: 1 serving, with 13 grams of carbohydrate and 3 grams of fibre, for a total of 10 grams of usable carbs and 18 grams of protein.

Hearty Piperade: Make just as you would the basic Piperade, but add 50 g diced ham for each serving. (This is a great time to use up any left-overs you've been saving.) Sauté the ham with the vegetables, then add the eggs and scramble as usual.

Yield: 1 serving, with 14 grams of carbohydrate and 3 grams of fibre, for a total of 11 grams of usable carbs and 24 grams of protein.

☉ Italian Scramble

This is a good quick supper. Serve it with a green salad and some garlic bread for the kids.

>   2 Tbsp olive oil
>   30 g diced green pepper
>   30 g chopped onion
>   1 clove garlic, crushed
>   3 eggs
>   1 Tbsp grated Parmesan cheese

1. Heat the olive oil in a heavy frying pan over a medium heat and sauté the pepper, onion and garlic for 5 to 7 minutes, or until the onion is translucent.
2. Beat the eggs with the Parmesan and pour into the frying pan. Scramble until the eggs are set, and serve.

   Yield: 1 serving, with 8 grams of carbohydrate and 1 gram of fibre, for a total of 7 grams of usable carbs and 17 grams of protein.

ʘ Mushroom Scramble

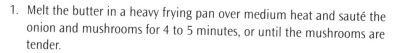

> 1 to 2 tsp butter
>
> 1 Tbsp minced onion
>
> 30 g cup sliced mushrooms
>
> 3 eggs, beaten

1. Melt the butter in a heavy frying pan over medium heat and sauté the onion and mushrooms for 4 to 5 minutes, or until the mushrooms are tender.

2. Add the eggs, scramble until set, and serve.

   Yield: 1 serving, with 3 grams of carbohydrate, a trace of fibre and 17 grams of protein.

ʘ Greek Scramble

> 2 Tbsp olive oil
>
> 1 Tbsp finely chopped onion
>
> 6 black Greek olives, chopped
>
> 3 eggs, beaten
>
> 30 g crumbled feta cheese

1. Heat the oil in heavy frying pan over medium heat. Sauté the onion for a minute or two, then add the olives and sauté for a minute more.

2. Pour in the eggs and add the feta. Scramble until set and serve.

   Yield: 1 serving, with 6 grams of carbohydrate, a trace of fibre and 22 grams of protein.

⌒ Chicken Liver Scramble

    1 Tbsp butter

    1/4 small onion, sliced

    1 chicken liver, cut into bite-sized pieces

    3 eggs, beaten

    Salt and freshly ground black pepper

1. Melt the butter in a heavy frying pan over a low heat. Sauté the onion for 2 to 3 minutes, then add the cut-up chicken liver.

2. Sauté, stirring frequently, until the chicken livers are no longer red but are still pinkish. Keep the heat very low and don't overcook!

3. When the chicken liver pieces are cooked through, pour in the eggs and scramble until they're set. Add salt and pepper to taste and serve.

    Yield: 1 serving, with 5 grams carbohydrates, a trace of fibre and 23 grams of protein.

⌒ Hot Dog Scramble

This is something your kids will eat without complaining.

    1 Tbsp butter

    1 hot dog, sliced into rounds

    1/2 small onion, chopped

    3 eggs, beaten

    30 g grated Cheddar cheese

1. Melt the butter in a heavy frying pan over a medium heat. Add the hot dog slices and onion and sauté until the onion is limp and the hot dog slices are starting to brown.

2. Add the eggs and scramble until half-set. Add the cheese and continue to scramble until they are set and the cheese is melted. Serve right away.

   Yield: 1 serving, with 8 grams of carbohydrate and 1 gram of fibre, for a total of 7 grams of usable carbs and 31 grams of protein.

Fried Eggs

Tired of all that scrambling? These next few recipes are, in one form or another, good old fried eggs.

☉ Fried Eggs Not Over Really Easy

If you're like me, you like your eggs over-easy, so that the whites are entirely set, but the yolks are still soft – but you find it maddeningly difficult to flip a fried egg without breaking the yolk. Here's the solution!

> 3 eggs
> 1/2 Tbsp butter or oil
> 1 tsp water

1. Spray your frying pan with nonstick cooking spray and place it over a medium to high heat. When the frying pan's hot, add the butter and coat the bottom of the pan with it. Crack your eggs into the frying pan – careful not to break the yolks! – and immediately cover them with a lid or some foil.

2. Wait about 2 minutes and check your eggs. They should be well set on the bottom, but still a bit runny on top. Add a teaspoon of water for each serving (you can guess this, as the quantity isn't vital), turn the heat down to low and cover the pan again.

3. Check after a minute; the steam will have cooked the tops of the eggs. If there's still a bit of uncooked white, give it another 30 seconds to 1 minute. Lift out and serve.

Yield: 1 serving, with about 1.5 grams of carbohydrate, no fibre and 16 grams of protein.

🍓 For the easiest eggs, use a frying pan that fits the number of eggs you're frying. A 20-cm job is just right for a single serving, but if you're doing two servings, use a big frying pan.

↻ Huevos Rancheros

1 Tbsp butter or oil

2 eggs

50 g Monterey Jack cheese, grated

3 Tbsp salsa (hot or mild, as you prefer)

1. Spray a heavy frying pan with nonstick cooking spray and set it over a medium heat. Add the butter or oil and crack the eggs into the frying pan. Turn down the heat and cover with a lid or some foil. Let the eggs fry for 4 to 5 minutes.

2. While the eggs are frying, warm the salsa in a saucepan or in the microwave.

3. When your fried eggs are set on the bottom but still a little underdone on top, scatter the cheese evenly over the eggs, add a teaspoon or two of water to the pan and cover it again. In a minute or two, the tops of the eggs should be set (but the yolks still soft) and the cheese melted.

4. Transfer the eggs to a plate with a fish slice, top with warmed salsa and serve.

Yield: 1 serving, with 4 grams of carbohydrate and 1 gram of fibre, for a total of 3 grams of usable carbohydrates and 25 grams of protein.

↻ Rodeo Eggs

This was originally a sandwich recipe, but it works just as well without the bread.

> 4 rashers bacon, chopped into 2.5-cm pieces
>
> 4 thin slices onion
>
> 4 eggs
>
> 4 thin slices Cheddar cheese

1. Begin frying the bacon in a heavy frying pan over a medium heat. When some fat has cooked out of it, push it aside and put the onion slices in beside it. Fry the onion on each side, turning carefully to keep the slices together, until it starts to look translucent. Remove the onion from the frying pan and set aside.

2. Continue frying the bacon until it's crisp. Pour off most of the fat and distribute the bacon bits evenly over the bottom of the frying pan. Break in the eggs and fry for a minute or two, until the bottoms are set but the tops are still soft. (If you like your yolks hard, break them with a fork; if you like them soft, leave them unbroken.)

3. Place a slice of onion over each yolk, then cover the onion with a slice of cheese. Add a teaspoon of water to the pan, cover and cook for 2 to 3 minutes, or until the cheese is thoroughly melted.

4. Cut into four separate eggs with the edge of a fish slice and serve.

Yield: This serves 2 if they're really hungry or 4 if they're only a bit peckish, or if they're kids. In 2 servings, each will have 4 grams of carbohydrate, a trace of fibre and 27 grams of protein.

↷ Gruyère Eggs

> 1 Tbsp butter
>
> 2 eggs
>
> 30 g grated Gruyère cheese
>
> 1 spring onion, sliced

1. Spray a heavy frying pan with nonstick cooking spray and melt the butter in it over a medium to high heat. Crack the eggs into the frying pan and fry them until the bottoms are done, but the tops are still a little soft.

2. Scatter the Gruyère over the eggs. Add a couple of teaspoons of water to the pan, cover and cook for another couple of minutes, until the cheese is melted and the whites are set.

3. Move the eggs to a serving plate, scatter the sliced spring onion on top and serve.

   Yield: 1 serving, with 2 grams of carbohydrate, a trace of fibre and 19 grams of protein.

↷ Oeufs avec le Beurre Noir

This just might be the easiest French cooking you'll ever do and it lends new interest to good old fried eggs.

> 1 Tbsp butter
>
> 3 eggs
>
> 1/2 tsp lemon juice

1. Spray a frying pan with nonstick cooking spray, put it over medium heat and melt half the butter in it. Crack the eggs into the pan and fry as desired. Remove the eggs to a plate and keep them warm.

2. Add the rest of the butter to the frying pan and let it cook until the foam on the butter shows a few flecks of brown. Stir in the lemon juice, pour the mixture over the eggs and serve.

   Yield: 1 serving, with 2 grams of carbohydrate, virtually no fibre and 17 grams of protein.

ᐭ Chilli Egg Puff

Serve this versatile dish for lunch or supper. And don't be afraid of those chillies: the mild ones aren't hot, just very flavourful. (If you like hot foods, feel free to use hotter chillies.)

> 5 eggs
>
> 3 Tbsp soya powder or rice protein powder
>
> 1/2 tsp salt
>
> 1/2 tsp baking powder
>
> 225 g cottage cheese
>
> 225 g Monterey Jack cheese, grated
>
> 3 Tbsp melted butter
>
> 100 g tinned mild green chillies, drained and diced

1. Preheat the oven to 180°C/Gas Mark 4. Spray a 11/2-litre casserole with nonstick cooking spray, or butter it generously.

2. Break the eggs into a bowl and beat them with a whisk. Whisk in the soya powder, salt and baking powder, mixing very well.

3. Beat in the cottage cheese, Monterey Jack, melted butter and chillies. Pour the whole thing into the prepared casserole, put it in the oven and bake for about 35 minutes. (It's all right if it's a little runny in the very centre when you spoon into it; that part acts as a sauce for the rest.)

Yield: 4 servings, each with 7 grams of carbohydrate and 1 gram of fibre, for a total of 6 grams of usable carbohydrates and 30 grams of protein.

 🍓 To find out how big your casserole is, fill it with water using a measuring cup. You want one that just holds 11/2 litres of water, although a little bigger or smaller won't matter.

ᕫ Ham and Cheese Puff

This dish reheats particularly well, making it the perfect left-over meal.

> 100 g ham
>
> 100 g Cheddar cheese
>
> 1 green pepper
>
> 100 g tinned mushrooms, well drained
>
> 5 eggs
>
> 3 Tbsp soya powder or unflavoured protein powder
>
> 1/2 tsp baking powder
>
> 1/2 tsp salt
>
> 225 g cottage cheese
>
> 2 Tbsp grated horseradish

1. Preheat the oven to 180°C/Gas Mark 4. Spray a 1 1/2-litre casserole with nonstick cooking spray, or butter it generously.

2. Use a food processor with the S-blade in place to mince the ham, cheese, green pepper and mushrooms together until finely chopped (no chunks of pepper or ham bigger than, say, a 1-cm cube).

3. In a large bowl, beat the eggs well. Add the soy or protein powder, baking powder and salt and beat well again.

4. Beat in the cottage cheese and horseradish and then add the chopped ham mixture.

5. Pour the egg mixture into the casserole. Bake for about 40 minutes, or until it's puffy and set but still jiggles a bit in the middle when you shake it.

Yield: 4 servings, each with 10 grams of carbohydrate and 2 grams of fibre, for a total of 8 grams of usable carbohydrates and 29 grams of protein.

🍓 The carb analysis of your recipe may vary from mine, depending on the ham, Cheddar and cottage cheese you use. As always, you can trim this carb count by using the lowest-carbohydrate ingredients you can find. And watch out when you buy your horseradish: I had to read a lot of labels to find one that had no added sugar.

♍ Turkey Club Puff

Disguise your Christmas left-overs in this delicious puff.

> 5 eggs
>
> 30 g soya powder or unflavoured protein powder
>
> 1/2 tsp salt
>
> 1/2 tsp baking powder
>
> 225 g cottage cheese
>
> 225 g Swiss cheese, cubed
>
> 75 ml melted butter
>
> 130 g cubed cooked turkey
>
> 6 rashers bacon, cooked until crisp

1. Preheat the oven to 180°C/Gas Mark 4. Spray a 1 1/2-litre casserole with nonstick cooking spray, or butter generously.
2. Break the eggs into a bowl and beat them with a whisk. Whisk in the soya powder, salt and baking powder, mixing very well.
3. Beat in the cottage cheese, Swiss cheese, melted butter and cubed turkey. Pour the whole thing into the greased casserole and crumble the bacon over the top. Bake for 35 to 40 minutes, or until set.

Yield: 5 servings, each with 5 grams of carbohydrate, a trace of fibre and 33 grams of protein.

Sausage, Egg and Cheese Bake

450 g pork sausagemeat (spicy or plain, as you prefer)

50 g diced green pepper

50 g diced onion

8 eggs

1/4 tsp freshly ground black pepper

100 g grated Cheddar cheese

100 g grated Swiss cheese

1. Preheat the oven to 180°C/Gas Mark 4.
2. In a large, heavy, ovenproof frying pan, start browning and crumbling the sausage over medium heat.
3. When some grease has cooked out of the sausage, add the green pepper and the onion and continue cooking, stirring frequently, until the sausage is no longer pink.
4. In a large bowl, beat the eggs and pepper together and stir in the cheeses.
5. Spread the sausage and vegetables evenly on the bottom of the frying pan and pour the egg and cheese mixture over it. Bake for 25 to 30 minutes, or until mostly firm but still just a little soft in the centre.

Yield: 6 servings, each with 4 grams of carbohydrate, a trace of fibre and 26 grams of protein.

⌒ Eggs Florentine

This is a great quick-and-simple supper for a tired night.

> 1 batch Creamed Spinach (see page 193)
> 4 eggs

1. Make Creamed Spinach according to the directions. After you've stirred in the cream and Parmesan cheese, spread the spinach on the bottom of your frying pan in an even layer.
2. Using the back of a spoon, make four evenly spaced hollows in the spinach and break an egg into each one. Turn the heat down to low and cover the frying pan.
3. Cook until the eggs are done (about 5 minutes). Divide into four sections with a fish slice to make serving easier.

Yield: 2 generous servings, each with 8 grams of carbohydrate and 4 grams of fibre, for a total of 4 grams of usable carbs and 20 grams of protein.

↻ Fried Mush

This idea would never have occurred to me, but it did occur to my friend Diana Lee. Ricotta cheese has a texture that's remarkably similar to that of cooked cornmeal. Based on that, she came up with this breakfast recipe, which she's allowed me to reprint from her book *Bread and Breakfast: Baking Low Carb II*.

> 4 large eggs
> 120 g ricotta cheese
> 75 ml double cream
> 2 Tbsp Splenda
> 1/2 tsp cinnamon
> 1/4 tsp nutmeg
> 1 tsp oil

1. Preheat the oven to 180°C/Gas Mark 4. Coat a 20 x 20-cm baking dish with nonstick cooking spray.

2. Mix all the ingredients together and pour the mixture into the prepared baking dish.

3. Bake for 20 to 30 minutes, until a knife inserted in the middle comes out clean. Cut into quarters.

4. Heat the oil in a frying pan and fry the four pieces until they're brown on both sides. Serve with your favourite topping.

   Yield: 4 servings, each with 2 grams of carbohydrate, a trace of fibre and 9 grams of protein.

↻ Yoghurt

When I tell people I make my own yoghurt, they react as if I'd said I could transmute base metals into gold. But as you'll see, it's easy to make and considerably cheaper than buying the commercial stuff. 'Officially', plain yoghurt has 12 grams of carbohydrate per 225 ml, but Dr Goldberg and Dr O'Mara point out in *GO-Diet* that most of the lactose (milk sugar) is converted to lactic acid, leaving only about 4 grams per cup. So if you like yoghurt, enjoy!

> 1 Tbsp plain yoghurt
> 180 to 225 g instant dried milk

🍓 For your first batch, you'll use store-bought plain yoghurt as a starter, but after that you can use a spoonful from the previous batch. Every so often it's good to start over with fresh, store-bought yoghurt, though.

1. Half-fill a clean 1-litre, snap-top container with water.
2. Put the plain yoghurt in the water and stir. Add the powdered milk and whisk until the lumps are gone.
3. Fill the container to the top with water, whisk it one last time and put the lid on.
4. Put your yoghurt-to-be in a warm place. I use a bowl lined with an old electric heating pad set on low, but any warm spot will do, such as inside an old-fashioned gas oven with a pilot light, or on the cooker top directly over the pilot light.
5. Leave for 12 hours or so. It should be thick and creamy at the end of this time, but if it's still a little thin, give it a few more hours. When it's ready, put it in the refrigerator and use it just like store-bought plain yoghurt. Or flavour it with vanilla or lemon extract and some Splenda. You can also stir in a spoonful of sugar-free preserves, or mash a few berries with a fork and stir them in.

Regarding those two different amounts of dry milk: using the full 225 g will give you richer, creamier yoghurt, with more protein and more calcium, but with a couple of extra grams of carbohydrate, as well. It's up to you. If you'd prefer, you could add 75 ml of double cream in place of 75 ml of the water, to make a higher-fat 'whole milk' yoghurt.

You could also make your yoghurt from liquid milk, but it's less easy. You have to scald the milk first and then cool it again before adding the 'starter' yoghurt, which seems like a lot of bother to me.

One last useful tip: if you find you use a lot of buttermilk – for example, if you decide you really enjoy low-carb muffins and such – you can make your own buttermilk exactly the same way you'd make yoghurt. Simply substitute a couple of tablespoons of commercial buttermilk for a 'starter' instead of the yoghurt.

CHAPTER FOUR

Breads, Muffins, Cereals and Other Grainy Things

Baked goods and other grain products, such as bread, cereal, pancakes, waffles and so on, are among the foods that new low-carb dieters miss most. They are also among the foods that sell best for the low-carb speciality outlets. Many of these products are quite good, but they're often quite expensive. With these recipes, you can make your own far more cheaply than you could buy them and they'll often taste even better, too. When you know you can have a slice of toast or a toasted cheese sandwich now and then, your worries about your ability to stay low carb for the long haul will fade.

About Low-Carb Bread

If you're regularly buying commercially made low-carbohydrate bread, it's time you bought a bread machine! Given the price of low-carb speciality products, you'll make your money back in no time.

All of the recipes below are designed for a 500-g bread machine, for the simple reason that that's the size I own. If you own a 750-g or a 1-kg machine, you can simply multiply the ingredients by one and a half or two, respectively. If your machine has a 'quick' option, don't use this – give your bread the longer, 'normal' cooking time. If it has 'white' and 'wholemeal' cycles, use 'wholemeal'.

If you're an experienced bread baker who doesn't own a bread machine but wants to try to make these recipes by hand, you certainly may, although I don't have all the instructions for you. What I can tell you is that tripling these quantities should give you the right amount for two average-size hand-made loaves.

All these breads will be far easier to slice evenly if you wait until they cool and use a good, sharp, serrated bread knife. But don't be surprised if the smell of freshly baked bread makes it impossible to wait!

One other note: as mentioned in Chapter 1, these recipes all use plain old activated yeast – not 'bread machine' or rapid-rise yeast. I can't guarantee the results if you use another sort of yeast.

◌ White Bread

This bread has a firm, fine texture and a great flavour.

> 250 ml water
>
> 30 g oat bran
>
> 2 Tbsp psyllium husks
>
> 75 g vital wheat gluten
>
> 50 g vanilla-flavoured whey protein powder
>
> 30 g rice protein powder
>
> 1 tsp salt
>
> 1 Tbsp oil
>
> 1 Tbsp Splenda
>
> 2 tsp yeast

Put the ingredients in your bread machine in the order given and run the machine. Remove the loaf from the machine and bread pan promptly, to cool.

Yield: About 10 slices, each with 5 grams of carbohydrate and 1 gram of fibre, for a total of 4 grams of usable carbs and 24 grams of protein.

꩜ 'Wholewheat' Bread

Slice this extra-thin so you can 'afford' two slices and it makes a great grilled cheese sandwich.

125 ml water

125 ml double cream

1 Tbsp soft butter

1 egg

1 tsp salt

75 g vital wheat gluten

2 Tbsp raw wheat germ

2 Tbsp wheat bran

30 g psyllium husks

50 g oat flour

50 g vanilla-flavoured whey protein powder

2 tsp yeast

Put the ingredients in your bread machine in the order given and run the machine. Remove the loaf from the machine and bread pan promptly, to cool.

Yield: About 10 slices, each with 13 grams of carbohydrate and 7.5 grams of fibre, for a total of 5.5 grams of usable carbs and 19 grams of protein (more than two eggs!).

◯ Seed Bread

Nutty and filling! Make sure you chop the sunflower seeds, though, or they'll mostly sink to the bottom of your loaf.

>125 ml warm water
>
>125 ml double cream
>
>1 Tbsp oil
>
>1 egg
>
>1/2 tsp salt
>
>75 g vital wheat gluten
>
>50 g oat bran
>
>50 g ground almonds
>
>50 g sunflower seeds, coarsely chopped
>
>30 g rice protein powder
>
>2 Tbsp flax seed
>
>1/2 tsp black treacle
>
>1 tsp Splenda
>
>2 tsp yeast

Put the ingredients in your bread machine in the order given and run the machine. Remove the loaf from the machine and bread pan promptly, to cool.

Yield: About 10 slices, each with 8 grams of carbohydrate and 2 grams of fibre, for a total of 6 grams of usable carbs and 21 grams of protein.

↻ My Mother's Oatmeal Treacle Bread

My de-carbed version of the bread that won my mother first prize at the county fair. This has the best texture of any low-carb bread I know!

   30 g rolled oats

   2 Tbsp raw wheatgerm

   75 ml boiling water

   1 Tbsp black treacle

   1 Tbsp Splenda

   1 Tbsp soft butter

   1 tsp salt

   50 g ground almonds

   75 g vital wheat gluten

   30 g vanilla-flavoured whey protein powder

   2 Tbsp water

   2 tsp yeast

1. Put the rolled oats and wheatgerm in the bread pan of your bread machine. Pour the boiling water over them and let them sit for at least 15 minutes.

2. Add everything else in the order given and run the machine. Remove the loaf from the machine and bread pan promptly, to cool.

   Yield: 8 slices, each with 5.5 grams of carbohydrate and 0.5 gram of fibre, for a total of 5 grams of usable carbs and 25 grams of protein.

⌒ Sesame Seed Bread

I like to eat this toasted, along with a bowl of soup.

> 250 ml warm water
>
> 30 g oat bran
>
> 30 g wheat bran
>
> 30 g sesame seeds
>
> 30 g vanilla-flavoured whey protein powder
>
> 100 g vital wheat gluten
>
> 1 1/4 tsp salt
>
> 1 Tbsp black treacle
>
> 2 tsp yeast

Put the ingredients in your bread machine in the order given and run the machine. Remove the loaf from the machine and bread pan promptly, to cool.

Yield: 12 slices, each with 6.5 grams of carbohydrate and 1.7 grams of fibre, for a total of 4.8 grams of usable carbs and 18 grams of protein.

⌒ Rye Bread

I love rye bread and it's so nice to be able to have it again! Leave out the caraway if you don't like it, but to many of us, it's just not proper rye bread without it.

> 250 ml warm water
>
> 50 g wheat bran
>
> 50 g whole grain rye flour
>
> 30 g rice protein powder
>
> 75 g vital wheat gluten
>
> 1 tsp salt
>
> 1 Tbsp oil
>
> 1 Tbsp caraway seeds
>
> 1 1/2 tsp yeast

Put the ingredients in your bread machine in the order given and run the machine. Remove the loaf from the machine and bread pan promptly, to cool.

Yield: 12 slices, each with 6.8 grams of carbohydrate and 2 grams of fibre, for a total of 4.8 grams of usable carbs and 14 grams of protein.

꩜ Cinnamon Raisin Bread

Sweet and cinnamony! Have a slice of this toasted and spread with butter for breakfast and you'll never know you're on a low-carb diet!

> 180 ml plus 2 Tbsp warm water
>
> 30 g oat bran
>
> 50 g ground almonds
>
> 40 g vanilla-flavoured whey protein powder
>
> 1 1/2 tsp cinnamon
>
> 75 g plus 3 Tbsp vital wheat gluten
>
> 30 g Splenda
>
> 1 Tbsp oil
>
> 1 tsp salt
>
> 2 tsp yeast
>
> 2 Tbsp raisins, each snipped in half

Put the ingredients in your bread machine in the order given and run the machine. Remove the loaf from the machine and bread pan promptly, to cool.

Yield: 12 slices, each with 6 grams of carbohydrate and 0.6 gram of fibre, for a total of 5.4 grams of usable carbs and 19 grams of protein.

🍓 The reason you cut the raisins in half is to let them distribute more evenly throughout the bread; even so, there aren't a lot of them, I'll admit. That's because the raisins are the highest-carb part of this bread. If you prefer, you can leave them whole so each one will be more noticeable.

⌒ Heart-y Bread

So named because both rice bran and flax are known to lower cholesterol. Want more good news? This bread tastes as good as it is good for you.

> 250 ml plus 2 Tbsp water
>
> 30 g rice bran
>
> 30 g flax seed meal
>
> 100 g vital wheat gluten
>
> 40 g vanilla-flavoured whey protein powder
>
> 2 tsp black treacle
>
> 1 tsp salt
>
> 1 Tbsp oil
>
> 2 tsp yeast

Put the ingredients in your bread machine in the order given and run the machine. Remove the loaf from the machine and bread pan promptly, to cool.

Yield: 11 slices, each with 6.7 grams of carbohydrate and 2.6 grams of fibre, for a total of 4.1 grams of usable carbs and 19 grams of protein.

◯ French Toast

Make this for breakfast some lazy weekend morning and the family will think you're cheating on your diet!

> 4 eggs
>
> 125 ml double cream
>
> 125 ml water
>
> 1 tsp vanilla extract (optional)
>
> 6 slices low-carb bread of your choice (white, 'whole wheat', cinnamon raisin and oatmeal treacle are all good choices)
>
> Butter

1. Beat together the eggs, double cream, water and vanilla extract (if using) and place the mixture in a shallow dish, such as a pie plate.
2. Soak the slices of bread in the mixture until they're well saturated; you'll have to do them one or two at a time. Let each slice soak for at least 5 minutes, turning once.
3. Fry each soaked piece of bread in plenty of butter over a medium heat in a heavy frying pan or griddle. Brown well on each side.
4. Serve with sugar-free syrup, cinnamon and Splenda, or sugar-free jam, as you choose.

Yield: 6 servings. The carb count will vary with the type of bread you use, but the egg and cream add only 2 grams of carbs, no fibre and 4 grams of protein per slice.

↻ English Muffins

Yes, you can make your own low-carb English Muffins. The yoghurt is what gives them that characteristic, mildly sour taste.

  125 ml warm water

  125 ml yoghurt

  1 tsp salt

  70 g vital wheat gluten

  30 g psyllium husks

  2 Tbsp raw wheat germ

  30 g wheat bran

  50 g oat flour

  50 g vanilla-flavoured whey protein powder

  1 1/2 tsp yeast

1. Put the ingredients in your bread machine in the order given and run until the end of the 'rise' cycle. Remove the dough from the machine.

2. Using just enough oat flour on your work surface to keep the dough from sticking, pat the dough out to 1 cm thick.

3. Using a washed tin can with both ends removed as a cutter, cut rounds from the dough. Cover them with a clean cloth, set them aside in a warm place and let them rise for about 1 hour, or until they've doubled in bulk.

4. Heat a heavy frying pan or griddle over a medium to low heat. Scatter the surface lightly with wheat germ to prevent sticking and place as many muffins in the frying pan as will fit easily. Let them cook for about 6 minutes per side, or until they're browned. Eat these just like you would traditional English muffins – split them, toast them and butter them.

Yield: About 6 muffins, or 12 servings, each with 13 grams of carbohydrate and 6.5 grams of fibre, for a total of 6.5 grams of usable carbs and 14 grams of protein.

⌒ Crunchy Protein Waffles

    50 g raw wheatgerm

    100 g soya powder

    100 g vanilla-flavoured whey protein powder

    1/2 tsp salt

    1 Tbsp Splenda

    50 g sesame seeds

    3 eggs

    200 ml double cream

    125 ml water

    4 to 6 Tbsp oil or melted butter

1. Preheat a waffle iron.
2. Combine the wheatgerm, soya powder, whey protein powder, salt, Splenda and sesame seeds in a large bowl.
3. Separate the eggs, reserving the yolks. Whip the whites until they're stiff, and set them aside.
4. Whisk the cream, water and oil together with the egg yolks and pour them into the dry ingredients. Mix well and gently fold in the egg whites.
5. Use a cup to pour the batter on to your waffle iron and bake until they're golden brown and crispy. Serve with butter and sugar-free syrup, sugar-free jam, cinnamon and Splenda, or – my favourite – thawed, frozen strawberries and whipped cream.

Yield: This depends on the size of your waffle iron; mine makes average waffles and I get about 10 servings, each with 8 grams of carbohydrate and 2 grams of fibre, for a total of 6 grams of usable carbs and 10 grams of protein.

Kim's Dutch Baby

A Dutch Baby is a big, puffy, eggy, baked pancake and my sister Kim adores them, so I came up with this recipe for her. It's great for a late Sunday breakfast.

> 2 Tbsp butter
>
> 50 g low-carb bake mix
>
> 30 g rice protein powder
>
> 30 g Splenda
>
> 1/2 tsp salt
>
> 1/2 tsp cinnamon
>
> 4 eggs
>
> 250 ml milk and cream mixed
>
> 2 tsp canola (rapeseed) or other vegetable oil
>
> 1 tsp vanilla extract

1. Preheat the oven to 220°C/Gas Mark 7. It is essential that the oven be up to temperature before putting your Dutch Baby in, so don't combine the wet and dry ingredients until the oven's ready.

2. Spray a large, cast-iron frying pan or a 25-cm pie tin with nonstick cooking spray and melt the butter in the bottom. Set aside.

3. In a bowl, combine the bake mix, protein powder, Splenda, salt and cinnamon.

4. In a separate bowl, beat together the eggs, milk and cream mixture, oil and vanilla extract and whisk it vigorously for a couple of minutes. (Beating air into it will make the Dutch Baby puff more.)

5. Beat in the dry ingredients just until well-mixed and pour the batter into the prepared tin.

6. Bake for 20 minutes; reduce the temperature to 180°C/Gas Mark 4 and bake for another 3 to 5 minutes.

🍓 Your Dutch Baby will come out gloriously puffed, but it will quickly sink in the middle. That's fine – it's supposed to. It will be crunchy around the edges and soft in the middle.

The traditional accompaniment for a Dutch Baby is a sprinkle of lemon juice and icing sugar, but lemon and Splenda works well. You could also try cinnamon and Splenda, plain Splenda, some thawed frozen berries or sugar-free jam. Delicious!

Yield: 2 big servings, or 4 small ones (if you serve 4, you'll want some sausage or something along with it, I think). Depending on the brand of low-carb bake mix and protein powder you use, calculate 20 to 25 grams of carbohydrate in the whole Dutch Baby and 3 to 4 grams of fibre. 2 servings would each have about 10 grams of usable carbs and about 38 grams of protein.

ᓂ Muesli

This isn't super-low in carbs and it's really more for eating during maintenance than during weight loss. But it's far lower in carbs than standard muesli, high in protein, very filling and best of all, it tastes like real cereal!

> 250 g rolled oats
>
> 150 g sunflower seeds
>
> 100 g sesame seeds
>
> 70 g wheatgerm
>
> 50 g unsweetened desiccated coconut
>
> 50 g chopped walnuts
>
> 50 g slivered almonds
>
> 50 g wheat bran
>
> 30 g flax seeds
>
> 1 tsp cinnamon
>
> 50 g Splenda
>
> 75 g vanilla-flavoured whey protein powder
>
> 1/4 tsp black treacle
>
> 125 ml canola (rapeseed) oil

1. Preheat the oven to 130ºC/Gas Mark 1/2.

2. In a large, shallow roasting tin, combine the rolled oats, sunflower seeds, sesame seeds, wheatgerm, coconut, walnuts, almonds, bran, flax seeds, cinnamon, Splenda and protein powder, mixing them very well.

3. Stir the treacle into the oil; it won't really blend with it, but it will help the treacle get distributed evenly. Pour the mixture over the dry ingredients and stir until it's uniformly distributed.

4. Place in the oven and toast for an hour, stirring once or twice. Store in a tightly covered container. Serve topped with cream or half milk and half cream.

Yield: Makes about 16 servings of 60 g, each with 21.8 grams of carbohydrate and 6 grams of fibre, for a total of 15.8 grams of usable carbs and 11.6 grams of protein.

↻ Evelyn's Muesli

From *Lowcarbezine!* reader Evelyn Nordahl, a much lower-carbohydrate muesli recipe.

> 100 g Textured Vegetable Protein granules
> (available at health food stores)
>
> 1 tsp cinnamon
>
> 2 Tbsp Splenda
>
> 50 g unsweetened desiccated coconut
>
> 50 g chopped pecans
>
> 50 g chopped, sliced or slivered almonds

1. Combine the Textured Vegetable Protein granules, cinnamon and Splenda in a plastic or glass container, large enough to hold all the ingredients.

2. Spread the coconut, pecans and almonds on a baking tray and toast under grill just until the coconut starts to brown. Remove from the grill and cool.

3. Add the toasted nuts to the granule mixture, attach the lid and shake to mix.

Yield: About 10 servings of 25 g, each with 9 grams of carbohydrate and 6 grams of fibre, for a total of 3 grams of usable carbs and 17 grams of protein.

🍓 Evelyn eats this muesli topped with about 2 tablespoons of water and 2 tablespoons of double cream; she says it's 'satisfying, crunchy and delicious'.

ᓚ Almond Pancake and Waffle Mix

This makes nice, tender pancakes and waffles that have a nutty taste and a texture similar to cornmeal pancakes and waffles.

> 250 g almond meal
>
> 50 g oat bran
>
> 50 g vanilla-flavoured whey protein powder
>
> 50 g rice protein powder
>
> 2 Tbsp wheat bran
>
> 2 Tbsp raw wheatgerm
>
> 2 Tbsp vital wheat gluten
>
> 2 1/2 Tbsp baking powder
>
> 1 1/2 tsp salt

1. Assemble all the ingredients in a food processor with the S-blade in place. Run the processor for a minute or so, stopping once or twice to shake it so everything will be well combined.

2. Store the mix in an airtight container in the refrigerator.

Yield: Makes about 4 servings of 100 g, each with 33 grams of carbohydrate and 3 grams of fibre, for a total of 30 grams of usable carbs and 36 grams of protein.

↻ Pancakes from Almond Mix

I like to eat these topped with sugar-free grape jelly, but you could also serve them with sugar-free syrup, sugar-free jam, thawed sugar-free frozen fruit, or Splenda and cinnamon.

> 200 g Almond Pancake and Waffle Mix (see left)
>
> 2 eggs
>
> 250 ml water
>
> 1 Tbsp canola (rapeseed), peanut or sunflower oil

1. Spray a frying pan or griddle with nonstick cooking spray and set it over a medium heat.

2. Mix all the ingredients with a whisk and drop the batter by the tablespoonful on to the griddle or frying pan. Cook as you would traditional pancakes, turning to brown lightly on each side. Stir the batter between batches to prevent it from settling.

Yield: About 16 pancakes, each with 4 grams of carbohydrate, a trace of fibre and 6 grams of protein.

🍓 For a little added flavour, melt a little butter on the griddle or frying pan before you cook the batter.

◯ Waffles from Almond Mix

These remind me a lot of cornmeal waffles and they're really good with bacon on the side.

>100 g Almond Pancake and Waffle Mix (see page 138)
>
>1 tsp Splenda
>
>125 ml half milk and half cream, mixed
>
>1 egg
>
>75 ml oil

1. Preheat a waffle iron.
2. In a mixing bowl, stir together the mix and Splenda.
3. In a separate bowl, stir together the milk and cream mixture, egg and oil, and pour the mixture into the dry ingredients. Stir only until everything's wet and there are no big lumps of dry mix.
4. Bake in the waffle iron according to the machine's directions. Serve with butter and sugar-free syrup, cinnamon and Splenda, sugar-free jam, or another low-carb topping of your choice.

Yield: In my waffle iron, this makes 6 servings, each with 5 grams of carbohydrate, a trace of fibre and 6 grams of protein.

ꙩ Perfect Protein Pancakes

These taste just like our mothers used to make – you'd never guess they were low carb.

> 2 eggs
> 100 g ricotta cheese
> 30 g vanilla-flavoured whey protein powder
> 1/2 tsp baking powder
> 1/8 tsp salt

1. Spray a heavy frying pan or griddle with nonstick cooking spray and place it over a medium heat.
2. In a mixing bowl, whisk together the eggs and ricotta until quite smooth. Whisk in the whey protein powder, baking powder and salt, only mixing until well combined.
3. Drop batter on to the frying pan or griddle by the tablespoonful. When the bubbles on the surface of the pancakes are breaking and staying broken, flip them and cook the other side.
4. Serve with butter and sugar-free syrup, sugar-free jam, Splenda and cinnamon, or a few mashed berries sweetened with Splenda.

Yield: 14 'mini' pancakes, each with about 0.6 gram of carbohydrate, no fibre and 2.5 grams of protein.

> ꙮ I'd call five of these tiny pancakes a 'serving', so double or triple your batches accordingly. Even better, make extras to freeze and you can warm them up in the oven for a healthy breakfast on a hurried morning.

⟲ Courgette Pancakes

I know the name sounds strange, but if you like courgette bread you should really try Vicki Cash's pancakes.

3 eggs (or 2 eggs and 2 egg whites)
2 Tbsp half milk and half cream, mixed
75 ml canola (rapeseed) oil
100 g low-carb bake mix
1 tsp cinnamon
1/2 tsp salt
1/2 tsp nutmeg
1 small courgette, grated

1. Mix the eggs, milk and cream mixture, oil, bake mix, cinnamon, salt and nutmeg together until no longer lumpy. Mix in the courgette and let the batter sit for 5 minutes.

2. Meanwhile, spray a nonstick griddle or frying pan with canola cooking spray and place it over a medium to high heat.

3. Pour the batter on to the griddle about 75 ml at a time. Flip the pancakes when their edges are slightly brown and cook thoroughly on both sides. Serve with butter or puréed berries or peaches.

Yield: 3 servings. The carb count will vary with the brand of low-carb bake mix you use, but calculate about 5 grams of usable carbs and about 20 grams of protein.

↻ Cheese Popovers

These are from *Lo-Carb Cooking*, by Debra Rowland and they are tasty!

> 100 g almond flour
>
> 1/2 tsp salt
>
> 250 ml cream
>
> 2 eggs
>
> 1 Tbsp melted butter
>
> 30 g grated Cheddar cheese

1. Preheat the oven to 220°C/Gas Mark 7.
2. Beat the flour, salt, cream, eggs and butter until smooth. Stir in the cheese.
3. Spoon the mixture into 8 muffin cups. Bake for 15 minutes, reduce heat to 180°C/Gas Mark 4 and bake for 25 additional minutes, or until golden brown. Serve immediately.

Yield: 8 servings, each with 6 grams of carbohydrate, a trace of fibre and 10 grams of protein.

↻ Buttermilk Bran Muffins

Tender, moist, sweet and perfumed with cinnamon. And, using the *GO-Diet's* figure of 4 grams of carbohydrate per 250 ml of buttermilk, not a bad deal, carbohydrate-wise.

> 80 g wheat bran
>
> 80 g plus 2 Tbsp vanilla-flavoured whey protein powder
>
> 2 Tbsp vital wheat gluten
>
> 1/4 tsp salt
>
> 1 tsp baking soda
>
> 30 g Splenda
>
> 1/2 tsp cinnamon
>
> 50 g chopped walnuts or pecans (optional)
>
> 250 ml buttermilk
>
> 1 egg
>
> 3 Tbsp oil
>
> 1 Tbsp black treacle

1. Preheat the oven to 180°C/Gas Mark 4.
2. In a mixing bowl, combine the wheat bran, protein powder, wheat gluten, salt, baking soda, Splenda, cinnamon and nuts, and stir until well combined.
3. In a measuring jug, stir together the buttermilk, egg, oil and treacle.
4. Spray 10 cups of a muffin tin well with nonstick cooking spray.
5. Give the wet ingredients one last stir and pour them into the dry ingredients. With a spoon, stir just long enough to moisten all the dry ingredients. Do not over-mix! The batter should look rough and a few lumps are fine.
6. Spoon into the prepared muffin cups, dividing the mixture evenly (the muffin cups should be about two-thirds full).
7. Bake for 20 to 25 minutes and turn out of the muffin cups on to a wire rack to cool.

Yield: 10 muffins, each with 13.5 carbohydrates and 6 grams of fibre, for a total of 7.5 grams of usable carbs and 9 grams of protein.

🍓 Try doubling this recipe and freezing the left-overs. Thaw the muffins a few at a time to grab on those mornings when you need a quick, nutritious breakfast.

◔ Soured Cream, Lemon and Poppy Seed Muffins

120 g almond meal

100 g vanilla-flavoured whey protein powder

1 1/2 tsp baking powder

1/2 tsp salt

30 g Splenda

1 tsp baking soda

2 Tbsp poppy seeds

225 ml soured cream

2 eggs

2 Tbsp water

2 tsp lemon extract

Grated peel of 1 lemon

1. Preheat the oven to 200°C/Gas Mark 6.
2. In a mixing bowl, combine the almond meal, protein powder, baking powder, salt, Splenda, baking soda and poppy seeds and stir until well combined.
3. In a separate bowl, combine the soured cream, eggs, water, lemon extract and lemon peel, and whisk together well.
4. Spray 16 muffin tins well with nonstick cooking spray. (You can use paper liners, if you prefer.)
5. Pour the soured cream mixture into the dry ingredients and stir together with just a few strokes – just enough to make the mixture evenly moist. Do not over-mix.
6. Spoon the batter evenly into muffin cups and bake for 20 minutes.

Yield: Makes 16 muffins, each with 5.25 grams of carbohydrate and 1 gram of fibre, for a total of 4.25 grams of usable carbs and 7.75 grams of protein.

⟳ Soured Cream Coffee Cake

Here's a coffee cake for you, from Diana Lee's invaluable *Baking Low Carb*. Notice that this has enough protein to be a satisfying breakfast all by itself.

Cake
225 ml soured cream
150 ml oil
125 ml water
3 eggs
2 tsp almond extract
130 g vanilla-flavoured whey protein powder
30 g oat flour
2 Tbsp vital wheat gluten
1 tsp baking soda
1 Tbsp baking powder
2 tsp cinnamon
60 g Splenda
1 Tbsp liquid sweetener (such as Sweet 'n' Low liquid)

Topping
50 g chopped nuts
2 Tbsp Splenda
1/4 tsp cinnamon

1. Preheat the oven to 180°C/Gas Mark 4 and grease a springform tin.

2. Combine the soured cream, oil, water, eggs and almond extract. Mix these ingredients together well.

3. Add the protein powder, oat flour, vital wheat gluten, baking soda, baking powder, cinnamon, Splenda and liquid sweetener. Mix until blended and pour into the prepared tin.

4. Combine the nuts, Splenda and cinnamon to make the topping and sprinkle it over the batter in the springform tin. Bake for 30 to 35 minutes.

   Yield: 12 slices, each with 9 grams of carbohydrate and 1 gram of fibre, for a total of 8 grams of usable carbs and 24 grams of protein.

ꙮ 'Corn Bread'

This low-carb alternative comes from Debra Rowland's *Lo-Carb Cooking*.

> 225 g butter, softened
>
> 2 tsp Splenda
>
> 5 eggs
>
> 150 g almond flour
>
> 50 g hazelnut flour
>
> 1 tsp baking powder
>
> 2 tsp liquified butter

1. Preheat the oven to 180ºC/Gas Mark 4.
2. Cream butter and sweetener well. Add the eggs one at a time, beating well after each.
3. Mix the almond and hazelnut flours with baking powder and add this dry mixture to the egg mixture a little at a time while continuously beating.
4. Mix in the liquified butter and pour the batter into a 25-cm springform or cake tin. Bake for 50 to 55 minutes.

   🍓 Debra Rowland is lucky enough to have access to a shop that sells almond and hazelnut flours. I'm not so lucky, so I make my own by grinding almonds and hazelnuts in my food processor, and it works fine. So don't be afraid to try it 'from scratch'.

↻ Hot Almond Cereal

Here's a recipe for all of you who miss hot cereal in the morning. Loaded with fibre, it's a great way to get the health benefits of flax – not to mention that it's really, really tasty

> 130 g flax seeds
>
> 115 g ground almonds
>
> 50 g oat bran
>
> 150 g wheat bran
>
> 115 g vanilla-flavoured whey protein powder

1. Preheat the oven to 150ºC/Gas Mark 2.

2. Grind your flax seeds in a food processor with the S-blade in place. They take a while to grind up, so you may have to run the processor for several minutes. (You can buy flax seed meal if you prefer, but flax seed oil spoils pretty quickly after the seeds are ground, so I much prefer to grind my own.)

3. While the food processor is running, lightly toast your ground almonds by putting them in a shallow baking tin in the oven for 5 minutes or so.

4. When the flax seed is ground and the almonds are toasted, combine them with the oat bran, wheat bran and protein powder and store in an airtight container.

5. To make a bowl of cereal, put 50 g of the mixture in a bowl and add 150 ml of boiling water and a pinch of salt. Stir and let your cereal sit for a few minutes before eating.

Yield: About 9 servings, each with about 16 grams of carbohydrate and 9 grams of fibre, for a total of 7 grams of usable carbs and 11 grams of protein.

> 🍓 Try this with a little Splenda and cream, or even a little cinnamon. Personally, I like to add just a drop or two of black treacle to give it a brown-sugar flavour without many extra carbs.

⟲ Cinnamon Hot Cereal

For those of you who used to eat your oatmeal with cinnamon and sugar. Add Splenda and cream to taste.

> 115 g ground flax seeds
>
> 115 g ground almonds
>
> 50 g oat bran
>
> 150 g wheat bran
>
> 50 g vanilla-flavoured whey protein powder
>
> 2 tsp cinnamon

1. Combine all the ingredients well and store in an airtight container.
2. To make a bowl of cereal, put 50 g of the mixture in a bowl and add 150 ml boiling water and a pinch of salt. Stir and let your cereal sit for a few minutes before eating.

   Yield: About 5 servings, each with 15 grams of carbohydrate and 9.5 grams of fibre, for a total of 5.5 grams of usable carbs and 11 grams of protein.

◌ Hot Chocolate Bran Cereal

Remember Cocopops? Here's a chocolate hot cereal for the kid in you, from Diana Lee's *Bread and Breakfast: Baking Low Carb II.*

> 30 g toasted wheat bran
>
> 1 sachet low-carb, sugar-free hot chocolate mix
>
> 30 g vanilla-flavoured whey protein powder
>
> 1 Tbsp ground almonds
>
> 100 ml water

1. Whisk the bran, hot chocolate mix, whey protein and almonds together. Add the water and mix until combined.

2. Microwave on full power for 30 seconds and stir. Microwave for another 30 seconds (if you want this thicker, microwave it longer) and serve with cream.

   Yield: 1 serving. With the lowest-carb cocoa mix, this has 17 grams of carbohydrate and 9 grams of fibre, for a total of 8 grams of usable carbs and 20 grams of protein.

About Making Low-Carb Crackers

To make all these cracker recipes, you will need a roll of nonstick baking parchment, available at kitchen shops or supermarkets everywhere. Do not try to make these crackers direct on a baking tray, no matter how well greased, or you will be sorry – it will take you hours to scrape them off!

◌ Sunflower Parmesan Crackers

These have a great, crunchy texture and a wonderful flavour.

> 200 g raw, hulled sunflower seeds
>
> 75 g grated Parmesan cheese
>
> 75 ml water

1. Preheat the oven to 170°C/Gas Mark 3.

2. Put the sunflower seeds and Parmesan in a food processor with the S-blade in place and process until the sunflower seeds are a fine meal with almost a flour consistency. Add the water and pulse the processor until the dough is well blended, soft and sticky.

3. Cover your baking tray with a piece of baking parchment. Turn the dough out on to the parchment, tear off another sheet of parchment and put it on top of the dough.

4. Through the top sheet of parchment, use your hands to press the dough into as thin and even a sheet as you can. Take the time to get the dough quite thin – the thinner the better, so long as there are no holes in the dough. Peel off the top layer of parchment and use a thin, sharp, straight-bladed knife or a pizza cutter to score the dough into squares or diamonds.

5. Bake for about 30 minutes, or until evenly browned. Peel off the parchment, break along the scored lines and let the crackers cool. Store them in a container with a tight lid.

Yield: How many carbs per cracker? It will vary with the size and thickness of your crackers. I get about 6 dozen, each with just a trace of carbohydrate, a trace of fibre and 1 gram of protein. But you could eat the whole batch for just 13 grams of usable carbohydrates, so who's counting?

⟳ Sunflower Sesame Crackers

200 g raw, hulled sunflower seeds

75 g sesame seeds

1/2 tsp salt

75 ml water

1. Preheat the oven to 170°C/Gas Mark 3.
2. In a food processor with the S-blade attached, grind the sunflower seeds to a fine meal.
3. Add the sesame seeds and salt, and pulse the food processor just long enough to combine. (You want the sesame seeds to stay whole.) Add the water and pulse to make a dough.
4. Cover your baking tray with a piece of baking parchment. Turn the dough out on to the parchment, tear off another sheet of parchment and put it on top of the dough.
5. Through the top sheet of parchment, use your hands to press the dough into as thin and even a sheet as you can. Take the time to get the dough quite thin – the thinner the better, so long as there are no holes in the dough. Peel off the top layer of parchment and use a thin, sharp, straight-bladed knife or a pizza cutter to score the dough into squares or diamonds.
6. Bake for about 30 minutes, or until they're a light golden colour. Peel off the parchment, break along the scored lines and let the crackers cool. Store them in a container with a tight lid.

🍓 If you like, you could sprinkle a little salt over the surface and gently press it into the dough before scoring the crackers.

Yield: About 6 dozen small crackers, each with 1 gram of carbohydrate and about 0.5 grams of fibre, for a total of 0.5 gram of usable carbs and 1 gram of protein.

⟲ Sunflower Cheddar Crackers

Are you missing cheesy nibbles? Try these!

> 300 g raw, hulled sunflower seeds
>
> 150 g grated Cheddar cheese
>
> 1/2 tsp salt, plus additional for sprinkling
>
> 75 ml water

1. Preheat the oven to 170ºC/Gas Mark 3.

2. In a food processor with the S-blade attached, grind the sunflower seeds to a fine meal.

3. Add the Cheddar and salt, and pulse the processor six to eight times to blend. Add the water and pulse until a dough ball forms.

4. Cover your baking tray with a piece of baking parchment. Turn the dough out on to the parchment, tear off another sheet of parchment and put it on top of the dough.

5. Through the top sheet of parchment, use your hands to press the dough into as thin and even a sheet as you can. Take the time to get the dough quite thin – the thinner the better, so long as there are no holes in the dough. Peel off the top layer of parchment. Sprinkle a little salt over the surface and gently press it in into place. Use a thin, sharp, straight-bladed knife or a pizza cutter to score the dough into squares or diamonds.

6. Bake for about 30 minutes. Peel off the parchment, break along the scored lines and let the crackers cool. Store them in a container with a tight lid.

Yield: About 6 dozen crackers, each with 1 gram of carbohydrate and 0.5 gram of fibre, for a total of 0.5 gram of usable carbs and 1 gram of protein.

🍓 Thanks to the cheese, these crackers come with a bonus: 21 milligrams of calcium!

Bran Crackers

These are thinner, crispier and lower-carb than many purchased fibre-rich crackers – and a whole lot cheaper. And they're great with dips, patés and tuna or egg salad.

> 150 g wheat bran
>
> 50 g rice protein powder
>
> 1 tsp salt
>
> 350 ml water

1. Preheat the oven to 180°C/Gas Mark 4.
2. Combine the wheat bran, protein powder and salt, stirring them together well. Stir in the water, making sure everything's wet, and let the mixture stand for about 5 minutes.
3. Cover a baking tray with baking parchment and turn the dough out on to the parchment (the dough will be very soft). Using the back of a spoon, pat and smooth this out into a thin, even, unbroken sheet.
4. Bake for 10 minutes and use a pizza cutter or a knife with a thin, sharp blade to score the sheet of dough into crackers. Put them back in the oven and bake for another 20 minutes.
5. Turn the oven to its lowest temperature and let the crackers sit in the warm oven for at least 3 hours, until they're good and dry and crisp. Allow to cool thoroughly, then break them apart and store in an air-tight container.

Yield: 3 dozen crackers, each with just over 2 grams of carbohydrate and 1 gram of fibre, for a total of about 1 gram of usable carbs and just a trace of protein.

Pizza

A big thank-you to Jennifer Eloff at **sweety.com** for this recipe from *Splendid Low-Carbing*! To make these pizza crusts, you first have to make her Almond Bake Mix No. 1:

ᴑ Almond Whey Bake Mix No. 1

> 150 g ground almonds
>
> 75 g natural whey protein powder
>
> 50 g unbleached spelt flour or 50 g unbleached plain flour
>
> 1 Tbsp vital wheat gluten

In a medium bowl, combine all the ingredients and stir well. Store in an airtight container at room temperature.

ᴑ Whey Pizza Crusts

Now, use the bake mix above to make your Pizza Crusts.

> 170 ml water, less 1 Tbsp
>
> 2 Tbsp olive oil
>
> 170 g Almond Whey Bake Mix No. 1 (see above)
>
> 70 g vital wheat gluten
>
> 50 g wheat bran
>
> 30 g natural whey protein powder
>
> 2 Tbsp Splenda
>
> 1 Tbsp spelt flour or plain flour
>
> 1 Tbsp sugar
>
> 1 Tbsp skimmed milk powder
>
> 1 Tbsp bread machine yeast
>
> 1 tsp salt

1. Preheat the oven to 190°C/Gas Mark 5 and warm the water in the microwave for 30 seconds.

2. Place the water, olive oil, Bake Mix No. 1, wheat gluten, wheat bran, protein powder, Splenda, flour, sugar, skimmed milk powder, yeast and salt in the bread machine.

3. Programme the bread machine for pizza dough, or knead and first rise.

4. When the dough's ready, remove it from the machine and divide it in half. On a lightly floured surface, roll out each ball of dough as far as possible. Cover with a tea towel and allow to stand for 10 to 20 minutes. Grease two 30-cm pizza pans.

5. Roll the dough again. Place it on the pizza pans and roll it out to fit each pan, using a small rolling pin or another small cylindrical object.

6. Cover the crusts with pizza sauce, toppings and grated cheese. Bake on lowest oven shelf for 20 to 25 minutes, or until the crusts are browned.

Yield: 2 pizzas with 12 slices each, or 24 servings. The carb count of your toppings will vary, depending on what you use, but the crust will add just 2.6 grams of carbohydrate, no fibre and 6 grams of protein.

🍓 A fan oven bakes pizza evenly and more quickly, so if you have one of these be sure to adjust your baking time accordingly.

Yet another great recipe from *Splendid Low-Carbing* by Jennifer Eloff at sweety.com. Again, you start this recipe by making a bake mix:

◌ Almond Whey Bake Mix No. 2

> 150 g ground almonds
>
> 75 g spelt flour
>
> 50 g natural whey protein powder
>
> 30 g vital wheat gluten

In a medium bowl, combine all ingredients. Mix with a wooden spoon until well combined. Store in an airtight container.

◌ Whey Tortillas

Jen Eloff at sweety.com says, 'These, in my humble opinion, taste better than the regular, almost tasteless white flour tortillas we used to buy.'

> 170 ml warm water (40 to 45°C)
>
> 1 Tbsp sugar
>
> 1 Tbsp yeast
>
> 2 Tbsp olive oil
>
> 150 g Almond Whey Bake Mix No. 2 (see above)
>
> 70 g vital wheat gluten
>
> 50 g wheat bran
>
> 40 g spelt flour or plain flour
>
> 2 Tbsp Splenda
>
> 1 Tbsp sugar
>
> 1 Tbsp skimmed milk powder
>
> 1 tsp salt

1. Preheat the oven to the lowest setting.

2. Pour the warm water in a large electric mixer bowl. Dissolve the sugar in the water and then sprinkle yeast over the water's surface.

3. Allow the mixture to stand for 3 to 5 minutes, then stir to dissolve completely.

4. Add the olive oil, Almond Whey Bake Mix No. 2, wheat gluten, wheat bran, flour, Splenda, sugar, skimmed milk powder and salt. Using the dough hook attachment on an electric mixer, mix, scraping the sides of the bowl occasionally, until the dough is moist and elastic. (If you don't have an electric mixer, you can do this by hand, with a wooden spoon.)

5. On a lightly floured surface, knead the dough briefly and place it in a greased bowl. Cover loosely with foil and place it in the oven. Turn the oven off and allow the dough to double in size (this will take about 1 hour).

6. When the dough has risen, remove from the bowl, punch it down and break into 20 small balls. Cover the dough balls with a clean tea towel to keep them from drying out.

7. Roll each dough ball into a paper-thin circle on a lightly floured surface.

8. In a dry, nonstick frying pan, cook each dough round briefly on both sides, until brown spots appear. Place your tortillas in a plastic bag to keep them supple, or refrigerate or freeze for longer storage.

Yield: 20 tortillas, each with 4.4 grams of carbohydrate, no fibre and 6.2 grams of protein.

CHAPTER FIVE

Hot Vegetable Dishes

When people first go low-carb, they suddenly don't know what to serve for side dishes. The answer is vegetables. If you're used to thinking of vegetables as something that sits between the meat and the potato, going rather unnoticed, read this chapter and think again! Here, to begin with, are three recipes that every low-carber needs:

↻ Cauliflower Purée (aka 'Fauxtatoes')

This is a wonderful substitute for mashed potatoes if you want something to put a fabulous soured cream gravy on! Feel free, by the way, to use frozen cauliflower instead; it works quite well with this recipe.

> 1 head fresh or 650 g frozen cauliflower
>
> 4 Tbsp butter
>
> Salt and freshly ground black pepper

1. Steam or microwave the cauliflower until it's soft.
2. Drain it thoroughly and put it through the blender or food processor until it's well puréed. Add the butter and salt and pepper to taste.

Yield: 6 generous servings, each with 5 grams of carbohydrate and 2 grams of fibre, for a total of 3 grams of usable carbs and 2 grams of protein.

↻ Fauxtatoes Deluxe

This extra-rich Fauxtatoes recipe comes from Adele Hite and it is the basis for the 'grits' part of her Low-Carb Prawns and 'Grits' recipe (see page 306).

1 large head cauliflower

100 ml cream

100 g cream cheese

1 Tbsp butter

Salt and freshly ground black pepper

1. Simmer the cauliflower in water with the cream added to it. (This keeps the cauliflower sweet and prevents it from turning an unappetising grey colour.) When the cauliflower is very soft, drain thoroughly.

2. Put the still-warm cauliflower in a food processor with the cream cheese, butter, and salt and pepper to taste, and process until smooth. (You may have to do this in more than one batch.)

Yield: 6 generous servings, each with 6 grams of carbohydrate and 2 grams of fibre, for a total of 4 grams of usable carbs and 4 grams of protein.

🍓 Give your Fauxtatoes a little zing by adding a few cloves of sliced garlic to the cooking water or some roasted garlic to the food processor when blending the cauliflower with the other ingredients. Each clove of garlic added will add just 1 gram of carbohydrate to the carb count for the batch.

↻ Cauliflower Rice

Many thanks to Fran McCullough! I got this idea from her book *Living Low Carb* and it's served me very well.

1/2 head cauliflower

Simply put the cauliflower through your food processor using the shredding blade. This gives the cauliflower a texture that's remarkably similar to rice. You can steam, microwave or even sauté it in butter. Whatever you do, though, don't overcook it!

Yield: About 3 servings, each with 5 grams of carbohydrate and 2 grams of fibre, for a total of 3 grams of usable carbs and 2 grams of protein.

↻ Cauliflower Rice Deluxe

This is higher-carb than plain Cauliflower Rice, but the wild rice adds a grain flavour that makes it quite convincing. And it has about 25 per cent less carbohydrate than most other kinds of rice. I only use this for special occasions, but it's wonderful.

1 recipe Cauliflower Rice (see above)

50 g wild rice

170 ml water

1. Cook your cauliflower rice as desired (I steam mine when making this), taking care not to overcook, so that it's tender but not mushy.
2. Put the wild rice and water in a saucepan, cover it and set it on the lowest heat until all the water is gone (half an hour, maybe a bit more).
3. Toss together the cooked cauliflower rice and wild rice, and season as desired.

Yield: 8 servings, each with 6 grams of carbohydrate and 1 gram of fibre, for a total of 5 grams of usable carbs and 2 grams of protein.

༄ Company Dinner 'Rice'

This is my favourite way to season the cauliflower-wild rice blend above. A big hit at dinner parties!

> 1 small onion, chopped
>
> 110 g butter, melted
>
> 1 recipe Cauliflower Rice Deluxe (see page 162)
>
> 6 rashers bacon, cooked until crisp and crumbled
>
> 1/4 tsp salt
>
> 1/4 tsp freshly ground black pepper
>
> 75 g grated Parmesan cheese

Sauté the onion in the butter until it's golden and limp. Toss the Cauliflower Rice Deluxe with the sautéed onion and the bacon, salt, pepper and cheese. Serve.

Yield: 8 servings, each with 8 grams of carbohydrate and 2 grams of fibre, for a total of 6 grams of usable carbs and 5 grams of protein.

༄ Sautéed Mushrooms

What could be better with a steak? Feel free to experiment with this recipe – use all butter or all olive oil, throw in a clove of garlic – try a few variations until you find what you like.

> 2 Tbsp butter
>
> 2 Tbsp olive oil
>
> 225 g mushrooms, thickly sliced
>
> Salt and freshly ground black pepper

1. Melt the butter and heat the olive oil over a medium to high heat in a heavy frying pan.
2. Add the mushrooms and sauté, stirring frequently, for 5 to 7 minutes, or until the mushrooms are limp and brown. Salt and pepper lightly and serve.

Yield: 3 generous servings, each with 4 grams of carbohydrate and 1 gram of fibre, for a total of 3 grams of usable carbs and 2 grams of protein.

🍓 Try this recipe with mushrooms other than the familiar 'button' ones. Portobellos are delicious prepared this way, for instance. Avoid shitakes, however; they are much higher in carbohydrates.

↶ Mushrooms in Sherry Cream

This is rich and flavourful and best served with a simple roast or the like.

>225 g small, very fresh mushrooms
>
>75 ml dry sherry
>
>1/4 tsp salt, divided
>
>125 ml soured cream
>
>1 clove garlic
>
>1/8 tsp freshly ground black pepper

1. Wipe the mushrooms clean and trim the woody ends off the stems. Place in a small saucepan with the sherry and sprinkle with half of the salt.

2. Bring the water to the boil, turn the heat down to low, cover the pan and let the mushrooms simmer for just 3 to 4 minutes, shaking the pan once or twice while they're cooking.

3. In another saucepan, over a very low heat, stir together the remaining salt and the soured cream, garlic and pepper. Heat the soured cream through, but don't let it boil or it will separate.

4. When the mushrooms are done, pour off the liquid into a small bowl. As soon as the cream is heated through, spoon it over the mushrooms and stir everything around over a medium-low heat. If it seems a bit thick, add a teaspoon or two of the reserved liquid.

5. Stir the mushrooms and soured cream together for 2 to 3 minutes, again making sure that the cream does not boil, and serve.

Yield: 3 servings, each with 4 grams carbohydrates and 1 gram of fibre, for a total of 3 grams of usable carbs and 2 grams of protein.

◯ Slice of Mushroom Heaven

This is so good. Thanks to my friend Kay for the name!

4 Tbsp butter

450 g mushrooms, sliced

1/2 medium onion, finely chopped

1 clove garlic, crushed

75 ml dry white wine

1 tsp lemon juice

350 ml half milk and half cream

3 eggs

1 tsp salt

1/4 tsp freshly ground black pepper

225 g grated Gruyère cheese

1. Preheat the oven to 180°C/Gas Mark 4.
2. Melt the butter in a heavy frying pan over medium heat and begin frying the mushrooms, onion and garlic. When the mushrooms are limp, turn the heat up a little and boil off the liquid. Stir in the white wine and cook until that's boiled away, too.
3. Stir in the lemon juice and turn off the heat. Transfer the mixture to a large mixing bowl and stir in the milk and cream mixture, eggs, salt, pepper and 150 g of the cheese.
4. Spray a 20 x 20-cm baking dish with nonstick cooking spray and spread the mixture from step 3 evenly over the bottom. Sprinkle the rest of the cheese on top and bake for 50 minutes, or until the cheese on top is golden.

Yield: 9 generous servings, each with 5 grams of carbohydrate and 1 gram of fibre, for a total of 4 grams of usable carbs and 13 grams of protein.

🍓 This dish is good hot, but I actually like it better cold – and when it's cold, it cuts in nice, neat squares. I think it makes a nice breakfast or lunch and it's definitely an excellent side dish. It would even make a good vegetarian main course.

Kolokythia Krokettes

These are rapidly becoming one of our favourite side dishes. They're Greek and very, very tasty. A delicious side dish with roast lamb or Greek Roasted Chicken (see page 276).

> 3 medium courgettes, grated
>
> 1 tsp salt
>
> 3 eggs
>
> 100 g crumbled feta cheese
>
> 1 tsp dried oregano
>
> 1/2 medium onion, finely diced
>
> 1/8 tsp freshly ground black pepper
>
> 3 Tbsp soya powder or rice protein powder
>
> Butter

Save some time preparing the ingredients for this dish by running the courgette and the onion through a food processor.

1. Mix the grated courgette with the salt in a bowl and let it stand for an hour or so. Squeeze out and drain the liquid.

2. Mix in the eggs, feta cheese, oregano, onion, pepper and soya powder, and combine well.

3. Spray a heavy frying pan with nonstick cooking spray, add a healthy tablespooon of butter and melt over medium heat. Fry the batter by the tablespoonful, turning once. Add more butter between batches, as needed, and keep the cooked krokettes warm. The trick to these is to let them get quite brown on the bottom before trying to turn them, or they tend to fall apart. If a few do fall apart, don't fret – the pieces will still taste incredible.

Yield: 6 servings, each with 6 grams of carbohydrate and 2 grams of fibre, for a total of 4 grams usable carbs and 8 grams of protein.

◯ Courgette with Soured Cream for People Who Don't Love Courgettes

Marilee Wellersdick sent me this recipe. My sister, who tested it, says the name is no joke – it went over well with non-courgette-loving in-laws.

> 4 Tbsp butter
>
> 1 medium onion, chopped
>
> 8 small courgettes, sliced very thinly
>
> Salt and freshly ground black pepper
>
> 225 ml soured cream

1. Melt the butter in a large, preferably nonstick, frying pan. Add the onion and courgettes, and salt and pepper to taste.
2. Cover and cook on medium heat, stirring occasionally, until the courgette is translucent (15 to 20 minutes).
3. Remove from the heat and stir in the soured cream. Serve.

   Yield: 6 servings, each with 11 grams of carbohydrate and 3 grams of fibre, for a total of 8 grams of usable carbs and no protein.

ꙮ Courgette Casserole

Jodee Rushton, who contributed this recipe, says, 'Since each serving has protein as well as vegetable, it's great as part of a lunch with some other veggies. It's also a great snack.'

> 2 Tbsp butter
>
> 650 g courgettes, unpeeled, washed and sliced
>
> 2 eggs, beaten
>
> 1 Tbsp unbleached flour
>
> 1/2 tsp dry mustard
>
> 1/2 tsp ground nutmeg
>
> 1/2 tsp salt
>
> Freshly ground black pepper
>
> 1 packet Splenda
>
> 225 ml double cream
>
> 175 g strong Cheddar cheese, grated

1. Preheat the oven to 170ºC/Gas Mark 3 and spray a large casserole with nonstick cooking spray.

2. Melt the butter in a large, heavy frying pan. Add the sliced courgettes and sauté over a medium to high heat until tender, stirring frequently. When done, remove from the heat and allow to cool until lukewarm. Place in the prepared casserole.

3. Combine the eggs, flour, mustard, nutmeg, salt, pepper to taste, and the Splenda, in a large mixing bowl; whisk together well. Add the double cream and Cheddar and mix well.

4. Add the egg mixture to the cooled courgettes and mix well. Place in the oven and bake for 30 minutes or until set. Cool and serve.

Yield: 6 servings, each with 6 grams of carbohydrate and 1 gram of fibre, for a total of 5 grams of usable carbs and 11 grams of protein.

᠀ Courgette-Crusted Pizza

This is like a somewhat-more-substantial quiche on the bottom and pizza on top.

> 400 g grated courgette
>
> 3 eggs
>
> 30 g rice protein powder or soya powder
>
> 150 g grated mozzarella
>
> 75 g grated Parmesan cheese
>
> A pinch or two of dried basil
>
> 1/2 tsp salt
>
> 1/4 tsp freshly ground black pepper
>
> 1 cup sugar-free pizza sauce
>
> Toppings as desired (such as sausage, pepperoni, peppers, mushrooms)

1. Preheat the oven to 180°C/Gas Mark 4.
2. Sprinkle the courgette with a little salt and leave it to stand for 15 to 30 minutes. Put it in a strainer and press out the excess moisture.
3. Beat together the strained courgette, eggs, protein powder, 50 g of the mozzarella, Parmesan, basil, salt and pepper.
4. Spray a 25 x 32-cm baking dish with nonstick cooking spray and spread the courgette mixture in it.
5. Bake for about 25 minutes, or until firm. Brush it with a little oil and grill it for about 5 minutes, until it's golden.
6. Next, spread on the pizza sauce, then add the remaining mozzarella and the other toppings.
7. Bake for another 25 minutes, then cut into squares and serve.

   🍓 If you're using vegetables as toppings, you may want to sauté them a little first.

   Yield: 4 generous servings, each with 14 grams of carbohydrate and 2 grams of fibre, for a total of 12 grams of usable carbs and 22 grams of protein. (Analysis does not include toppings.)

⌒ Aubergine Parmesan Squared

When you use Parmesan cheese instead of breadcrumbs to 'bread' the aubergine slices, it becomes Aubergine Parmesan Squared! This takes a little doing, but it's delicious and it's easily filling enough for a main dish.

> 1 large aubergine, sliced no more than 5 mm thick
>
> 50 g low-carb bake mix or unflavoured protein powder
>
> 2 or 3 eggs*
>
> 180 to 250 g Parmesan cheese*
>
> Olive oil, for frying
>
> 1 clove garlic, cut in half
>
> 350 ml sugar-free spaghetti sauce
>
> 225 g grated mozzarella

🍓 How many eggs and how much Parmesan you will need depends on the size of the aubergine.

1. Preheat the oven to 180°C/Gas Mark 4.
2. Put the bake mix on a plate, break the eggs into a shallow bowl and beat well. Put 150 to 225 g of Parmesan on another plate.
3. Dip each aubergine slice in the bake mix so each side is well dusted.
4. Dip each 'floured' slice of aubergine in the beaten egg and then in the Parmesan, so that each slice has a good coating of the cheese. Refrigerate the 'breaded' slices of aubergine for at least half an hour, or up to an hour or two.
5. Pour 3 mm of olive oil in the bottom of a heavy frying pan over a medium heat. Add the garlic, letting it sizzle for a minute or two before removing. Now fry the refrigerated aubergine slices until they're golden brown on both sides (you'll need to add more olive oil as you go along).
6. Spread 125 ml of spaghetti sauce in the bottom of a 25 x 30-cm roasting tin. Arrange half of the aubergine slices to cover bottom of pan. Cover with the mozzarella and top with the remaining aubergine.

Pour the rest of the spaghetti sauce on and sprinkle the remaining Parmesan on top.

7. Bake for 30 minutes.

Yield: 6 servings, each with 13 grams of carbohydrate and 4.5 grams of fibre, for a total of 8.5 usable carbs and 24 grams of protein.

↻ Cauliflower-Green Bean Casserole

Reader Honey Ashton says her family loves this. It makes a great holiday side dish.

> 900 g frozen cauliflower
>
> 100 g sliced green beans
>
> 225 ml mayonnaise
>
> 225 g butter
>
> 1/4 small yellow or white onion, finely sliced
>
> 225 g freshly cooked, crumbled bacon
>
> 100 g grated mixture Mozzarella and Cheddar cheeses

1. Preheat the oven to 150°C/Gas Mark 2.
2. Follow the package directions to cook the cauliflower; add the beans to cook with cauliflower. Drain after cooking.
3. Place the cooked vegetables in a large casserole and stir in the mayonnaise, butter, onion and bacon; mix thoroughly.
4. Top the casserole with the cheese. Bake for 20 minutes or until the cheese has melted and serve immediately.

Yield: 8 servings, each with 10 grams of carbohydrate and 4 grams of fibre, for a total of 6 grams of usable carbs and 11 grams of protein.

Ꮞ Cauliflower Kugel

A kugel is a traditional Jewish casserole that comes in both sweet and savoury varieties. This savoury kugel makes a nice side dish with a simple meat course. It could also be served as a vegetarian main dish.

> 600 g frozen cauliflower, thawed
>
> 1 medium onion, chopped
>
> 225 g cottage cheese
>
> 100 g grated Cheddar cheese
>
> 4 eggs
>
> 1/2 tsp salt
>
> 1/4 tsp freshly ground black pepper
>
> Paprika

1. Preheat the oven to 180°C/Gas Mark 4.
2. Chop the cauliflower into 1-cm pieces. Combine with the onion, cottage cheese, Cheddar, eggs, salt and pepper in a large mixing bowl and mix very well.
3. Spray a 20 x 20-cm baking dish with nonstick cooking spray and spread the cauliflower mixture evenly on the bottom. Sprinkle paprika lightly over the top and bake for 50 to 60 minutes, or until the kugel is set and lightly browned.

Yield: 9 servings, each with 5 grams of carbohydrate and 2 grams of fibre, for a total of 3 grams of usable carbs and 10 grams of protein.

⌒ Smoky Cauliflower and Sausage

Holly Holder, who sent this recipe, says, 'My kids, who wouldn't touch cauliflower, loved this recipe. They had no idea what it was – and my lips are sealed!'

> 1 medium head cauliflower (or 450 g frozen)
>
> 225 g cream cheese, beaten to soften
>
> 225 g sausagemeat, cooked and crumbled
>
> 100 g smoked Gruyère, or any other smoked cheese,
>   cut into thin slices
>
> Salt and freshly ground black pepper

1. Preheat the oven to 180°C/Gas Mark 4.
2. Cut up the cauliflower and steam or microwave it until tender. Mash with a potato masher and mix in the cream cheese and cooked sausagemeat.
3. Spread half the cauliflower mixture in a 2-litre casserole. Top with half the cheese slices.
4. Add the remaining cauliflower and top with the remaining cheese. Bake until bubbly (about 30 minutes).

Yield: 6 servings, each with 5 grams of carbohydrate and 2 grams of fibre, for a total of 3 grams of usable carbs and 13 grams of protein.

🍓 Don't be fooled into overcooking your casserole: smoked Gruyère will not look melted, but it will be very creamy when dished up.

☽ Green Beans Almondine

My friend Tonya always thought this was a terribly complicated dish, because it's elegant and delicious. As if! It's child's play.

    450 g frozen French beans
    50 g slivered almonds
    4 Tbsp butter

1. Steam or microwave the beans according to the package directions.
2. While the beans are cooking, sauté the almonds in the butter over medium heat, stirring frequently.
3. When they are done and the almonds are golden, drain the water off the beans and pour the almonds and butter over them; use a scraper to get all the butter. Toss the mixture and serve.

Yield: 4 servings, each with 12 grams of carbohydrate and 4 grams of fibre, for a total of 8 grams of usable carbs and 6 grams of protein.

Green Beans Pecandine: Make this exactly as you would Green Beans Almondine, only substitute 50 g of chopped pecans for the slivered almonds. Just as good!

Yield: 4 servings, each with 11 grams of carbohydrate and 4 grams of fibre, for a total of 7 grams of usable carbs and 3 grams of protein.

Cashew Green Beans: This tasty twist comes from an anonymous reader – thanks, whoever you are! Make as you would Green Beans Almondine, but substitute 50 g of raw cashew pieces for the almonds.

Yield: 4 servings, each with 13 grams of carbohydrate and 4 grams of fibre, for a total of 9 grams usable carbs and 5 grams of protein.

↻ Lemon Pepper Beans

I think this makes a particularly good side dish with chicken or fish.

> 450 g frozen French beans, thawed and sliced
>
> 75 ml olive oil
>
> 1 clove garlic, crushed
>
> 1 Tbsp lemon juice
>
> 1/4 tsp freshly ground black pepper

Over a high heat, stir-fry the beans in the olive oil until they're tender-crisp. Stir in the garlic, lemon juice and pepper, cook another minute and serve.

Yield: 4 servings, each with 9 grams of carbohydrate and 3 grams of fibre, for a total of 6 grams of usable carbs and 2 grams of protein.

↻ Herby Green Beans

> 3 Tbsp butter
>
> 450 g frozen sliced green beans, thawed
>
> 30 g finely diced celery
>
> 30 g finely diced onion
>
> 1 clove garlic, crushed
>
> 1/2 tsp dried rosemary, slightly crushed
>
> 1/2 tsp dried basil, slightly crushed
>
> Salt

1. Melt the butter in a heavy frying pan over a medium heat. Add the beans, celery, onion and garlic to the pan and sauté until the beans are tender-crisp.

2. Stir in the rosemary and basil, and sauté another minute or so. Salt to taste and serve.

Yield: 4 servings, each with 10 grams of carbohydrate and 4 grams of fibre, for a total of 6 grams of usable carbs and 2 grams of protein.

⌒ Italian Bean Bake

If you're having a roast, simplify your life by serving this dish – it can cook right alongside the meat.

> 450 g frozen sliced fine beans, thawed
>
> 100 ml tomato sauce
>
> 1/4 small onion, finely chopped
>
> 1 clove garlic, crushed
>
> 1 tsp Dijon mustard
>
> Freshly ground black pepper
>
> 50 g grated mozzarella

1. Preheat the oven to 180°C/Gas Mark 4. Put the beans in a 2-litre casserole.
2. Combine the tomato sauce, onion, garlic, mustard and a dash of pepper in a mixing bowl; stir into the beans.
3. Bake for 1 hour, or until the beans are tender, and then top with mozzarella and bake for another 3 to 5 minutes, or until the cheese is melted. Serve.

Yield: 4 servings, each with 12 grams of carbohydrate and 4 grams of fibre, for a total of 8 grams of usable carbs and 6 grams of protein.

🍓 If you're not serving a roast and you'd like to take a half-hour off the baking time for this dish, microwave the beans until they're tender-crisp before you combine them with the sauce.

↻ Greek Beans

> 2 Tbsp olive oil
>
> 1/2 small onion, finely chopped
>
> 1 clove garlic, crushed
>
> 450 g frozen cut green beans, thawed
>
> 125 ml diced tinned tomatoes
>
> 75 ml beef stock
>
> 75 ml dry white wine

1. Heat the oil in a large, heavy frying pan over medium heat. Add the onion and garlic and sauté for a minute or two.
2. Drain the beans and add them to the pan, stirring to coat. Sauté the beans for 6 to 7 minutes, adding another tablespoon of oil if the pan starts to get dry.
3. Stir in the tomatoes, stock and wine. Turn up the heat to medium-high and let everything simmer until the beans are just tender-crisp and most of the liquid has cooked off (about 5 minutes).

Yield: 4 servings, each with 11 grams of carbohydrate and 3 grams of fibre, for a total of 8 grams of usable carbs and 3 grams of protein.

↻ Green Beans Vinaigrette

> 450 g frozen, cut green beans, thawed
>
> 4 Tbsp butter
>
> 4 Tbsp Italian dressing (see page 236, or use bottled)

Sauté the green beans in the butter in a large, heavy frying pan set over a medium to high heat. When they're not quite tender-crisp, stir in the dressing and simmer for another 5 to 7 minutes. Serve.

Yield: 4 servings, each with 9 grams of carbohydrate and 3 grams of fibre, for a total of 6 grams of usable carbs and 2 grams of protein.

↻ Green Beans à la Carbonara

Bacon, cheese and garlic – if these three things won't get your family to eat green beans, nothing will. Another great recipe from the *Low Carb Success Calendar* by Vicki Cash, this has enough protein to be a main dish.

> 7 to 10 thick rashers of bacon
>
> 1 tsp olive oil
>
> 1/2 small onion, chopped
>
> 1 clove garlic, crushed
>
> 450 g frozen green beans
>
> 6 eggs
>
> 3 Tbsp cream
>
> 1/2 tsp chilli flakes
>
> 1/4 tsp nutmeg
>
> Salt and freshly ground black pepper
>
> 100 g grated Parmesan cheese

1. Fry the bacon in a large, nonstick frying pan over medium heat until not quite crisp. Drain on kitchen paper, and sauté the onions and garlic in the remaining bacon fat until brown.

2. Place the green beans in a 2-litre microwave-safe bowl with 1 table-spoon of water. Cover and microwave on high for 10 minutes, turning halfway through cooking.

3. While the beans are cooking, dice the bacon and add it to the onions and garlic. Keep the frying pan over a warm hob. Beat together the eggs, cream, chilli flakes, nutmeg and salt and pepper to taste, as if you were preparing scrambled eggs.

4. Turn the heat under the frying pan up to medium. Add the egg mixture, hot green beans and Parmesan to the frying pan, stirring until the eggs are thoroughly cooked. Serve immediately.

Yield: 4 servings, each with 12 grams of carbohydrate and 3 grams of fibre, for a total of 9 grams of usable carbs and 27 grams of protein.

↷ Fried Brussels Sprouts

We've served these to friends many times and they're always a hit, even with people who think they don't like Brussels sprouts. We didn't think we liked Brussels sprouts, either, until our dear friends John and Judy Horwitz served them to us this way – and suddenly we were addicted.

> 450 g Brussels sprouts (fresh is best, but frozen will do)
> Olive oil
> 3 or 4 cloves garlic, crushed

1. If you're using fresh Brussels sprouts, remove any bruised, wilted or discoloured outer leaves and trim the stems. If you're using frozen, just thaw them.

2. In a heavy-bottomed pot or frying pan, heat 1 cm of olive oil over a medium heat. Add the Brussels sprouts and fry them, stirring occasionally, until they are very dark brown all over – you really want them just about burned.

3. For the last minute or so, add the garlic and stir it around well. Remove the pan from the heat and serve the sprouts before the garlic burns.

Yield: Technically 4 servings, but my husband and I can easily eat 450 g of these between the two of us. Assuming you can bring yourself to share with 3 other people, you'll each get 10 grams of carbohydrate with 4 grams of fibre per serving, for a total of 6 grams of usable carbs and 4 grams of protein.

↷ Simple Sprouts

> 450 g Brussels sprouts
> 3 to 4 Tbsp butter

1. Trim the stems of your sprouts and remove any wilted or yellowed leaves. Thinly slice the sprouts using the slicing blade of a food processor.

2. Melt the butter in a heavy frying pan and sauté the sprouts over a medium to high heat until they're tender but not mushy (about 7 to 10

minutes). They should be getting a few brown spots around the edges to show they are ready to serve.

Yield: 4 servings, each with 9 grams of carbohydrate and 4 grams of fibre, for a total of 5 grams of usable carbs and 4 grams of protein.

↻ Nutty Brussels Sprouts

    450 g Brussels sprouts
    50 g hazelnuts
    6 Tbsp butter
    4 rashers bacon
    1/4 tsp salt
    1/8 tsp freshly ground black pepper

1. Trim the stems of the Brussels sprouts and remove any wilted or yellowed leaves. Thinly slice the sprouts using the slicing blade of a food processor.
2. Chop the hazelnuts to a medium texture in a food processor.
3. Melt 2 tablespoons of the butter in a heavy frying pan over medium heat and add the hazelnuts. Sauté, stirring frequently, for about 7 minutes or until golden. Remove from the frying pan and set aside.
4. Cook the bacon, either using a separate frying pan or in the microwave. While the bacon is cooking, melt the remaining 4 tablespoons of butter over a medium to high heat in the same frying pan you used for the hazelnuts. Add the sliced Brussels sprouts and sauté, stirring frequently, for 7 to 10 minutes, or until tender.
5. Stir in the toasted hazelnuts and the seasonings and transfer to a serving dish. Drain the bacon, crumble it over the top and serve.

Yield: 4 servings, each with 12 grams of carbohydrate and 5 grams of fibre, for a total of 7 grams of usable carbs and 8 grams of protein.

↻ Swede Crisps

Swedes are often given a wide berth, as people are convinced they don't like them. Well, everyone I know who tries these loves them!

>1 kg swede
>
>3 to 4 Tbsp butter

1. Peel your swede and cut it into strips the size of thick potato crisps, using a good, heavy knife with a sharp blade.

2. Steam the 'crisps' over boiling water in a pan with a tight lid until they're easily pierced with a fork but not mushy (about 10 to 15 minutes). You want them still to be al dente.

3. Melt the butter in a heavy-bottomed frying pan over a medium to high heat and fry the strips of swede until they're browned on all sides. Salt and serve.

Yield: 6 servings, each with 12 grams of carbohydrate and 4 grams of fibre, for a total of 8 grams of usable carbs and 2 grams of protein.

↻ Glazed Turnips

These make wonderful substitute for potatoes with a roast.

>500 g turnip, cut into small chunks
>
>2 Tbsp butter
>
>1/2 small onion
>
>1 tsp Splenda
>
>1/2 tsp liquid beef stock concentrate
>
>1/8 tsp paprika

1. Steam or microwave the turnip chunks until tender (I steam mine in the microwave for about 7 minutes on High), then drain.

2. Melt the butter in a heavy frying pan over a medium heat. Add the turnips and onion and sauté until the onion is limp.

3. Stir in the Splenda, stock concentrate and paprika, coating all the turnips, and sauté for just another minute or two.

Yield: 6 servings, each with 12 grams of carbohydrate and 3 grams of fibre, for a total of 9 grams of usable carbs and 2 grams of protein.

↺ Mashed Garlic Turnips

Great with a steak, a roast or chops.

> 1 kg turnips, peeled and cut into chunks
> 8 cloves garlic, peeled and sliced
> 2 Tbsp butter
> 2 Tbsp prepared horseradish
> 1 tsp salt
> 1/2 tsp freshly ground black pepper
> 1/8 tsp ground nutmeg
> 3 Tbsp chopped fresh chives

1. Place the turnips and the garlic in a saucepan with a tight-fitting lid. Add water to fill about halfway, cover and place over a medium to high heat. Bring to the boil, turn down the heat and simmer until quite soft (about 15 minutes). Drain the turnips and garlic very well.

2. Using a potato masher, mash the turnips and garlic together. Stir in the butter, horseradish, salt, pepper and nutmeg, and mix well. Just before serving, stir in the chives.

Yield: 6 servings, each with 10 grams of carbohydrate and 2 grams of fibre, for a total of 8 grams of usable carbs and 2 grams of protein.

↻ Turnips Au Gratin

This is sublime with top-quality Canadian Cheddar cheese, but you can make it with any good, mature Cheddar.

1 kg turnips, peeled and thinly sliced
1/2 medium onion, sliced
225 ml double cream
225 ml half milk and half cream, mixed
350 g grated mature Cheddar cheese
2 tsp prepared horseradish
1/4 tsp ground nutmeg
Salt and freshly ground black pepper

1. Preheat the oven to 180°C/Gas Mark 4.
2. Steam the turnips until they're just tender (I steam mine in the microwave for 7 minutes on High).
3. While the turnips are cooking, combine the double cream and milk-cream mixture in a saucepan over a very low heat. Bring to a simmer.
4. When the cream is up to temperature, whisk in 300 g of the cheese, a couple of tablespoons at a time. Stir each addition until it's completely melted before adding more. When the cheese is melted into the sauce, whisk in the horseradish and nutmeg. Turn off the heat.
5. Spray a 20 x 20-cm glass baking dish with nonstick cooking spray. Put about one-third of the turnips in the dish and scatter half of the sliced onion over it. Add another layer of one-third the turnips, half of the onions and the final third of the turnips on top. Pour the cheese sauce over the whole thing and scatter the remaining cheese over the top. Bake for 30 to 40 minutes, or until golden.

Yield: 6 servings, each with 12 grams of carbohydrate and 2 grams of fibre, for a total of 10 grams of usable carbs and 17 g of protein.

ᕤ Indian Cabbage

Good with anything curried. This combination of seasonings works well with green beans, too.

>Oil or butter
>
>1 tsp black mustard seed
>
>1 tsp turmeric
>
>300 g finely chopped cabbage
>
>1 tsp salt

1. Put a heavy frying pan over medium heat. Add a few tablespoons of oil or butter (I like to use coconut oil) and then the mustard seed and the turmeric. Sauté together for just a minute.

2. Stir in the cabbage, add the salt and stir-fry for a few minutes, combining the cabbage well with the spices.

3. Add a couple of tablespoons of water, cover and let the cabbage steam for a couple more minutes, until it is tender-crisp.

Yield: 4 servings, each with 4 grams of carbohydrate and 2 grams of fibre, for a total of 2 grams of usable carbs and 1 gram of protein.

ᕤ Sweet-and-Sour Cabbage

>3 rashers bacon
>
>300 g finely chopped cabbage
>
>2 Tbsp cider vinegar
>
>2 tsp Splenda

1. In a heavy frying pan, cook the bacon until crisp. Remove and drain.

2. Add the cabbage to the bacon fat and sauté it until tender-crisp.

3. Stir in the vinegar and Splenda, crumble in the bacon and serve.

Yield: 4 servings, each with 4 grams of carbohydrate and 2 grams of fibre, for a total of 2 grams of usable carbs and 2 grams of protein.

ᢙ Thai Stir-Fried Cabbage

This exotic and tasty dish cooks lightning-fast, so make sure you have everything cut up, mixed up and ready to go before you start stir-frying.

> 2 Tbsp lime juice
>
> 2 Tbsp Thai fish sauce (nam pla)
>
> 2/3 tsp chilli flakes
>
> Peanut, canola (rapeseed) or coconut oil
>
> 450 g finely chopped Chinese napa cabbage
>
> 6 spring onions, sliced
>
> 2 cloves garlic, crushed
>
> 30 g unsweetened desiccated coconut
>
> 30 g chopped, dry-roasted peanuts

1. Mix together the lime juice, fish sauce and chilli flakes. Set aside.
2. In a wok or heavy-bottomed frying pan, heat a few tablespoons of oil over a high heat. Add the cabbage, spring onions and garlic, and stir-fry for no more than 5 minutes, or just until the cabbage is heated through.
3. Add the step 1 mixture to the cabbage and stir to coat. Let it cook just another minute and stir in the coconut. Serve topped with peanuts.

Yield: 4 servings, each with 13 grams of carbohydrate and 4 grams of fibre, for a total of 9 grams of usable carbs and 5 grams of protein.

↻ Ratatouille

This French dish is so popular with almost everyone!

> 170 ml olive oil
>
> 450 g aubergine cut into 1-inch cubes
>
> 450 g sliced courgette
>
> 1 medium onion, sliced
>
> 2 green peppers, cut into strips
>
> 3 cloves garlic
>
> 400 g tinned sliced tomatoes
>
> 100 g tinned black olives, drained and sliced
>
> 1 1/2 tsp dried oregano
>
> 1/2 tsp salt
>
> 1/4 tsp freshly ground black pepper

1. Heat the oil in a heavy frying pan over medium heat. Add the aubergine, courgette, onion, peppers and garlic.

2. Sauté for 15 to 20 minutes, turning from time to time so it all comes in contact with the olive oil. Once the vegetables are all starting to look about half-cooked, add the tomatoes (including the liquid), olives, oregano, salt and pepper.

3. Stir it all together, cover, turn the heat down to low and let the whole thing simmer for 40 minutes or so.

Yield: 8 servings, each with 11 grams of carbohydrate and 3 grams of fibre, for a total of 8 grams of usable carbs and 2 grams of protein.

🍓 Use your largest frying pan for this dish – possibly even your wok, if you have one. This amount of vegetables will cause even a 25-cm frying pan almost to overflow. And don't be afraid to toss in a little more olive oil if you need it while you are sautéing.

⌒ Courgette-Mushroom Pan-Fry

1 large or 2 medium courgettes

225 g mushrooms

1 medium onion

125 ml olive oil

2 cloves garlic, crushed

1/2 tsp oregano

Salt

1. Halve the courgettes lengthways, then cut into 2.5-cm sections. Wipe the mushrooms clean with a damp cloth, then quarter them vertically. Halve the onion and cut it into slices about 5 mm thick.

2. Heat the olive oil in a heavy frying pan over a medium to high heat. Add the courgette, mushrooms, onion and garlic, and stir-fry until the courgette and mushrooms are just barely tender and the onion is tender-crisp (about 10 minutes).

3. Stir in the oregano, salt to taste and serve.

Yield: 4 servings, each with 7 grams of carbohydrate and 2 grams of fibre, for a total of 5 grams of usable carbs and 2 grams of protein.

ᗌ Snow Peas, Mushrooms and Beansprouts

The combination of flavours here is magical, somehow; these three vegetables seem to be made for each other.

> 3 Tbsp peanut oil
>
> 100 g fresh snow peas
>
> 100 g fresh mushrooms, sliced
>
> 100 g fresh beansprouts
>
> 1 tsp soy sauce

1. Heat the oil in a wok or heavy frying pan over a high heat. Add the snow peas and mushrooms and stir-fry until the peas are almost tender-crisp (3 to 4 minutes).
2. Add the beansprouts and stir-fry for just another 30 seconds to 1 minute.
3. Stir in the soy sauce and serve.

   Yield: 3 servings, each with 7 grams of carbohydrate and 2 grams of fibre, for a total of 5 grams of usable carbs and 3 grams of protein.

ᗌ Buttered Snow Peas

If you've only had sugar snap peas in Chinese food, try them this way. They're really wonderful.

> 4 Tbsp butter
>
> 350 g fresh snow peas

1. Melt the butter in a heavy frying pan over a medium to high heat.
2. Add the snow peas and sauté just until tender-crisp.

   Yield: 3 servings, each with 9 grams of carbohydrate and 3 grams of fibre, for a total of 6 grams of usable carbs and 3 grams of protein.

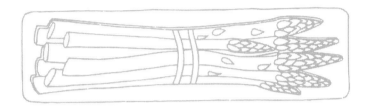

About Cooking Asparagus

Asparagus is divine if cooked correctly, and mushy and nasty if overcooked – and it's extremely easy to overcook. If you're cooking it on the cooker top, the best way, believe it or not, is standing up in an old cooker-top coffee percolator with the middle bits removed. This lets the tougher ends boil while the tender tips steam. I put my asparagus in the coffee pot, add about 10 cm of water and put on the lid. Set it over a medium-high heat and bring the water to the boil. Once it's boiling, 5 minutes is plenty!

If you don't have a coffee percolator (or an asparagus pot, for that matter, which lets you do the same thing), I'd recommend that you microwave your asparagus. Place the stems in a microwave-safe casserole or on a glass pie plate. If you're using a pie plate or a round casserole, arrange the asparagus with the tips toward the centre. (I've microwaved asparagus in a rectangular casserole and it's come out fine.) Add a tablespoon or two of water and cover with clingfilm, or a lid if your casserole has one. Microwave it on High for 5 to 6 minutes, then remove the clingfilm or lid immediately or the trapped steam will keep cooking your asparagus.

One last thing: believe it or not, the proper way to eat asparagus is with your fingers, dipping it in whatever sauce may be provided. This is according to all the best authorities on etiquette. It's definitely more fun than using a fork – the kids may even take to asparagus this way – and it's amusing to see people look at you, thinking 'with her fingers?', knowing all along that you are correct and they are not!

↻ Asparagus with Lemon Butter

To me, this is the taste of springtime.

> 450 g asparagus
>
> 50 g butter
>
> 1 Tbsp lemon juice

1. Break the ends off the asparagus where they snap naturally. Steam or microwave asparagus until just barely tender-crisp.
2. While the asparagus is cooking, melt the butter and stir in the lemon juice. Put the lemon butter in a pretty little jug and let each diner pour a pool of it on to his or her plate for dipping.

Yield: 4 servings, each with 5 grams of carbohydrate and 2 grams of fibre, for a total of 3 grams of usable carbs and 3 grams of protein.

↻ Asparagus with Aioli and Parmesan

Cold asparagus, dipped in garlic sauce and cheese – wonderful.

> 1 kg asparagus
>
> Aioli (see page 424)
>
> 75 g grated Parmesan cheese

1. Break the ends off the asparagus where they snap naturally. Steam or microwave the asparagus for barely 3 to 4 minutes, or just until the colour brightens. (They should be even less done than tender-crisp.) Chill the asparagus.
2. At dinnertime, give each diner a couple of tablespoons of Aioli and a little hill of Parmesan. Dip each asparagus stalk in the Aioli, then in the Parmesan, and eat.

Yield: 4 servings, each with 6 grams of carbohydrate and 2 grams of fibre, for a total of 4 grams of usable carbs and 5 grams of protein.

↻ Asparagus Pecandine

I never thought anything could be as good with asparagus as lemon butter is – and then I tried this.

 5 Tbsp butter

 50 g chopped pecans

 1 1/2 tsp tarragon vinegar

 450 g asparagus, steamed just until tender-crisp

1. Melt the butter in a heavy frying pan over a medium to high heat. Stir in the pecans and sauté, stirring frequently, for 5 to 7 minutes, or until they are golden and crisp through. Stir in the tarragon vinegar.
2. Place the asparagus on serving plates and spoon the sauce over it. Serve immediately.

 Yield: 4 servings, each with 8 grams of carbohydrate and 4 grams of fibre, for a total of 4 grams of usable carbs and 4 grams of protein.

↻ Garlic Asparagus

 450 g fresh asparagus

 75 ml olive oil

 2 cloves garlic, crushed

1. Break the ends off the asparagus where they snap naturally. Cut asparagus on the diagonal into 2.5-cm lengths.
2. Heat the olive oil in a heavy frying pan over a medium to high heat. Add the asparagus and sauté, stirring occasionally, until it is tender-crisp (6 to 8 minutes).
3. Stir in the garlic, sauté 1 minute more and serve.

 Yield: 4 servings, each with 6 grams of carbohydrate and 2 grams of fibre, for a total of 4 grams of usable carbs and 3 grams of protein.

↻ Fried Artichoke

This is one of the fastest ways I know to cook artichokes.

> 1 large artichoke
> Olive oil
> Lemon wedges
> Salt

1. Cut about 2.5 cm off the top of your artichoke, trim the stem and pull off the bottom few rows of leaves. Now slice it vertically down the centre. You'll see the 'choke' – the fuzzy, inedible part at the centre. Using the tip of a spoon, scrape every last bit of this out (it pulls off the tasty part of the artichoke quite easily).

2. In a large, heavy frying pan, heat 2.5 cm of olive oil over a medium to high heat. When the oil is hot, add your cleaned artichoke, flat side down. Fry for about 10 minutes, turning over halfway through. It should be tender and just starting to brown. Drain on kitchen paper.

3. Serve the artichoke halves with lemon wedges to squeeze over them and salt to sprinkle on them to taste.

Yield: 1 serving, with 13 grams of carbohydrate and a whopping 7 grams of fibre, for a total of 6 grams of usable carbs (a couple of teaspoons of lemon juice add just 1 more gram) and 4 grams of protein.

🍓 If you've never eaten one of these before, peel off the leaves, one by one, and drag the base of each one between your teeth, scraping off the little bit of edible stuff at the bottom of each leaf. When you've finished doing that and you have a big pile of artichoke leaves on your plate, use a fork and knife to eat the delectable heart.

↻ Artichokes with Aioli

Artichokes with a rich, garlicky sauce – what's not to like?

> 6 artichokes
>
> Salt
>
> 1 batch Aioli (see page 424)

1. Cut about 2.5 cm off the top of each artichoke, trim the stems and pull off the bottom few rows of leaves.
2. Put enough water to cover the artichokes in a good-size pan and bring it to the boil. Add a couple of teaspoons of salt and drop in your artichokes.
3. Turn the heat down and let the artichokes simmer until they're tender. Depending on how big they are, this could take anywhere from 15 to 45 minutes. When the artichokes are done, drain them well.
4. Divide the Aioli between four small dishes and put a dish of Aioli and an artichoke on each serving plate.
5. Peel off the leaves, one by one, and dip the tender, edible bottom ends in the Aioli, then scrape them between your teeth. Each diner will need to cut or scrape off the fuzzy 'choke' after eating all the leaves. They can then use a knife and fork to cut up the artichoke's heart and dip it in the remaining Aioli.

Yield: 6 servings, each with 15 grams of carbohydrate and 7 grams of fibre, for a total of 8 grams of usable carbs and 5 grams of protein.

↻ Stir-Fried Spinach

Spinach originated in Asia, so stir-frying it is a very traditional way of preparing it.

> 75 ml peanut oil
>
> 1 kg fresh spinach, washed and dried
>
> 2 cloves garlic, crushed

Heat the oil in a heavy frying pan or wok over a high heat. Add the spinach and garlic and stir-fry for only a minute or two, then serve.

Yield: 6 servings, each with 6 grams of carbohydrate and 4 grams of fibre, for a total of 2 grams of usable carbs and 4 grams of protein.

⤳ Sicilian Spinach

> 3 Tbsp butter
>
> 1 kg fresh spinach, washed and dried
>
> 1 clove garlic, crushed
>
> 1 or 2 anchovy fillets, finely chopped

1. Heat the butter in a heavy frying pan. Add the spinach and garlic, and sauté until the spinach is just limp.
2. Stir in the anchovies and serve.

Yield: 6 servings, each with 5 grams of carbohydrate and 4 grams of fibre, for a total of just 1 gram of usable carbs and 5 grams of protein.

> 🍓 Not everyone likes anchovies and if you're among those who don't, just leave them out.

⤳ Creamed Spinach

> 300 g frozen, chopped spinach, thawed
>
> 30 g double cream
>
> 30 g grated Parmesan cheese
>
> 1 clove garlic, crushed

Put all the ingredients in a heavy-bottomed saucepan over a medium-low heat and simmer for 7 to 8 minutes.

Yield: 3 servings, each with 5 grams of carbohydrate and 3 grams of fibre, for a total of 2 grams of usable carbs and 6 grams of protein.

♻ Greek Spinach

    1 Tbsp butter
    1/4 small onion, finely chopped
    300 g frozen, chopped spinach, thawed
    30 g crumbled feta cheese
    50 g cottage cheese

1. Melt the butter in a heavy frying pan over medium heat. Add the onion and let it sizzle for just a minute. Add the spinach and sauté, stirring now and then, for 5 to 7 minutes.

2. Add in the cheeses and stir until they start to melt. Let the spinach cook for another minute or so, then serve.

    Yield: 3 servings, each with 6 grams of carbohydrate and 3 grams of fibre, for a total of 3 grams of usable carbs and 7 grams of protein.

♻ Sag Paneer

With cottage cheese, this isn't totally authentic, but it's mighty tasty.

    2 Tbsp butter
    1 tsp curry powder
    300 g frozen, chopped spinach, thawed
    1 tsp salt
    75 g cottage cheese
    2 tsp soured cream

1. Melt the butter in a heavy frying pan over low heat and stir in the curry powder. Let the curry powder cook in the butter for 3 to 4 minutes.

2. Stir in the spinach and the salt. Cover the frying pan and let the spinach cook for 4 to 5 minutes, or until heated through.

3. Stir in the cottage cheese and soured cream, and cook, stirring, until the cheese has completely melted.

    Yield: 3 servings, each with 5 grams of carbohydrate and 3 grams of fibre, for a total of 2 grams of usable carbs and 6 grams of protein.

About Cooking Broccoli

If you're using fresh broccoli, cut it up and peel the stems. If you've been discarding the stems, you'll be startled to discover that they're the best part of the broccoli once you've peeled off the tough skin.

Broccoli is another vegetable that's great when it's cooked just barely enough, but revolting when it's overcooked. I often think that the reason there are so many broccoli-haters in the world is because they've only been exposed to the mushy, grey, overcooked version. So above all, don't overcook your broccoli!

You can steam or microwave broccoli. If you're steaming, start timing after the water comes to the boil. Fresh broccoli needs about 7 minutes and frozen broccoli (assuming you start with it still frozen) needs closer to 10 or 11 minutes. If you're microwaving (my favourite way to cook it), put it in a microwave-safe casserole, add a tablespoon or two of water and cover with clingfilm or a lid. Microwave on High for about 5 minutes for fresh broccoli or closer to 10 minutes for frozen, stirring halfway through to make sure it cooks evenly. However you cook your broccoli, uncover it as soon as it is done to your liking, or it will continue to cook and end up mushy.

ᖆ Broccoli with Lemon Butter

I'm always bemused when I see frozen broccoli with lemon butter at my grocery store. I mean, how hard is it to add butter and
lemon juice to your broccoli?

> 450 g frozen, or 1 large head fresh broccoli
>
> 4 Tbsp butter
>
> 1 Tbsp lemon juice

Steam or microwave your broccoli. When it's cooked, drain off the water
and toss the broccoli with the butter and lemon juice until the butter is
melted. That's it!

Yield: 4 servings, each with 6 grams of carbohydrate and 3 grams of
fibre, for a total of 3 grams of usable carbs and 3 grams of protein.

ᖆ Broccoli Piquant

This is a country-style dish that's good with pork chops.

> 450 g frozen broccoli florets
>
> 4 rashers bacon
>
> 1 clove garlic, crushed
>
> 3 Tbsp cider vinegar

1. Steam or microwave the broccoli until just tender-crisp.
2. While the broccoli is cooking, fry the bacon until crisp, remove from the
   pan and drain. Pour off all but a couple of tablespoons of the fat.
3. When the broccoli is cooked, drain and add it to the bacon fat in the
   frying pan. Add the garlic and vinegar and stir over a medium heat for
   a minute or two.
4. Crumble the bacon over the broccoli, stir for another minute or so
   and serve.

Yield: 4 servings, each with 7 grams of carbohydrate and 3 grams of
fibre, for a total of 4 grams of usable carbs and 5 grams of protein.

↻ Ginger Stir-Fry Broccoli

2 or 3 Tbsp peanut oil, or other bland oil

2 cloves garlic, crushed

450 g frozen broccoli florets, thawed

1 Tbsp grated fresh ginger

1 Tbsp soy sauce

1. Heat the oil in a wok or heavy frying pan over a high heat. Add the garlic and the broccoli, and stir-fry for 7 to 10 minutes, or until the broccoli is tender-crisp.

2. Stir in the ginger and soy sauce, stir-fry for just another minute and serve.

Yield: 4 servings, each with 7 grams of carbohydrate and 3 grams of fibre, for a total of 4 grams of usable carbs and 4 grams of protein.

About Cooking Spaghetti Squash

If you've never cooked a spaghetti squash, you may be puzzled as to how to go about it, but it's really easy: just stab it several times (to keep it from exploding) and put it in your microwave on High for 12 to 15 minutes. Then slice it open and scoop out and discard the seeds. Now take a fork and start scraping at the flesh of the squash. You will be surprised and charmed to discover that it separates into strands very much like spaghetti, only yellow-orange in colour.

Spaghetti squash is not a terribly low-carb vegetable, but it's much lower-carb than spaghetti, so it's a useful substitute in many recipes – especially casseroles. If you only need half of your cooked spaghetti squash right away, the rest will live happily in a sealed bag in your fridge for 3 or 4 days.

◯ Spaghetti Squash Alfredo

We love this! My husband is a Spaghetti Alfredo fiend, so by using spaghetti squash instead of pasta, he gets his fix without all those additional carbs.

> 500 g cooked spaghetti squash
>
> 3 Tbsp butter
>
> 3 Tbsp double cream
>
> 1 clove garlic, crushed
>
> 40 g grated or shaved Parmesan cheese

Simply heat up your squash and stir in everything else. Stir until the butter's melted and serve!

Yield: 4 servings, each with 4 grams of carbohydrate, a trace of fibre and 3 grams of protein.

This makes a very nice side dish with some chicken sautéed in olive oil and garlic.

○ Spaghetti Squash Carbonara

This makes a very filling side dish.

> 8 rashers bacon
>
> 4 eggs
>
> 100 g grated Parmesan cheese
>
> 700 g cooked spaghetti squash
>
> 1 clove garlic, crushed

1. Fry the bacon until crisp. Remove from pan and pour off all but a couple tablespoons of fat.
2. Beat the eggs with the cheese and toss with the spaghetti squash. Pour the squash mixture into the hot fat in the frying pan and add the garlic. Toss for 2 to 3 minutes.
3. Crumble in the bacon, toss and serve.

Yield: 6 servings, each with 6 grams of carbohydrate and 1 gram of fibre, for a total of 5 grams of usable carbs and 11 grams of protein.

> 🍓 You can make this dish higher in protein by using diced, leftover ham in place of the bacon. Brown the ham in olive oil, remove from the pan, cook the squash mixture in the oil and then toss in the ham just before serving.

ʕ Spicy Sesame 'Noodles' with Vegetables

This isn't terribly low-carb, but it does make a rather splendid dinner for a mixed group of vegetarian and non-vegetarian friends and family.

700 g cooked spaghetti squash

75 ml water

3 Tbsp soy sauce

5 Tbsp tahini

1 1/2 Tbsp rice vinegar

1/2 tsp chilli flakes

1 Tbsp sesame seeds

2 to 3 Tbsp peanut or other bland oil

100 g mushrooms, thickly sliced

100 g diced green pepper

100 g diced celery

50 g chopped onion

100 g sugar snap peas, cut into 2.5-cm lengths

2 Tbsp grated fresh ginger

2 cloves garlic, crushed

80 g cooked prawns, or diced left-over chicken, pork or ham per serving (optional)

1. Place the spaghetti squash in a large mixing bowl.

2. In a separate bowl, combine the water, soy sauce, tahini, rice vinegar and chilli flakes, mixing well. Pour over the spaghetti squash and set aside.

3. Place the sesame seeds in a small, heavy frying pan over a high heat and shake the frying pan constantly until the seeds start to 'pop'. Immediately turn off the heat and shake the seeds out on to a small plate to cool. Set aside.

4. Just before you're ready to serve the dish, heat the oil in a large frying pan or wok. Add the mushrooms, pepper, celery, onion, sugar snap peas, ginger and garlic, and stir-fry over high heat for 7 to 10 minutes or until tender-crisp.

5. When the vegetables are done, add them to the large mixing bowl with the spaghetti squash mixture and toss until well combined.

6. Pile the vegetables and 'noodles' on serving plates. Top the meat-eaters' servings with the prawns, chicken, pork or ham (if using), and scatter sesame seeds over each serving.

Yield: 4 servings, each with 19 grams of carbohydrate and 4 grams of fibre, for a total of 15 grams of usable carbs and 7 grams of protein. (Analysis does not include optional meat.)

🍓 This is a great dish to make for guests, because so much of it can be done ahead of time. You can prepare the noodles (step 2) and the garnish (step 3) before your company arrives and then just stir-fry the vegetables and garnish the plates when it's time to eat.

CHAPTER SIX

Side Dish Salads

Salad isn't always afforded the regard it deserves. Many people dump some 'iceberg mix' in a bowl, throw in a few dismal winter tomatoes, slosh some gooey bottled dressing on top and are then surprised that their families show no enthusiasm for it.

Made with just a little extra imagination, salad really can be one of the most delicious, exciting foods. It is, of course, one of the most nutritious as well, so learn to pay attention to your salads.

First of all, abandon the iceberg lettuce; not only is it the least-nutritious lettuce on the market, it's also the blandest. Try all sorts of other green and leafy things, such as romaine lettuce, round lettuce, radicchio, frisée, fresh spinach, rocket, or whatever else you can find. Try making some fresh dressings, too. And unless all the members of your family have violently opposing opinions on salad dressing, try actually tossing your salad with the dressing, instead of just sloshing it on top. I think you'll be surprised at the difference it makes to the end product.

The dressings, by the way, are at the end of this chapter. But first let's get to the salads themselves.

Greek Salad

This is a wonderful, filling, fresh-tasting salad we never get tired of.

> 1 large romaine lettuce
>
> 50 g chopped fresh parsley
>
> 1/2 cucumber, sliced
>
> 1 green pepper, sliced
>
> Greek Lemon Dressing (see page 237)
>
> 1/4 sweet red onion, thinly sliced into rings
>
> 12 to 15 Greek olives
>
> 2 ripe tomatoes, cut into wedges
>
> 100 to 150 g feta cheese, crumbled
>
> Anchovy fillets packed in olive oil (optional)

You can do step 1 ahead of time, if you like, which makes this salad very servable on a weeknight.

1. Wash and dry your romaine and break or cut it into bite-sized pieces. Cut up and add the parsley, cucumber and green pepper.
2. Just before serving, pour on the Greek dressing and toss the salad well.
3. Arrange the onions, olives and tomatoes artistically on top and sprinkle the crumbled feta in the middle. You can also add the anchovies at this point, if you know that everybody likes them, but I prefer to serve them separately, for those who like them.

Yield: 4 servings, each with 16 grams of carbohydrate and 6 grams of fibre, for a total of 10 grams of usable carbs and 11 grams of protein.

Ꙩ Autumn Salad

The flavour contrasts in this salad are lovely and I've kept the pear to a quantity that won't add too many carbs.

2 Tbsp butter

50 g chopped walnuts

200 g assorted salad greens

1/4 sweet red onion, thinly sliced

75 ml olive oil

2 tsp wine vinegar

2 tsp lemon juice

1/4 tsp Dijon mustard

1/8 tsp salt

1/8 tsp freshly ground black pepper

1/2 ripe pear, chopped

30 g crumbled blue cheese

1. Melt the butter in a small, heavy frying pan over medium heat. Add the walnuts and let them toast in the butter, stirring occasionally, for about 5 minutes.

2. While the walnuts are toasting – and make sure you keep an eye on them so they don't burn – wash and dry your greens and put them in salad bowl with the onion. Toss with the oil first, then combine the vinegar, lemon juice, mustard, salt and pepper, and add that to the salad bowl. Toss until everything is well covered.

3. Top the salad with the pear, the warm toasted walnuts and the crumbled blue cheese, and serve.

Yield: 4 generous servings, each with 13 grams of carbohydrate and 6 grams of fibre, for a total of 7 grams of usable carbs and 10 grams of protein.

↻ Rocket-Pear Salad

An extraordinary combination of flavours. If you've never tried rocket, you'll be surprised: it tastes almost as if it's been roasted. You could use grated Parmesan cheese, but I think the bigger pieces of thinly sliced Parmesan make a difference in the salad's flavour.

> 100 g washed, dried, torn-up rocket
>
> 1/2 ripe pear, cut in small chunks or slices
>
> 3 Tbsp extra-virgin olive oil
>
> Juice of 1 lemon
>
> Salt and freshly ground black pepper
>
> 2 Tbsp shavings of Parmesan cheese

Combine the rocket and pear in a salad bowl. Add the olive oil and toss well. Add the lemon juice, salt and pepper lightly, and toss again. Top with Parmesan and serve.

Yield: 2 generous servings, each with 9 grams of carbohydrate and 2 grams of fibre, for a total of 7 grams of usable carbs and 3 grams of protein.

◌ Spinach Pecan Salad

> 1 kg fresh spinach
>
> Salt
>
> 10 spring onions, thinly sliced, including about 10 cm of the green part
>
> 75 ml extra-virgin olive oil
>
> 75 ml lemon juice
>
> 100 g toasted, salted pecans, chopped

1. Wash and dry the spinach until you're absolutely sure it's clean – spinach can hold a lot of grit! When you're sure it's clean and dry, put it in a salad bowl and sprinkle it with a little salt – maybe a teaspoonful – and squeeze the leaves gently with your hands. You'll find that the spinach becomes limp and reduces in volume. Add the spring onions to the bowl.
2. Pour on the olive oil and toss the salad thoroughly. Add the lemon juice and toss again. Top with the pecans and serve.

Yield: 6 servings, each with 12 grams of carbohydrate and 6 grams of fibre, for a total of 6 grams of usable carbs and 6 grams of protein.

◌ Classic Spinach Salad

> 100 g fresh spinach
>
> 1/8 large, sweet red onion, thinly sliced
>
> 3 Tbsp oil
>
> 2 Tbsp cider vinegar
>
> 2 tsp tomato purée
>
> 1 1/2 tsp Splenda
>
> 1/4 small onion, grated
>
> 1/8 tsp dry mustard
>
> Salt and freshly ground black pepper
>
> 2 rashers bacon, cooked until crisp, and crumbled
>
> 1 hard-boiled egg, chopped

1. Wash the spinach very well, and dry. Tear up larger leaves. Combine with the onion in a salad bowl.
2. In a separate bowl, mix up the oil, vinegar, tomato purée, Splenda, onion, mustard, and salt and pepper to taste. Pour the mixture over the spinach and onion, and toss.
3. Top the salad with the bacon and egg, and serve.

   Yield: 2 generous servings, each with 7 grams of carbohydrate and 2 grams of fibre, for a total of 5 grams of usable carbs and 2 grams of protein.

○ Summer Treat Spinach Salad

Where will you get your potassium now that you're not eating bananas? Each serving of this salad has more potassium than three bananas!

> 1 kg fresh spinach
>
> 1 ripe avocado
>
> 1/4 cantaloupe melon
>
> 2 Tbsp alfalfa sprouts
>
> 2 spring onions, sliced
>
> French Vinaigrette Dressing (see page 235)

1. Wash the spinach very well, and dry. Tear up larger leaves.
2. Cut the avocado in half, remove the stone and the peel, and cut into chunks.
3. Peel and cube the cantaloupe, or use a melon baller.
4. Add the avocado and cantaloupe to the spinach, along with the alfalfa sprouts and spring onions. Toss with the vinaigrette just before serving.

   Yield: 6 servings, each with 11 grams of carbohydrate and 5 grams of fibre, for a total of 6 grams of usable carbs and 5 grams of protein.

☽ Mixed Salad Greens with Warm Brie Dressing

This elegant dinner party fare is a carbohydrate bargain with lots of flavour.

> 170 g romaine lettuce, washed, dried and broken up
>
> 170 g red leaf lettuce, washed, dried and broken up
>
> 50 g radicchio, washed, dried and broken up
>
> 50 g fresh parsley, chopped
>
> 4 spring onions, thinly sliced, including the crisp green part
>
> 125 ml extra-virgin olive oil
>
> 1/2 small onion, finely chopped
>
> 3 cloves garlic, crushed
>
> 170 g Brie, rind removed, cut into small chunks
>
> 75 ml sherry vinegar
>
> 1 Tbsp lemon juice
>
> 1 1/2 tsp Dijon mustard

1. Put the lettuce, radicchio, parsley and spring onions in a large salad bowl and keep cold.
2. Put the olive oil in a heavy-bottomed saucepan over a medium-low heat. Add the onion and garlic and let them cook for 2 to 3 minutes.
3. Melt in the Brie, one chunk at a time, continuously stirring with a whisk. (It'll look dreadful at first, but don't worry.)
4. When all the cheese is melted in, whisk in the sherry vinegar, lemon juice and Dijon mustard. Let it cook for a few minutes, stirring all the while, until your dressing is smooth and thick. Pour over the salad, and toss.

Yield: 6 servings, each with 7 grams of carbohydrate and 3 of fibre, for a total of 4 grams of usable carbs and 8 grams of protein.

◯ Bayside Salad

This is my version of a fantastic salad I had at a restaurant called The Bayside Grill, down near the sea. The combination of greens isn't vital – you can put in what you prefer, as long as you make sure to include some bitter greens, such as chicory.

> 30 g chopped pecans
>
> 2 Tbsp butter
>
> 50 g torn romaine
>
> 30 g torn radicchio
>
> 30 g torn frisée
>
> 30 g torn English round lettuce
>
> 30 g torn curly endive
>
> 1/4 sweet red onion, thinly sliced
>
> Raspberry Vinaigrette (see page 241)
>
> 30 g crumbled blue cheese
>
> 4 rashers bacon, cooked until crisp, and crumbled

1. Melt the butter in a heavy frying pan. Add the pecans and toast them over medium heat, stirring for 5 minutes or so, until brown and crisp.

2. Toss the salad leaves and onion with the Raspberry Vinaigrette.

3. Pile the salad on 4 serving plates and top each with 1 tablespoon of pecans, 1 tablespoon of blue cheese and 1 strip of crumbled bacon.

Yield: 4 servings, each with 6 grams of carbohydrate and 2 grams of fibre, for a total of 4 grams of usable carbs and 2 grams of protein.

↻ Caesar Salad

This is the salad that made Tijuana restaurateur Caesar Cardini famous. If you've only had that wilted stuff that sometimes passes for Caesar salad, you have to try this.

> 1 large romaine lettuce
> Caesar Dressing (see page 243)

Wash, dry and tear up an entire romaine lettuce. Toss it with the dressing. That's it!

Yield: 6 servings, each with 5 grams of carbohydrate and 2 grams of fibre, for a total of 3 grams of usable carbs and 6 grams of protein.

🍓 If you have some low-carb bread on hand, you could dice up a couple of slices, put them in a pan with 75 ml of olive oil and a couple of cloves of garlic, and sauté them for a few minutes, until they're brown and crispy. I'd probably only bother with that for company, though.

◌ Our Favourite Salad

We've served this salad over and over and we never tire of it. The dressing tastes a lot like Caesar, but it's less trouble and there's no blender to wash afterwards

> 1 clove garlic
>
> 125 ml extra-virgin olive oil
>
> 1 romaine lettuce
>
> 30 g chopped fresh parsley
>
> 1/2 green pepper, diced
>
> 1/4 cucumber, quartered and sliced
>
> 1/4 sweet red onion
>
> 2 to 3 Tbsp lemon juice
>
> 2 to 3 tsp Worcestershire sauce
>
> 30 g Parmesan cheese
>
> 1 medium ripe tomato, cut into thin wedges

1. Crush the clove of garlic in a small bowl, cover it with the olive oil and set it aside.

2. Wash and dry your romaine, break it up into a bowl and add the parsley, pepper, cucumber and onion. Pour the garlic-flavoured oil over the salad and toss until every leaf is covered.

3. Sprinkle on the lemon juice and toss again. Then sprinkle on the Worcestershire sauce and toss again. Finally, sprinkle on the Parmesan and toss one last time. Top with the tomatoes and serve.

Yield: 6 servings, each with 7 grams of carbohydrate and 3 grams of fibre, for a total of 4 grams of usable carbs and 4 grams of protein.

↻ Update Salad

This recipe went around in the 1960s, using curly endive instead of this mixture of bitter greens and, of course, using sugar in the dressing. I like to think I've brought it into the 21st century – hence the name.

Salad

2 medium green peppers, cut in smallish strips

6 Tbsp chopped parsley

30 g torn radicchio

30 g chopped curly endive

30 g chopped frisée

3 tomatoes, each cut in 8 lengthways wedges

1/8 large, sweet red onion, thinly sliced

2 Tbsp chopped black olives

Dressing

75 ml water

125 ml tarragon vinegar

1/2 tsp salt

1 1/2 Tbsp lemon juice

1 Tbsp Splenda

1/8 tsp black treacle

Topping

6 Tbsp soured cream

1. Put the peppers, parsley, salad leaves, tomatoes, onion and olives in a big bowl and set aside.
2. In a separate bowl, combine the water, vinegar, salt, lemon juice, Splenda and treacle. Pour it all over the salad and toss.
3. Put the whole thing in the refrigerator and leave it there for a few hours, stirring it now and then.
4. To serve, put a 1-tablespoon dollop of soured cream on each serving.

Yield: 6 servings, each with 9 grams of carbohydrate and 2 grams of fibre, for a total of 7 grams of usable carbs and 2 grams of protein.

↶ Parsley Salad

If you've always thought of parsley as a garnish, it's time to start thinking of it as a food. It's delicious and very, very nutritious.

> 3 tomatoes, diced
>
> 1 cucumber, peeled (if desired) and diced
>
> 3 spring onions, sliced
>
> 6 Tbsp chopped parsley
>
> 75 ml fresh lemon juice
>
> 125 ml extra-virgin olive oil
>
> Salt and freshly ground black pepper
>
> Small tin black olives, drained and sliced

1. Combine the tomatoes, cucumber, spring onions and parsley, and chill.
2. Combine the lemon juice, olive oil, and salt and pepper to taste, and toss with the vegetables.
3. Top with the olives and serve.

Yield: 4 servings, each with 10 grams of carbohydrate and 3 grams of fibre, for a total of 7 grams of usable carbs and 2 grams of protein.

℧ California Salad

　　100 g torn romaine lettuce

　　100 g torn red leaf lettuce

　　1 ripe black avocado

　　3 Tbsp extra-virgin olive oil

　　2 Tbsp lemon juice

　　Salt and freshly ground black pepper

　　2 Tbsp alfalfa sprouts

1. Combine the lettuces in a salad bowl. Peel the avocado, cut it into small chunks (or just scoop it all out with a spoon) and add it to the bowl.
2. Toss the salad first with the oil, then the lemon juice, then finally with salt and pepper to taste. Top with the alfalfa and serve.

Yield: 4 servings, each with 12 grams of carbohydrate and 5 grams of fibre, for a total of 7 grams of usable carbs and 4 grams of protein.

> 🍓 If you're thinking about substituting a green avocado for the black one in this recipe, remember that the little black avocados are substantially lower in carbs.

℧ Tomatoes Basilico

This is a simple, elegant summer classic, but you shouldn't even bother trying it with second-rate tomatoes.

　　4 medium-sized ripe tomatoes

　　2 Tbsp fresh basil, coarsely chopped

Slice the tomatoes and arrange them on a platter. Sprinkle the basil over them and let the salad stand for half an hour or so before serving.

Yield: 4 generous servings, each with 6 grams of carbohydrate and 2 grams of fibre, for a total of 4 grams of usable carbs and 1 gram of protein.

☌ Tomato-Mozzarella Plate

It's hard to know whether this is a salad or a starter. All that really matters is that it's good and remarkably easy. The tomatoes you use must be superb and you must use fresh mozzarella, not the cheap kind sold for pizza. Look for it in a bowl of water on the fancy cheese counter.

> 2 Tbsp fresh basil, finely chopped
>
> 75 ml extra-virgin olive oil
>
> 450 g fresh mozzarella
>
> 3 ripe tomatoes, sliced
>
> Fresh coarsely ground black pepper

1. Mix the basil with the olive oil and set aside.
2. Cut 18 slices of mozzarella and tomatoes (6 slices from each tomato). Arrange three slices of tomato and three slices of mozzarella on each serving plate.
3. Spoon a couple of teaspoons of the basil and olive oil over each plate. Scatter just a tiny bit of pepper over, and serve.

Yield: 6 servings, each with 5 grams of carbohydrate and 1 gram of fibre, for a total of 4 grams of usable carbs and 17 grams of protein.

☌ Melon with Prosciutto

Undoubtedly an Italian classic.

> 1 ripe cantaloupe melon
>
> 12 very thin slices prosciutto

Cut your melon into 12 wedges, removing seeds and rind. Wrap each melon wedge in a slice of prosciutto. Serve and enjoy!

Yield: 12 servings, each with 4 grams of carbohydrate, a trace of fibre and 6 grams of protein.

ᴼ Melon Prosciutto Salad

1/2 ripe cantaloupe melon
1/2 ripe honeydew melon
225 g prosciutto

1. Seed and peel the melon and cut it into 2.5-cm cubes (or use a melon baller).
2. Chop the prosciutto, toss everything together and serve.

Yield: 10 servings, each with 8 grams of carbohydrate and 1 gram of fibre, for a total of 7 grams of usable carbs and 7 grams of protein.

🍓 If you can't get real Italian prosciutto, you could use any good, thinly sliced deli ham.

Make-Ahead Salads

I just love deli-style salads – you know, the kind you can make ahead and just pull out of the refrigerator when you want them. There are so many varieties and they are so, so convenient. I like to make them in big batches. That way I have fast, easy vegetables for a few days.

Our first several make-ahead salads here feature cucumbers – not only because cucumbers are delicious, but also because they're about the lowest-carb vegetable around!

⌒ Soured Cream and Cuke Salad

1 green pepper

2 cucumbers, scrubbed but not peeled

1/2 large sweet red onion

1/2 cauliflower

2 tsp salt

225 ml soured cream

2 Tbsp vinegar (cider vinegar is best, but wine vinegar will do)

2 rounded tsp dried dill

1. Slice the pepper, cucumbers, onion and cauliflower as thinly as you possibly can. The slicing blade on a food processor works nicely and it saves you time, but I've also done it with a good, sharp knife.

2. Toss the vegetables well with the salt and chill them in the refrigerator for an hour or two.

3. In a separate bowl, mix the soured cream, vinegar and dill, combining them well.

4. Remove the vegetables from the fridge, drain off the water that will have collected at the bottom of the bowl and stir in the soured cream mixture.

Yield: 10 servings, each with 4 grams of carbohydrate and 1 gram of fibre, for a total of 3 grams of usable carbs and 1 gram of protein.

🍓 You can eat this right away and it will be great, but it improves overnight.

Monica's In-Laws' Cucumber Salad

Monica is a reader who didn't send me her last name, but she did send me this great salad recipe.

> 3 medium cucumbers, thinly sliced
> 3 tsp salt
> 30 g Splenda
> 75 ml vinegar
> 225 ml soured cream
> 50 g finely chopped onion
> 1 tsp chopped fresh dill
> Salt and freshly ground black pepper

1. Put the cucumber slices in a large bowl and sprinkle with the salt. Refrigerate for 1 to 2 hours.

2. Drain off the water that will have collected at the bottom of the bowl, rinse and drain again.

3. Dissolve the Splenda in the vinegar, whisk in the soured cream, onion and dill, and fold the mixture into the cucumber slices. Salt and pepper to taste, and serve.

Yield: 8 servings, each with 7 grams of carbohydrate and 1 gram of fibre, for a total of 6 grams of usable carbs and 2 grams of protein.

↺ Gorkensalad

From reader Heather Firth, who says this is 'a really amazing cucumber salad. The cucumbers are limp – but still crunchy'.

> 4 peeled cucumbers, thinly sliced
> 1 1/2 Tbsp salt
> 75 ml water
> 3 Tbsp cider vinegar
> 3 Tbsp oil
> 2 Tbsp Splenda
> Freshly ground black pepper

1. Peel and slice the cucumbers. Put them in a large bowl, sprinkle the salt over them and stir it in. Cover and refrigerate overnight.

2. An hour or so before serving, take the cucumbers from the refrigerator and squeeze the water out of them, using your hands and working in small batches. The slices will go from kind of stiff and opaque to limp and almost translucent.

3. Mix together the fresh water, vinegar, oil, Splenda and pepper to taste. This is the 'dressing' – it should be light, tangy and just slightly sweet. Pour this over the cucumbers and mix them up. Chill until ready to serve.

Yield: 10 servings, each with 4 grams of carbohydrate and 1 gram of fibre, for a total of 3 grams of usable carbs and 1 gram of protein.

↻ Thai Cucumber Salad

Sweet and hot and so good! This, by the way, is one of those magnificent recipes that is low-carb, low-fat, low-calorie, fine for vegetarians and tastes great.

1/2 small red onion

1 small fresh jalapeño chilli, seeds removed

3 medium cucumbers

2 or 3 cloves fresh garlic, crushed

2 Tbsp grated fresh ginger

125 ml rice vinegar

1/2 tsp salt

1/4 tsp freshly ground black pepper

2 Tbsp Splenda

🍓 If you're not using a food processor, you should dice the onion and finely chop the chilli, then slice the cucumber as thinly as you can.

1. Using a food processor with the S-blade in place, put the onion and chilli in the food processor and pulse until they are both finely chopped.

2. Remove the S-blade and put on the slicing disk. Quarter the cucumbers lengthways, then run them through processer.

3. Put the onion, chilli and cucumbers in a big bowl. In a separate bowl, thoroughly combine the garlic, ginger, vinegar, salt, pepper and Splenda. Pour over the vegetables and mix well.

4. Chill for a few hours before serving, for the best flavour.

Yield: 8 generous servings, each with 6 grams of carbohydrate and 1 gram of fibre, for a total of 5 grams of usable carbs and 1 gram of protein.

⌒ Broccoli Salad

>1 kg frozen broccoli florets
>
>125 ml olive oil
>
>75 ml vinegar
>
>1 clove garlic, crushed
>
>1/2 tsp Italian seasoning herb blend
>
>1/2 tsp salt
>
>1/8 tsp freshly ground black pepper

1. Whisk the olive oil, vinegar, garlic, herbs, salt and pepper together.
2. Don't even bother to thaw the broccoli – just put it in a bowl and pour the olive oil mixture on top of it. Mix well and leave it in the fridge for several hours, stirring it now and then. Serve it just as it is or on salad greens.

Yield: 6 servings, each with 7 grams of carbohydrate and 4 grams of fibre, for a total of 3 grams of usable carbs and 4 grams of protein.

🍓 Of course, if you prefer, you can use fresh broccoli to make this salad. You'll have to peel the stems, cut it up and steam it for about 5 minutes first. And at that point, it will be very much like thawed frozen broccoli! Personally, I take the easy route.

↷ Parmesan Bean Salad

This salad is filling enough to make a nice light lunch.

> 450 g frozen sliced green beans
> 50 g finely chopped red onion
> 4 Tbsp extra-virgin olive oil
> 5 Tbsp cider vinegar
> 1/2 tsp salt
> 1/2 tsp paprika
> 1/4 tsp ground ginger
> 100 g grated Parmesan cheese

1. Steam or microwave the green beans until they're tender-crisp.
2. Let them cool a little, then stir in the onion, oil, vinegar, salt, paprika and ginger, then finally the Parmesan cheese. Chill well and serve.

   Yield: 4 servings, each with 12 grams of carbohydrate and 4 grams of fibre, for a total of 8 grams of usable carbs and 9 grams of protein.

↷ Low-Carb Rosy Radish Salad

This looks very pretty and tastes surprisingly mild.

> 450 g frozen sliced green beans
> 4 rashers bacon, cooked until crisp, and crumbled
> 1 small onion, chopped
> 100 g sliced radishes
> 3 Tbsp cider vinegar
> 1 1/2 Tbsp Splenda
> 3/4 tsp salt
> 1/4 tsp freshly ground black pepper

1. Steam or microwave the beans until they're tender-crisp.
2. Combine the beans, bacon, onion and radishes in a mixing bowl. In a separate bowl, combine the vinegar, Splenda, salt and pepper.

3. Pour the mixture over the salad, toss and serve.

Yield: 5 servings, each with 10 grams of carbohydrate and 3 grams of fibre, for a total of 7 grams of usable carbs and 4 grams of protein.

ᕲ Green Bean Salad

> 800 g frozen or fresh green beans
> 50 g chopped sweet red onion
> 100 g Splenda
> 1 tsp salt
> 1/2 tsp freshly ground black pepper
> 125 ml canola (rapeseed) oil
> 150 ml cider vinegar

1. Drain the beans and combine them in a bowl with the onion.
2. In a separate bowl, combine the Splenda, salt, pepper, oil and vinegar; pour the mixture over the vegetables.
3. Let it marinate for several hours at least; overnight would be fine. Drain off the marinade and serve.

Yield: 4 generous servings. If you were to eat all the marinade, this would have 17 grams of carbohydrate per serving, but since you don't, each serving actually has about 10 grams of carbohydrate and 4 grams of fibre, for a total of 6 grams of usable carbs and 2 grams of protein.

🍓 If you like, you can make this with frozen green beans, cooked tender-crisp. This is certainly preferable to pouring the vitamins down the sink, the way you do with tinned ones. Or, of course, you could do it with fresh beans.

↻ Dilled Beans

Hard to say if this is a salad or a pickle, but whatever you call it, it's tasty.

> 450 g frozen sliced green beans
>
> 125 ml wine vinegar
>
> 125 ml water
>
> 1 clove garlic
>
> 2 tsp salt
>
> 2 tsp chilli flakes
>
> 3 Tbsp dried dill

1. Steam or microwave the beans until they're tender-crisp.
2. While they are cooking, combine the vinegar, water, garlic, salt, chilli flakes and dill in a small saucepan and bring to the boil.
3. Drain the beans, leave to cool and put them in a jar. Pour the vinegar mixture over the beans and cover with a tight-fitting lid. Refrigerate for a day or two, shaking the jar occasionally. Serve cold.

Yield: 8 servings, each with 6 grams of carbohydrate and 2 grams of fibre, for a total of 4 grams of usable carbs and 1 gram of protein.

↻ Sesame Asparagus Salad

This is from Jennifer Eloff's wonderful cookbook *Splendid Low-Carbing*. Jen, of sweety.com, says it's simple, yet it has an eye-catching presentation.

> 450 g fresh asparagus
>
> 1 litre water
>
> 4 tsp soy sauce
>
> 2 tsp sesame or olive oil
>
> 1 Tbsp sesame seeds

1. Break off the tough ends of the asparagus by bending each stalk back until it snaps.

2. Bring the water to the boil in a large saucepan and drop the asparagus stalks into the rapidly boiling water. Parboil for 5 minutes, drain immediately and rinse in cold water. Pat dry with kitchen paper.

3. Combine the soy sauce and oil in a small bowl. Lay the asparagus stalks in a casserole and toss with the soy sauce mixture.

4. Sprinkle with the sesame seeds and chill in the refrigerator for an hour or two before serving.

Yield: 6 servings, each with 2 grams of carbohydrate and 1 gram of fibre, for a total of 1 gram of usable carbs and 1 gram of protein.

�◌ Coleslaw

This is my standard coleslaw recipe and it always draws compliments. The tiny bit of onion really sparks the flavour.

> 1 green cabbage
> 1/4 sweet red onion
> Coleslaw Dressing (see page 244)

1. Using a food processor's slicing blade or a sharp knife, reduce your cabbage to shreds and put them in a very large bowl.

2. Chop the onion really finely and put that in the bowl, too.

3. Pour on the dressing and toss well.

Yield: 10 servings, each with 1 gram of carbohydrate, a trace of fibre and 1 gram of protein.

🍓 Just got invited to a picnic and short on time for making something that'll feed a crowd? This recipe makes a veritable bucketful and it's a wonderful side dish to almost any plain meat, including chops and chicken. You could even use ready-prepared coleslaw vegetables from the supermarket and just add my dressing – I promise not to tell!

◌ Coleslaw for Company

The colours in this slaw are so intense, it's almost too beautiful to eat.

> 1 red cabbage
> 1 small carrot, grated
> 1/4 sweet red onion, finely chopped
> Coleslaw Dressing (see page 244)

1. Using a food processor's slicing blade or a sharp knife, shred the cabbage and put it in a big bowl.
2. Add the carrot and onion, and toss with the dressing. Admire and enjoy.

   Yield: 10 servings, each with 2 grams of carbohydrate, a trace of fibre and 1 gram of protein.

◌ Coleslaw Italiano

My sister makes this recipe – and it's pretty good.

> 300 g finely chopped cabbage
> 125 ml Italian Vinaigrette Dressing (see page 236), or use bottled

Toss the cabbage with the Italian dressing and serve.

Yield: 8 servings, each with 3 grams of carbohydrate and 1 gram of fibre, for a total of 2 grams of usable carbs and 1 gram of protein.

↻ Asian Ginger Slaw

Even my slaw-hating husband likes this! A very different texture and flavour from standard slaws.

300 g finely chopped Chinese napa cabbage

30 g grated carrot

2 spring onions, thinly sliced

30 g pale inner celery stalk, thinly sliced

75 ml mayonnaise

1 tsp grated fresh ginger

2 Tbsp rice vinegar

1 tsp soy sauce

1 tsp Splenda

1. Combine the cabbage, carrot, spring onions and celery in a salad bowl.
2. In a separate bowl, combine the mayonnaise, ginger, vinegar, soy sauce and Splenda. Beat together until smooth, pour over the vegetables, toss and serve.

Yield: 8 servings, each with 4 grams of carbohydrate and 1 gram of fibre, for a total of 3 grams of usable carbs and 1 gram of protein.

⟲ Confetti UnSlaw

This may be a raw cabbage salad, but it's not much like coleslaw. Actually, it's utterly gorgeous on the plate.

> 150 g finely chopped green cabbage
>
> 150 g finely chopped red cabbage
>
> 1/2 red pepper, chopped
>
> 1/2 green pepper, chopped
>
> 4 spring onions, sliced, including the crisp green part
>
> 30 g grated carrot
>
> 1 small celery stick, thinly sliced
>
> 2 Tbsp finely chopped fresh parsley
>
> Creamy Garlic Dressing (see page 242)

Just cut up and combine all these vegetables and toss with the Creamy Garlic Dressing.

Yield: 8 servings, each with 6 grams of carbohydrate and 2 grams of fibre, for a total of 4 grams of usable carbs and 1 gram of protein.

◌ Cauliflower-Olive Salad

Unusual, and unusually good.

> 1/2 cauliflower, broken into small florets
>
> 50 g diced red onion
>
> 50 g tinned ripe olives, drained and sliced
>
> 30 g chopped fresh parsley
>
> 75 ml lemon juice
>
> 75 ml olive oil
>
> 75 ml mayonnaise
>
> 1/2 tsp salt
>
> About a dozen cherry tomatoes
>
> Lettuce (optional)

1. Combine the cauliflower, onion, olives and parsley in a bowl.
2. Combine the lemon juice, olive oil, mayonnaise and salt in a separate bowl. Pour over the vegetables and toss well.
3. Chill for at least an hour – a whole day would be even better. When you're ready to serve the salad, cut the tomatoes in half and add them to the salad. Serve on a bed of lettuce if you wish, but it's wonderful alone, too.

Yield: 4 servings, each with 7 grams of carbohydrate and 2 grams of fibre, for a total of 5 grams of usable carbs and 1 gram of protein.

☌ UnPotato Salad

You are going to be so surprised; this is amazingly like potato salad.

> 1 large cauliflower, cut into small chunks
>
> 225 g diced celery
>
> 110 g diced red onion
>
> 500 ml mayonnaise
>
> 75 ml cider vinegar
>
> 2 tsp salt
>
> 2 tsp Splenda
>
> 1/2 tsp freshly ground black pepper
>
> 4 hard-boiled eggs, chopped

🍓 Use the time while the cauliflower cooks to dice your celery and onions.

1. Put the cauliflower in a microwave-safe casserole, add just a tablespoon or so of water and cover. Cook it on High for 7 minutes, then leave it to stand, covered, for another 3 to 5 minutes. The cauliflower should be tender, but not mushy. (And you may steam it, if you prefer.)

2. Drain the cooked cauliflower and combine it with the celery and onions. (You'll need a big bowl.)

3. Combine the mayonnaise, vinegar, salt, Splenda and pepper. Pour the mixture over the vegetables and mix well. Mix in the chopped eggs last and stir only lightly, to preserve some small bits of yolk. Chill and serve.

Yield: 12 servings, each with 3 grams of carbohydrate and 1 gram of fibre, for a total of 2 grams of usable carbs and 3 grams of protein.

⌒ Bacon, Tomato and Cauliflower Salad

This recipe originally called for cooked rice, so I thought I'd try it with cauliflower 'rice'. I liked it so much, I made it again the very next day.

>   1/2 cauliflower
>   225 g bacon, cooked until crisp, and crumbled
>   2 medium tomatoes, chopped
>   10 to 12 spring onions, sliced, including the crisp green part
>   125 ml mayonnaise
>   Salt and freshly ground black pepper
>   Lettuce (optional)

1. Put the cauliflower through a food processor with the shredding disk. Steam or microwave it until it's tender-crisp.

2. Combine the cooked cauliflower with the bacon, tomatoes, onions and mayonnaise in a big bowl. Season to taste and mix again.

   🍓 This salad holds a moulded shape really well, so pack it into a suitably sized bowl, then unmould it on to a plate lined with lettuce; it looks quite pretty served this way.

Yield: 5 servings, each with 6 grams of carbohydrate and 2 grams of fibre, for a total of 4 grams of usable carbs and 15 grams of protein.

ᴖ Cauliflower-Mozzarella Salad Basilico

Just like the Bacon, Tomato and Cauliflower Salad, this originally called for rice, but it works very well with cauliflower. Make your own pesto or use purchased, whichever you prefer.

> 1/2 cauliflower, run through the shredding blade
>   of a food processor
>
> 15 cherry tomatoes, halved
>
> 15 strong black olives, stoned and coarsely chopped
>
> 150 g mozzarella, cut in 1-cm cubes
>
> 1 Tbsp finely chopped sweet red onion
>
> 2 Tbsp olive oil
>
> 75 ml Tootsie's Pesto (see page 435)
>
> 1 Tbsp wine vinegar
>
> 1/2 tsp salt
>
> 1/4 tsp freshly ground black pepper

1. Cook the cauliflower 'rice' until tender-crisp (about 5 minutes on High in a microwave). Let it cool.

2. When the 'rice' is cool, add the tomatoes, olives, mozzarella and onion, and toss well.

3. Whisk together the olive oil, pesto, vinegar, salt and pepper, pour over the salad and toss.

4. Let the salad stand for at least half an hour for the flavours to blend; overnight would be better still.

Yield: 5 servings, each with 6 grams of carbohydrate and 1 gram of fibre, for a total of 5 grams of usable carbs and 9 grams of protein.

↷ Avocado-Lime Salad

When avocados are in season, there is no easier or more nutritious salad than this.

> 1 ripe, black avocado
> 2 big lettuce leaves
> 2 tsp lime juice
> Salt

Simply place a lettuce leaf on a salad plate, slice the avocado and arrange the slices attractively on the lettuce. Sprinkle a teaspoon of lime juice over each serving and salt lightly.

Yield: 2 servings, each with 8 grams of carbohydrate and 3 grams of fibre, for a total of 5 grams of usable carbs and 2 grams of protein. This is also loaded with healthy, monounsaturated fats and potassium.

↷ Guacamatoes

So pretty and just wonderful served with a simple grilled steak.

> 6 ripe smallish tomatoes
> 1 batch Guacamole (see page 53)

1. Cut the stems out of the tomatoes, leaving the skin intact at the very bottom. Slice each tomato into eight wedges, being careful not to cut through the tomato skin at the very bottom of the stem.
2. Place a lettuce leaf, or some other green leaf, on each salad plate and put a tomato on top, spreading the wedges out to look like a flower.
3. Spoon 2 to 3 heaped tablespoons of guacamole into the middle of the tomato flower and serve.

Yield: 6 servings. Depending on the size of your tomatoes, each will have about 17 grams of carbohydrate and 5 grams of fibre, for a total of 12 grams of usable carbs and 4 grams of protein.

🍓 Don't have a family of six? Why not halve the recipe and use the rest of the guacamole for omelettes, or something else? With over 1,000 mg of potassium in a serving, you're going to want to find a way to serve Guacamatoes often.

↻ Mayonnaise

If you have a blender, making your own sugar-free mayonnaise is so easy. If you're on a paleo diet or a yeast-free diet, use 3 table-spoons of lemon juice and omit the vinegar. (Don't feel, by the way, that the presence of this recipe means that purchased mayon-naise is off-limits for most low-carbers; it isn't. I just thought you ought to know how easy and good it is when made from scratch.)

> 1 egg
> 1 tsp dry mustard
> 1 tsp salt
> Dash of Tabasco
> 1 1/2 Tbsp vinegar
> 1 1/2 Tbsp lemon juice
> 100 to 150 ml olive or other vegetable oil.

1. Place the egg, mustard, salt, Tabasco, vinegar and lemon juice in the blender. Have the oil ready in a measuring jug.

2. Turn on the blender and let it run for a second. With the blender run-ning, pour in oil in a very thin stream – no thicker than a pencil lead. The mayonnaise will start to thicken before your eyes. When it gets thick enough that the 'whirlpool' disappears and oil starts to collect on top, stop adding oil and turn off the blender.

3. Store your mayonnaise in a tightly covered jar in the refrigerator and keep in mind that home-made mayonnaise does not have the shelf life that the commercial kind does.

Yield: A little over 225 ml, with just a trace of carbohydrate, fibre and protein – it's mostly healthy fat!

Dressings

These dressings are a great place to use home-made mayonnaise, although purchased is fine, too. Some of these recipes will give you left-overs that you should store in your refrigerator, but not for as long as you would a commercial dressing. And my general rule is this: 6 servings is about what I'd put on a large, family-sized salad. So if you see '12 servings', you can get two salads out of it if you're a family of 6, more if you have a smaller family.

 French Vinaigrette Dressing

No, this is not that sweet, tomato-y stuff that somehow has taken the name 'French dressing'. No Frenchman would eat that stuff, even for a bet! This is a classic vinaigrette dressing.

> 1/2 tsp salt
> 1/4 tsp freshly ground black pepper
> 75 to 100 ml wine vinegar
> 1/2 tsp Dijon mustard
> 200 ml extra-virgin olive oil

Put all the ingredients in a container with a tight lid and shake well. Shake again before pouring over salad and tossing.

Yield: 12 servings, each with only a trace of carbohydrate, fibre and protein.

The French Vinaigrette and Italian Vinaigrette Dressing recipes make approximately enough for two big, family-size salads, but feel free to double them and keep them in the fridge.

Italian Vinaigrette Dressing

Add a little zip to the French Vinaigrette and you've got Italian Vinaigrette.

75 ml wine vinegar

2 cloves garlic, crushed

1/2 tsp oregano

1/4 tsp basil

1 or 2 drops Tabasco

150 ml extra-virgin olive oil

Put all the ingredients in a container with a tight lid-fitting and shake well.

Yield: 12 servings, each with 1 gram of carbohydrate, a trace of fibre and a trace of protein.

Creamy Italian Dressing. This is a simple variation on the Italian Vinaigrette. Just add 2 tablespoons of mayonnaise to the Italian Vinaigrette Dressing and whisk until smooth.

Yield: 12 servings, each with 1 gram of carbohydrate, a trace of fibre and a trace of protein.

Greek Lemon Dressing

The use of lemon juice in place of vinegar in salad dressings is distinctively Greek.

> 200 ml extra-virgin olive oil
>
> 75 ml lemon juice
>
> 2 Tbsp dried oregano, crushed
>
> 1 clove garlic, crushed
>
> Salt and freshly ground black pepper

Put all the ingredients in a container with a tight-fitting lid and shake well.

🍓 This is best made at least a few hours in advance, but don't try to double the recipe and keep it around. Lemon juice just doesn't hold its freshness the way vinegar does.

Yield: 12 servings, each with 1 gram of carbohydrate, a trace of fibre and a trace of protein.

Blue Cheese Dressing

> 500 ml mayonnaise
>
> 125 ml buttermilk
>
> 100 g cottage cheese
>
> 1/2 tsp Worcestershire sauce
>
> 1 clove garlic, crushed
>
> 1 tsp salt
>
> 75 g crumbled blue cheese

Whisk together the mayonnaise, buttermilk, cottage cheese, Worcestershire sauce, garlic and salt, mixing well. Stir in the blue cheese gently, to preserve some chunks. Store in a container with a tight-fitting lid.

Yield: Makes roughly 700 ml. A 2-tablespoon serving has 1 gram of carbohydrate, a trace of fibre and 2 grams of protein.

☽ Balsamic-Parmesan Dressing

> 3 Tbsp balsamic vinegar
>
> 75 ml extra-virgin olive oil
>
> 1 Tbsp mayonnaise
>
> 2 cloves garlic, crushed
>
> 1 tsp grated onion
>
> 1/4 tsp salt
>
> 1/4 tsp freshly ground black pepper
>
> 1 tsp Dijon mustard
>
> 1 Tbsp grated Parmesan cheese

Whisk all the ingredients together until smooth. Store in a container with a tight-fitting lid and shake or whisk again before tossing with salad.

Yield: 6 servings, each with 1 gram of carbohydrate, a trace of fibre and a trace of protein.

☽ Doreen's Dressing

My friend Doreen made this up and told me about it when I told her I was writing a cookbook. So I tried it and discovered that it's simple and wonderful.

> 125 ml mayonnaise
>
> 3 Tbsp balsamic vinegar
>
> 1 clove garlic, crushed

Simply combine all ingredients and store in the refrigerator, in a container with a tight-fitting lid.

Yield: 6 servings, each with 1 gram of carbohydrate, a trace of fibre and a trace of protein.

○ Ranch Dressing

225 ml mayonnaise

250 ml buttermilk

2 Tbsp finely chopped spring onion

1/4 tsp onion powder

2 Tbsp finely chopped fresh parsley

1 clove garlic, crushed

1/4 tsp paprika

1/8 tsp cayenne powder or a few drops of Tabasco

1/4 tsp salt

1/4 tsp freshly ground black pepper

Combine all ingredients well and store in the refrigerator, in a container with a tight-fitting lid.

Yield: Makes about 24 servings, each with 1 gram of carbohydrate, a trace of fibre and 1 gram of protein.

○ Tangy 'Honey' Mustard Dressing

You know that honey, despite being 'natural', is pure sugar, right? Make this instead.

75 ml canola (rapeseed) oil

2 Tbsp cider vinegar

2 Tbsp Dijon mustard

1 Tbsp plus 2 tsp Splenda

1/8 tsp freshly ground black pepper

1/8 tsp salt

Combine all ingredients and store in a container with a tight-fitting lid.

Yield: 6 servings, each with 1 gram of carbohydrate, a trace of fibre and a trace of protein.

🍓 This makes a little over 125 ml, or just enough for one big salad, but feel free to double, or even quadruple, this recipe.

᧒ Mellow 'Honey' Mustard Dressing

> 300 ml mayonnaise
> 75 ml Dijon mustard
> 30 g Splenda
> 4 Tbsp water
> 1 tsp salt

Combine all ingredients and store in the refrigerator, in a container with a tight-fitting lid.

Yield: 12 servings, each with 1 gram of carbohydrate, a trace of fibre and 1 gram of protein.

᧒ Raspberry Vinegar

Commercial raspberry vinegar has as much as 4 grams of carbohydrate per tablespoon, so keep a batch of this home-made dressing on hand.

> 125 ml white vinegar
> 1/4 tsp raspberry cake flavouring (this is a highly concentrated oil)
> 3 Tbsp Splenda

Just combine these ingredients and store in a container with a tight-fitting lid.

Yield: About 125 ml, with 11.5 grams of carbohydrate in the whole batch or 1.5 grams of carbohydrate per tablespoon, no fibre and no protein.

↻ Raspberry Vinaigrette Dressing

Sweet and tangy, raspberry vinaigrette is something you'll want to enjoy more often, once you're making your own low-carb variety.

> 75 ml Raspberry Vinegar (see left)
>
> 75 ml canola (rapeseed) or other bland oil
>
> 3 Tbsp plus 1 tsp mayonnaise
>
> 1 tsp Dijon mustard
>
> Pinch salt and freshly ground black pepper

Blend all the ingredients and store in the refrigerator, in a container with a tight-fitting lid.

Yield: 6 servings, each with a trace of carbohydrate, fibre and protein.

↻ Parmesan Peppercorn Dressing

> 2 Tbsp olive oil
>
> 3 Tbsp mayonnaise
>
> 2 Tbsp wine vinegar
>
> 3 Tbsp grated Parmesan cheese
>
> 1 tsp freshly ground black pepper
>   (or coarse cracked pepper would be fine)

Blend all the ingredients and store in the refrigerator, in a container with a tight-fitting lid.

Yield: 6 servings, each with 1 gram of carbohydrate, a trace of fibre and 1 gram of protein.

Creamy Garlic Dressing

Look at all that garlic! If you plan to get kissed, make sure you share this salad with the object of your affections.

125 ml mayonnaise

Pinch each of freshly ground black pepper and salt

8 cloves garlic, crushed

2 Tbsp olive oil

2 Tbsp wine vinegar

Combine all the ingredients well and store in the refrigerator, in a container with a tight-fitting lid.

Yield: 6 servings, each with 2 grams of carbohydrate, a trace of fibre and a trace of protein.

This is only enough for one big salad, but I wouldn't double it; I'd make each one fresh, so the garlic flavour will be better.

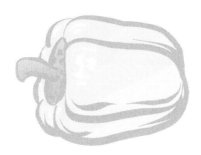

◌ Caesar Dressing

If you're dubious about using raw egg, you could check your supermarket for pasteurised eggs. Home-made Caesar Dressing is far better than any bottled version I've found, if it's not quite as wonderful as the one I had on my honeymoon in Mexico – although I suspect that the atmosphere had something to do with that.

4 Tbsp lemon juice

75 ml olive oil

1 tsp freshly ground black pepper

1 1/2 tsp Worcestershire sauce

1 clove garlic, crushed

1/2 tsp salt

1 raw egg

75 g grated Parmesan

5 cm anchovy paste (you could use an anchovy fillet or two if you prefer, but anchovy paste in a tube is handier and it keeps forever in the fridge)

Put everything in a blender, run it for a minute and toss with one really huge Caesar salad – dinner-party-sized – or a couple of smaller ones. Use it up pretty quickly and refrigerate it carefully because of the raw egg.

 If you'd like this a little thicker, you could add 1/4 teaspoon of guar or xanthan to the mix.

Yield: 8 servings, each with 1 gram of carbohydrate, a trace of fibre and 3 grams of protein.

☉ Coleslaw Dressing

Virtually all commercial coleslaw dressing is simply full of sugar, which is a shame, since cabbage is a very low-carb vegetable. I just love coleslaw, so I came up with a sugar-free dressing.

125 ml mayonnaise

125 ml soured cream

1 to 1 1/2 Tbsp cider vinegar

1 to 1 1/2 tsp prepared mustard

1/2 to 1 tsp salt

1 tsp Splenda

Combine all the ingredients well and toss with coleslaw. (See the recipes on page 226)

🍓 You may, of course, vary these proportions to taste. Also, a teaspoon or so of celery seed can be nice in this, for a little variety. I use the above amount of dressing for a whole head of cabbage. If you're used to purchased coleslaw, which tends to be simply swimming in dressing, you may want to double this, or use this recipe for half a cabbage.

Yield: 12 servings, each with 1 gram of carbohydrate, with a trace of fibre and a trace of protein.

CHAPTER SEVEN

Chicken and Turkey

We eat chicken a couple of times a week and many other families do the same. After all, chicken is inexpensive and it's always tasty. It also lends itself to infinite variation, as this chapter will prove. I often use just leg-and-thigh quarters, both because I like dark meat best and because they're usually inexpensive.

Turkey minced is also good to have on hand and it's a nice change from minced beef. You'll find some interesting ways to use it in this chapter.

⟲ Ranchhouse Chicken

> 4 chicken quarters
>
> 75 ml Ranch Dressing (see page 239)

1. Preheat the oven to 190°C/Gas Mark 5.

2. Arrange the chicken in a roasting tin and spoon the dressing over it, smearing it with the back of the spoon to cover each piece. Roast for 75 to 90 minutes.

   Yield: 4 servings, each with 1 gram of carbohydrate, no fibre and 44 grams of protein. (The dressing adds maybe 3 grams of carbs to the whole batch.)

◌ Tarragon Chicken

  4 chicken quarters

  2 Tbsp butter

  1 tsp salt

  Freshly ground black pepper

  3 Tbsp dried tarragon

  1 clove garlic, crushed

  125 ml dry white wine

1. Cut the chicken drumsticks from the thighs and the wings from the breasts (they will fit in your frying pan more easily this way).

2. Melt the butter in a heavy frying pan over a medium to high heat and brown the chicken, turning it once or twice, until it's golden all over.

3. Pour off most of the fat and sprinkle the chicken with the salt and just a dash of black pepper. Scatter the tarragon over the chicken, crushing it a little between your fingers to release the flavour, then add the garlic and the wine.

4. Cover the frying pan with a lid or some foil, turn the heat down to low and simmer for 30 minutes, turning the chicken at least once. Spoon a little of the pan juices over each piece of chicken when serving.

Yield: 4 servings, each with 2 grams of carbohydrate, a trace of fibre and 44 grams of protein.

◯ Curried Chicken

　　4 or 5 chicken quarters, skinned and cut up

　　1 medium onion

　　1 Tbsp butter

　　1 rounded Tbsp curry powder

　　225 ml double cream

　　3 or 4 cloves of garlic, crushed

　　125 ml water

1. Preheat the oven to 190ºC/Gas Mark 5.

2. Arrange the chicken in a shallow baking dish. Chop the onion and scatter it over the chicken.

3. Melt the butter in a small, heavy frying pan and sauté the curry powder in it for a couple of minutes – just until it starts to smell good.

4. Mix together the cream, garlic, water and sautéed curry powder, and pour this over the chicken. Bake it, uncovered, for 60 to 80 minutes, turning the chicken over every 20 to 30 minutes so that the sauce flavours both sides.

5. To serve, arrange the chicken on a platter. Take the sauce in the pan (it will look dreadful, almost curdled, but it will smell like heaven) and scrape it all into your blender. Blend it with a little more water or cream, if necessary, to get a nice, rich, golden sauce. Pour it over the chicken and serve.

Yield: 4 generous servings, each with 6 grams of carbohydrate and 1 gram of fibre, for a total of 5 grams of usable carbs and 42 grams of protein.

🍓 Take a look at the first ingredient in this recipe – the chicken is skinned, right? Now, that's not because you can't have chicken skin on a low-carb diet, it's because cooking chicken with the skin on in a recipe like this only results in flabby, uninteresting chicken skin. Do you enjoy crispy chicken skin, too? For what to do, check out Chicken Chips (see page 248).

◌ Chicken Crisps

Chicken skin

Salt

1. Preheat the oven to 190°C/Gas Mark 5.
2. Take any chicken skin you have on hand – chunks of chicken fat will work, too – and spread them out as flat as you can on the grill rack set inside a roasting tin.
3. Bake for 10 to 15 minutes, or until the skin gets brown and crunchy (thicker pieces take longer than thinner ones). Sprinkle with salt and eat like crisps – these are not to be believed!

Yield: This will totally depend on how much chicken skin you bake, but here's the info that really matters: There are no carbohydrates here at all.

◌ Pizza Chicken

This recipe is basically a frying pan cacciatore, except for the mozzarella – that's what makes it Pizza Chicken.

3 chicken leg-and-thigh quarters

1 to 2 Tbsp olive oil

225 ml tinned unflavoured tomato sauce

100 g tinned mushrooms, drained

125 ml dry red wine

1 green pepper, chopped

1 small onion, chopped

1 or 2 cloves garlic, crushed

1 to 1 1/2 tsp dried oregano

75 g grated mozzarella cheese

Parmesan cheese (optional)

1. Strip the skin off the chicken and cut leg and thigh quarters in two at the leg joint.
2. Warm the olive oil in a big, heavy frying pan and brown the chicken in it over a medium heat.
3. Pour in the tomato sauce, mushrooms and wine. Add the green pepper, onion, garlic and oregano. Cover the whole thing with a lid or some foil, turn the heat to the lowest setting and forget about it for 45 minutes to 1 hour.
4. When the chicken is cooked through, remove the pieces from the frying pan and put them on the serving plates. If the sauce isn't nicely thick by now, turn up the heat to medium-high and let it reduce for a few minutes.
5. While the sauce is thickening, sprinkle the grated mozzarella over the chicken and warm each plate in the microwave for 20 to 30 seconds on Low to melt the cheese. (Your microwave may take a little more or a little less time.)
6. Spoon the sauce over each piece of chicken and serve. Sprinkle a little Parmesan over your Pizza Chicken, if you like.

Yield: 3 servings, each with 16 grams of carbohydrate and 4 grams of fibre, for a total of 12 grams of usable carbs and 49 grams of protein.

◌ Looed Chicken

Traditionally looing is done on the cooker top, but this makes a terrific electric 'slow-cooker' recipe.

> 4 or 5 chicken quarters,
>   or 4 or 5 boneless, skinless chicken breasts
> 1 batch Chinese Looing Sauce (see page 428)
> Spring onions, sliced
> Toasted sesame oil

1. Put your chicken in your slow-cooker, pour the looing sauce over it, cover the slow-cooker, set it to Low and forget about it for 8 to 9 hours.
2. When it's time to eat, remove the chicken from the looing sauce, put each piece on a serving plate, scatter a few sliced spring onions over each serving and top with a few drops of toasted sesame oil.

Yield: 4 or 5 servings. The looing sauce adds no more than a gram or so of carbohydrate and no fibre, and each 100 g of meat will have 28 grams of protein.

ꙮ Roast Chicken with Balsamic Vinegar

Wonderfully crunchy skin, with a sweet-and-tangy sauce to dip bites of chicken in.

Bay leaves

4 chicken quarters

Salt

Freshly ground black pepper

3 to 4 Tbsp olive oil

3 to 4 Tbsp butter

125 ml dry white wine

3 Tbsp balsamic vinegar

1. Preheat the oven to 180ºC/Gas Mark 4.
2. Tuck a bay leaf or two under the skin of each piece of chicken. Sprinkle each piece with salt and pepper, and arrange them in a roasting tin.
3. Drizzle the chicken with olive oil and dot them with equal amounts of butter. Roast in the oven for 1 1/2 hours, turning each piece every 20 to 30 minutes. (This makes for gloriously crunchy, tasty skin.)
4. When the chicken is done, put it on a platter and pour off the fat from the pan. Put the pan over a medium heat and pour in the wine and balsamic vinegar. Stir this around, dissolving the tasty brown stuff stuck to the pan, to make a sauce. Boil this for just a minute or two, pour into a sauceboat or a jug and serve with the chicken.

Yield: 4 servings, each with 2 grams of carbohydrate, a trace of fibre and 44 grams of protein.

↻ Spicy Peanut Chicken

This takes 10 minutes to put together and only another 15 to cook. It's hot and spicy, with a definite Thai influence.

>	1 tsp ground cumin
>
>	1/2 tsp ground cinnamon
>
>	2 or 3 boneless, skinless chicken breasts
>
>	2 to 3 Tbsp peanut oil, for sautéing
>
>	1/2 smallish onion, thinly sliced
>
>	400 g tinned diced tomatoes
>
>	2 Tbsp natural peanut butter
>
>	1 Tbsp lemon juice
>
>	2 cloves garlic, crushed
>
>	1 fresh jalapeño chilli, cut in half and seeded

1. On a saucer or plate, stir the cumin and cinnamon together, then rub into both sides of chicken breasts.

2. Put 2 to 3 tablespoons of oil in a heavy frying pan over medium heat and add the chicken and sliced onion. Brown the chicken a little on both sides.

3. While that's happening, put all the tomato liquid, and half the tomatoes, in a blender or food processor, along with the peanut butter, lemon juice, garlic and chilli. (Wash your hands after handling that hot pepper, or you'll be sorry the next time you touch your eyes!) Blend or process until smooth.

4. Pour this rather thick sauce over the chicken (which you've turned at least once by now), add the rest of the tomatoes, cover, turn the heat down to low and leave to cook gently for 10 to 15 minutes, or until the chicken is cooked through.

Yield: About 3 servings, each with 14 grams of carbohydrate and 1 gram of fibre, for a total of 13 grams of usable carbs and 26 grams of protein.

🍓 Some like it hot and some a little bit less so. So when you're buying your ingredients, choose a small jalapeño chilli or a big one, depending on how hot you like your food. I use a big one and it definitely makes this dish hot. And don't forget, you can always use only half the jalapeño.

↻ Frying Pan Chicken Florentine

My husband took one bite of this and said, 'This is going to get you a lot of new readers!' I know of no other dish that's so quick and easy, yet so incredibly good.

> Olive oil
>
> 2 or 3 boneless, skinless chicken breasts
>
> 300 g frozen chopped spinach, thawed
>
> 2 cloves garlic, crushed
>
> 75 ml double cream
>
> 30 g grated Parmesan cheese

1. Warm a little olive oil in a heavy frying pan and brown the chicken breasts over a medium heat to the point where they just have a touch of gold. Remove the chicken from the frying pan.

2. Add a couple more tablespoons of olive oil, the spinach and the garlic and stir for 2 to 3 minutes. Stir in the cream and cheese and spread the mixture evenly over the bottom of the frying pan. Place the chicken breasts on top, cover, turn the heat down to low and simmer for 15 minutes.

3. Serve chicken breasts with the spinach on top.

Yield: 3 servings, each with 5 grams of carbohydrate and 3 grams of fibre, for a total of 2 grams of usable carbs and 33 grams of protein.

ͻ Those Chicken Things

Kate Sutherland sends this recipe and says this works best on a gas barbecue.

> 10 spring onions
>
> 225 g cream cheese, beaten to softened
>
> 8 boneless, skinless chicken breasts
>
> 16 to 24 rashers bacon

1. Clean, trim and chop the spring onions, including a generous portion of the green part. Mix the spring onions into the cream cheese and set aside.

2. Butterfly the chicken breasts from the thinner edge in toward the thicker. (The thicker edge will be the middle of the breast once it is opened up.) Working on one piece at a time, open the breast up and put it in a heavy freezer bag. Seal the bag and, with a rolling pin, pound the chicken breast to a depth of 5 mm. Repeat with the remaining chicken breasts.

3. Once all 8 breasts have been flattened, place an equal amount of the cream cheese and spring onion mixture on each. Wrap the chicken meat around the cheese mix so that it is completely enclosed.

4. Wrap a strip of bacon around the ball of chicken, stretching it to provide maximum overlap. Then wrap a second piece of bacon around the still-exposed portion of the chicken, again giving it a bit of a stretch. Secure with a few cocktail sticks. (Depending on the size of the chicken breasts, you may need a third piece of bacon. Most of the chicken should be covered by the bacon strips.)

5. Refrigerate for several hours or overnight. They should be well chilled before they go on the barbecue.

6. Cover the barbecue rack with a sheet of foil and spray it with nonstick cooking spray. (The foil helps prevent flare-ups from the bacon fat and also helps the chicken cook evenly.) Preheat the barbecue to High.

7. Place the chicken on the covered rack, reduce the heat to Medium and close the lid. Turn about every 5 minutes, until all sides are nicely browned. When the cheese starts to ooze out in a few places, they are done. (Depending on the size of the pieces and the overall temperature

of your barbecue, this should take 20 to 30 minutes.) Remove the cocktail sticks and serve.

Yield: 8 servings, each with 1 gram of carbohydrate, a trace of fibre and 36 grams of protein.

◌ Chicken and Artichoke Fry

This is quick and easy enough for a weeknight, but elegant enough for company.

> 3 Tbsp butter
>
> 4 boneless, skinless chicken breasts
>
> 400 g tinned artichoke hearts, drained and quartered
>
> 1/2 red pepper, cut into strips
>
> 1 medium onion, sliced
>
> 1 clove garlic, crushed
>
> 75 ml dry white wine
>
> 1 tsp dried thyme

1. Melt 2 tablespoons of butter in a heavy frying pan over medium heat and sauté the chicken breasts until they're golden (5 to 7 minutes per side). Remove from the pan.
2. Melt the remaining tablespoon of butter and toss the artichoke hearts, pepper, onion and garlic into the frying pan. Sauté for 3 minutes or so, stirring frequently.
3. Pour the wine and sprinkle the thyme over the vegetables. Place the chicken breasts over the vegetables, turn the heat to medium low, cover and simmer for 10 minutes.

Yield: 4 servings, each with 8 grams of carbohydrate and 4 grams of fibre, for a total of 4 grams of usable carbs and 26 grams of protein.

↺ Teriyaki Chicken

4 to 6 boneless, skinless chicken breasts

1 batch Teriyaki Sauce (see page 426)

1. Put the chicken breasts in a large freezer bag and pour the teriyaki sauce over them. Put the bag in the refrigerator and let the breasts marinate for at least 1 hour.

2. When you're ready to cook, pour off the marinade into a small saucepan. Barbecue or grill the chicken for 5 to 7 minutes per side, checking by cutting into one breast to see if it's white clear through. Don't overcook, or your chicken will be dry.

3. While the chicken is cooking, bring the marinade to the boil for a few minutes. It will then be safe to pour a little on each piece of chicken before serving.

Yield: 4 to 6 servings, each with 2 grams of carbohydrate, a trace of fibre and 26 grams of protein.

↺ Satay without a Stick

Here's a recipe for boneless, skinless chicken breasts that reminds me of satay, the popular Asian kebabs.

1 Tbsp oil

1 clove garlic, crushed

1 tsp curry powder

1 boneless, skinless chicken breast

Not-Very-Authentic Peanut Sauce (see page 417)

1. Put a heavy frying pan over medium heat. Add the oil, garlic and curry powder and stir for a few seconds to flavour the oil.

2. Add the chicken breasts and sauté for about 7 minutes on each side, or until done through.

3. Serve with the peanut sauce, warming it first, if desired.

Yield: 1 serving, with 2 grams of carbohydrate, with a trace of fibre and 28 grams of protein. (Analysis includes a serving of sauce.)

◌ Picnic Chicken

150 ml cider vinegar

3 Tbsp oil

2 tsp salt

1/4 tsp freshly ground black pepper

4 chicken quarters

1. Combine the vinegar, oil, salt and pepper and pour over the chicken in a large freezer bag. Marinate for at least an hour.

2. Preheat the grill to a high heat. Take the chicken out of the marinade and grill it about 20 cm from the flame. Baste it with the marinade every 10 to 15 minutes while cooking. Give it about 25 minutes per side, or until done through. (Pierce it to the bone; the juices should run clear, not pink.) You may need to rearrange the chicken pieces on your grill rack to get them to cook evenly, so they're all ready at the same time.

Yield: 4 servings, each with 3 grams of carbohydrate per serving if you consumed all the marinade, but of course you don't, so each serving has less than 1 gram of carbohydrate, no fibre and 44 grams of protein.

🍓 You may be wondering why this is called Picnic Chicken – it's because come summer, if you really were going on a picnic, you could bring the bag of chicken and marinade along in the cool box and grill it at the park or the beach. What a treat! But don't continue basting the chicken with the marinade once you're done cooking it: if you do, you're risking food poisoning.

⌒ Middle Eastern Fried Chicken

    3 boneless, skinless chicken breasts

    3 Tbsp olive oil

    1 medium onion, chopped

    1/2 tsp ground coriander

    1 tsp ground cumin

    1/4 tsp ground cinnamon

    1/2 tsp turmeric

    1/4 tsp freshly ground black pepper

    1 Tbsp freshly grated ginger

    400 g tinned diced tomatoes

    2 cloves garlic, crushed

    225 ml chicken stock

1. Cut the chicken breasts into cubes. Heat the olive oil over a medium heat in a heavy frying pan and add the chicken and onions.

2. Sauté for a couple of minutes, then stir in the coriander, cumin, cinnamon, turmeric and pepper. Cook until the chicken is white all over.

3. Add the ginger, tomatoes, garlic and stock; stir. Cover, turn the heat down to low and simmer for 15 minutes.

Yield: 3 servings, each with 14 grams of carbohydrate and 1 gram of fibre, for a total of 13 grams of usable carbs and 26 grams of protein.

ᔕ Chicken Paprikash

Making my Paprikash with soured cream is one of the great joys of low-carbing!

> 4 chicken quarters
>
> 3 Tbsp butter
>
> 1 small onion
>
> 2 Tbsp paprika
>
> 125 ml chicken stock
>
> 225 ml soured cream
>
> Salt and freshly ground black pepper

1. Melt the butter in a heavy frying pan and brown the chicken and onions over medium-high heat.
2. In a separate bowl, stir the paprika into the chicken stock. Pour the mixture over the chicken.
3. Cover the pan with a lid or some foil, turn the heat down to low and let it simmer for 30 to 45 minutes.
4. When the chicken is tender and cooked through, remove it from the frying pan and put it on a serving platter. Stir the soured cream into the liquid left in the pan and stir until smooth and well blended. Heat through, but do not let it boil, or it will curdle. Salt and pepper to taste and serve this gravy with the chicken.

Yield: 4 servings, each with 7 grams of carbohydrate and 1 gram of fibre, for a total of 6 grams of usable carbs and 53 grams of protein.

> 🍓 Be sure to serve plenty of Cauliflower Purée (see page 159) with it, to smother in the extra gravy!

☽ Homestyle Turkey Loaf

You may find turkey mince makes a nice change from beef for this meatloaf.

  450 g turkey mince

  1/2 cup crushed pork rinds

  1 stick celery, finely chopped

  1 small onion, finely chopped

  1 apple, finely chopped

  1 1/2 Tbsp Worcestershire sauce

  2 tsp poultry seasoning

  1 tsp salt

  1 egg

1. Preheat the oven to 180°C/Gas Mark 4.
2. Combine all the ingredients in a big bowl and – with clean hands – squeeze it together until it's very well combined.
3. Spray a loaf tin with nonstick cooking spray and pack the turkey mixture into the tin. Bake for 50 minutes.

Yield: 5 servings, each with 5 grams of carbohydrate and 1 gram of fibre, for a total of 4 grams of usable carbs and 32 grams of protein.

◯ Curried Turkey Loaf

This has a good, rich curry flavour and it's great with Cranberry Chutney (see page 430).

> 1 kg turkey mince
>
> 1 medium onion, finely chopped
>
> 2 eggs
>
> 2 cloves garlic, crushed
>
> 1 to 2 Tbsp curry powder
>
> 1 Tbsp salt
>
> 1 tsp freshly ground black pepper

1. Preheat the oven to 180ºC/Gas Mark 4.
2. Combine all the ingredients in a big bowl and – with clean hands – squeeze it together until it's very well combined.
3. Spray a loaf tin with nonstick cooking spray and pack the turkey mixture into the tin. Bake for 60 to 75 minutes.

Yield: 6 servings, each with 4 grams of carbohydrate and 1 gram of fibre, for a total of 3 grams of usable carbs and 29 grams of protein.

☉ Low-Carb Microwave Pasticchio

This has become my sister's standby recipe for pot-luck meals and other casserole occasions.

1/2 medium onion, chopped

1 clove garlic, crushed

450 g turkey mince

3/4 tsp ground cinnamon

1/8 tsp ground nutmeg

225 g ricotta cheese

1 Tbsp chopped fresh parsley

1/4 tsp salt

1/8 tsp freshly ground black pepper

Sauce

2 Tbsp butter

1/2 tsp salt

350 ml double cream

75 g Parmesan cheese

500 g cooked spaghetti squash

1. In a microwave-safe casserole, combine the onion and garlic; place the turkey mince on top. Microwave this, uncovered, for 5 minutes at full power. Stir it all together, breaking up the turkey mince in the process. Microwave for another 3 minutes, or until the turkey is done through.

2. Break up the turkey some more – it should be well crumbled – and drain off the fat. Stir in the cinnamon and nutmeg, and microwave it for just another minute, to blend the flavours. Transfer the mixture to a bowl.

3. In a separate bowl, combine the ricotta cheese, parsley and salt and pepper.

4. In yet another bowl, or a measuring jug, combine the butter, sauce, cream and cheese to make the sauce.

5. Spray your microwave-safe casserole with nonstick cooking spray. In the dish, layer half of the spaghetti squash, then half the turkey mixture,

then half the ricotta mixture, then half the sauce. Repeat the layers, ending with the sauce.

6. Microwave the pasticchio at full power for 6 to 8 minutes, or until it's bubbly and hot right through. Let it stand for 5 minutes or so and serve.

Yield: 6 servings, each with 7 grams of carbohydrate, a trace of fibre and 22 grams of protein.

☽ Asian Turkey Burgers

Turkey mince is handy, but by itself it can be bland. Here's a good way to liven it up.

> 450 g turkey mince
>
> 30 g finely chopped onion
>
> 3 Tbsp chopped fresh parsley
>
> 2 Tbsp Worcestershire sauce
>
> 2 Tbsp finely chopped green pepper
>
> 1 Tbsp soy sauce
>
> 1 Tbsp cold water
>
> 1 Tbsp grated fresh ginger
>
> 1/4 tsp freshly ground black pepper
>
> 2 cloves garlic, crushed

1. Combine all the ingredients in a large bowl and – with clean hands – squeeze the mixture together until it's very well combined.

2. Divide into three equal portions and form into burgers about 2 cm thick.

3. Spray a frying pan with nonstick cooking spray and place over medium to high heat. Cook the burgers for about 5 minutes per side, until cooked through.

Yield: 3 servings, each with 5 grams of carbohydrate and 1 gram of fibre, for a total of 4 grams of usable carbs and 27 grams of protein.

ᕚ Saltimbocca

Who says all Italian food involves pasta?

> 4 boneless, skinless chicken breasts
>
> 100 g prosciutto or good boiled ham, thinly sliced
>
> 40 leaves fresh or dry sage (fresh is preferable)
>
> 2 Tbsp butter
>
> 2 Tbsp olive oil
>
> 125 ml dry white wine

1. Place a chicken breast in a large, heavy, freezer bag and, using a rolling pin, pound it to a depth of 5 mm. Repeat with the remaining chicken breasts.

2. Once all your chicken breasts are pounded thin, place a layer of the prosciutto on each one, scatter about 10 sage leaves over each one and roll each breast up. Fasten with cocktail sticks.

3. Melt the butter with the olive oil in a heavy frying pan over a medium heat. Add the chicken rolls and sauté, turning occasionally, until golden all over.

4. Add the wine to the frying pan, turn the heat down to low, cover the pan with a lid or some foil and simmer for 15 minutes.

5. Remove the rolls to a serving plate and cover to keep warm. Turn the heat up to high and boil the liquid in the frying pan hard for 5 minutes, to reduce. Spoon over rolls and serve.

Yield: 4 servings, each with 2 grams of carbohydrate, no fibre and 37 grams of protein.

Saltimbocca Gruyère

I couldn't decide which version I liked best, so I included both!

4 boneless, skinless chicken breasts

100 g prosciutto or good boiled ham, thinly sliced

100 g grated Gruyère cheese

2 Tbsp butter

2 Tbsp olive oil

125 ml dry white wine

1. Place a chicken breast in a large, heavy, freezer bag and, using a rolling pin, pound it to a depth of 5 mm. Repeat with the remaining chicken breasts.

2. Once all your chicken breasts are pounded thin, place a layer of the prosciutto on each one, scatter the grated Gruyère over each one and roll each breast up. Fasten with cocktail sticks.

3. Melt the butter with the olive oil in a heavy frying pan over a medium heat. Add the chicken rolls and sauté, turning occasionally, until golden all over.

4. Add the wine to the pan, turn the heat down to low, cover with a lid or some foil and simmer for 15 minutes.

5. Remove the rolls to a serving plate and cover to keep warm. Turn the heat up to high and boil the liquid in the frying pan hard for 5 minutes, to reduce. Spoon over rolls and serve.

Yield: 4 servings, each with just a trace of carbohydrate, no fibre and 45 grams of protein.

↻ Key Lime Chicken

An unusual – and good! – combination of flavours.

4 chicken quarters
125 ml lime juice
125 ml olive oil
1 Tbsp grated onion
2 tsp tarragon
1 tsp seasoned salt
1/4 tsp freshly ground black pepper

1. Arrange the chicken pieces on the grill rack, skin-side down.
2. In a bowl, combine the lime juice, oil, onion, tarragon, salt and pepper, and brush the chicken well with the mixture.
3. Grill the chicken about 20 cm from the flame for 45 to 50 minutes, turning the chicken and basting with more lime mixture every 10 minutes or so.

Yield: 4 servings, each with 4 grams of carbohydrate, a trace of fibre and 44 grams of protein.

ᘔ Devilled Chicken

    4 Tbsp butter
    60 g Splenda
    75 ml Dijon mustard
    1 tsp salt
    1 tsp curry powder
    4 chicken quarters

1. Preheat the oven to 190°C/Gas Mark 5.
2. Melt the butter in a shallow roasting tin. Add the Splenda, mustard, salt and curry powder and stir until well combined.
3. Roll the chicken pieces in the butter mixture until coated, then arrange them skin side up in the tin. Bake for 1 hour.

Yield: 4 servings, each with 5 grams of carbohydrate, a trace of fibre and 44 grams of protein.

ᘔ Jerk Chicken

This hot-and-sweet Jamaican chicken is great for a special barbecue, but you have to remember to begin marinating the chicken the day before.

    1 batch Jerk Marinade (see page 427)
    4 chicken quarters

1. Smear the jerk marinade all over your chicken – even up under the skin. Coat it well and put the chicken in a freezer bag.
2. Wash your hands! You don't want the hot peppers to stay on them.
3. Leave the marinating chicken in the refrigerator overnight. When you're ready to eat, preheat the oven to 190°C/Gas Mark 5.
4. Pull the chicken out of the bag, but do not wipe the marinade off. Roast for about 40 minutes, then finish under the grill or on the barbecue. (This prevents the chicken from drying out and scorching.)

Yield: 4 servings, each with 4 grams of carbohydrate and 1 gram of fibre, for a total of 3 grams usable carbs and 44 grams of protein.

꩜ Tasty Roasted Chicken

  1 whole chicken (about 2 1/2 kg)
  1 heaped Tbsp mayonnaise
  Salt
  Freshly ground black pepper
  Paprika
  Onion powder

1. Preheat the oven to 190°C/Gas Mark 5.

2. If your chicken was frozen, make sure it's completely thawed.
   (If it's still a bit icy in the middle, run some hot water inside it to get
   rid of the ice.) Take out bag of giblets from the body cavity, if these
   have been included.

3. Dry the chicken and rub it all over with the mayonnaise. Sprinkle
   liberally with equal parts salt, pepper, paprika and onion powder,
   on all sides.

4. Put the chicken on a rack in a shallow roasting tin and roast for 1 1/2
   hours, or until the juices run clear when you put a fork in where the
   thigh joins the body.

5. Remove the chicken from the oven and let it stand for 10 to 15 minutes
   before carving, to let the juices settle.

Yield: 5 generous servings, each with a trace of carbohydrate, a trace
of fibre and 52 grams of protein.

○ Chicken Taco Filling

This is easy, versatile, and sure to be popular with the whole family.

> 450 g boneless, skinless chicken breasts
> (or 750 g to 1 kg chicken pieces)
> 225 ml chicken stock
> 2 Tbsp Taco Seasoning (see page 418)

1. If you're using chicken pieces (I like to make this with leg and thigh quarters), skin them first. Put your chicken in either a large, heavy-bottomed saucepan, or in your slow cooker.

2. Mix together the chicken stock and the taco seasoning and pour the mixture over the chicken. If you're cooking this on the cooker top, simply cover the pot, put it over a low heat and let it simmer for about 1 1/2 hours. If you're using a slow cooker, set the pot on Low and leave it for 6 to 8 hours.

3. With either method, when the chicken's done, use two forks to tear it into largish shreds. If you've used bone-in chicken parts, this is the time to remove the bones, as well. If you've cooked this on the cooker top, most of the liquid will have cooked away, but if you've used a slow cooker, there will be quite a lot of liquid, so turn the pot up to High, leave the cover off and let the liquid cook down. Stir the chicken back into the reduced seasoning liquid and it's ready to serve.

Yield: 4 servings, each with 1 gram of carbohydrate, a trace of fibre and 26 grams of protein.

> 🍓 Don't know what to do with your taco filling? See Cheesy Bowls and Taco Shells (page 80), Taco Salad (page 384) and Taco Omelette (page 91).

☙ Chicken Piccata

Meat cooked 'piccata' is traditionally floured first, but with all this flavour going on, who'll miss it?

4 boneless, skinless chicken breasts
75 ml olive oil
1 clove garlic, crushed
1 Tbsp lemon juice
125 ml dry white wine
1 Tbsp capers, chopped
3 Tbsp fresh parsley, chopped

1. Place a chicken breast in a large, heavy, freezer bag and, using a rolling pin, pound it to a depth of 5 mm. Repeat with the remaining chicken breasts.
2. Heat the olive oil in a large, heavy frying pan over a medium-high heat. Add the chicken; if it doesn't all fit at the same time, cook it in two batches, keeping the first batch warm while the second batch is cooking. Cook the chicken until it's well done (3 to 4 minutes per side).
3. Remove the chicken from the pan. Add the garlic, lemon juice, white wine and capers to the pan, stirring it all around and getting the tasty little brown bits off the bottom. Boil hard for about 1 minute, to reduce it a little.
4. Put the chicken back in the pan for another minute, sprinkle the parsley over it and serve.

Yield: 4 servings, each with 1 gram of carbohydrate, a trace of fibre and 29 grams of protein.

Pork Piccata: make this variation just like Chicken Piccatta, substituting 4 good, big pork steaks or chops for the chicken breasts. (Cut out and discard any bones from the pork steaks or chops.)

Yield: 4 servings, each with 1 gram of carbohydrate, a trace of fibre and 26 grams of protein.

↻ Chicken-Almond Stir-Fry

Serve this tasty stir-fry over brown rice for the carb-eaters in your family and enjoy yours straight.

2 Tbsp soy sauce

4 Tbsp dry sherry

1 clove garlic, crushed

2.5 cm fresh root ginger, grated

1/4 tsp guar (optional)

Peanut oil (rapeseed or coconut oil would work, too)

30 g slivered almonds

100 g snow peas, cut in half

100 g mushrooms, sliced

15 spring onions, cut into 2.5-cm pieces

50 g sliced water chestnuts (optional; they increase the carb count, but they're tasty)

3 large boneless, skinless chicken breasts, cut into 1-cm cubes

🍓 There's one hard-and-fast rule with stir-fries: make sure all your ingredients are chopped, sliced and grated before you begin cooking.

1. Stir together the soy, sherry, garlic and ginger. (If you're using the guar, put these seasonings through the blender with the guar.)

2. Heat a couple of teaspoons of the peanut oil in a wok or large, heavy frying pan over a high heat. Add the almonds and stir-fry them until they're light golden. Remove and set aside.

3. Heat another couple of tablespoons of oil in the pan and add the sugar snap peas, mushrooms, spring onions and water chestnuts (if using) to the pan. Stir-fry for about 5 minutes, or until just barely tender-crisp. Remove from the pan and set aside.

4. Heat another couple of tablespoons of oil in the pan and add the chicken. Stir-fry for 5 to 7 minutes, or until done; there should be no pink left.

5. Return the vegetables to the frying pan and add the soy sauce/sherry mixture from the first step. Toss everything together well. Cover and simmer for 3 to 4 minutes. Top with the almonds and serve.

Yield: 3 servings, each with 18 grams of carbohydrate and 6 grams of fibre, for a total of 12 grams of usable carbs and 36 grams of protein.

◌ Lemon-Pepper Chicken and Gravy

4 chicken quarters

1 1/4 tsp lemon pepper

1 1/4 tsp onion powder

1 tsp salt

75 ml chicken stock

125 ml double cream

1 1/2 tsp Dijon mustard

1. Preheat the oven to 190°C/Gas Mark 5.
2. Sprinkle the chicken pieces with 1 teaspoon of lemon pepper, 1 teaspoon of onion powder and the salt. Arrange in a roasting tin and roast, basting once or twice, for about 1 hour or until the juices run clear when the chicken is pierced.
3. Remove the chicken from the roasting tin and skim off the excess fat, leaving just the brown drippings. Place the roasting tin over a low heat, add the chicken stock to the tin and stir, scraping the tasty brown bits off the bottom of the pan. When the stock is simmering, add the cream, the rest of the lemon pepper and onion powder and the mustard. Stir well, heat through and pour over the chicken.

Yield: 4 servings, each with 2 grams of carbohydrate, a trace of fibre and 44 grams of protein.

↻ Thai-ish Chicken Basil Stir-Fry

You'll find this an interesting change from the more usual Chinese stir-fries.

2 Tbsp Thai fish sauce (nam pla)

2 Tbsp soy sauce

1 tsp Splenda

1/4 tsp guar or xanthan

2 tsp dried basil

1 1/2 tsp chilli flakes

Peanut, canola (rapeseed) or coconut oil

2 cloves garlic, crushed

3 boneless, skinless chicken breasts cut into 1-cm cubes

1 small onion, sliced

250 g frozen, sliced green beans, thawed

1. Combine the fish sauce, soy sauce, Splenda and guar in a blender. Blend for several seconds, then turn off the blender and add the basil and chilli flakes and set aside.

2. Heat a few tablespoons of oil in a wok or heavy frying pan over high heat. When the oil is hot, add the garlic, chicken and onion, and stir-fry for 3 to 4 minutes. Add the green beans and continue to stir-fry until the chicken is cooked through.

3. Stir the blended seasoning mixture into the stir-fry, turn the heat to medium, cover and let it simmer for 2 to 3 minutes (the beans should be tender-crisp).

Yield: 3 servings, each with 13 grams of carbohydrate and 3 grams of fibre, for a total of 10 grams of usable carbs and 31 grams of protein.

☺ Sautéed Sesame Chicken Breasts

Try serving this with a salad, a broccoli dish, or both.

> 4 boneless, skinless chicken breasts
> 40 g sesame seeds
> Salt
> 3 Tbsp peanut oil

1. Place a chicken breast in a large, heavy freezer bag and, using a rolling pin, pound it to a depth of 5 mm. Repeat with the remaining chicken breasts.
2. Sprinkle each side of each breast evenly with 1/2 tablespoon of sesame seeds and lightly salt.
3. Heat the peanut oil in a heavy frying pan over medium heat. Add the chicken breasts and sauté for about 5 minutes each side, or until lightly golden. (You may have to do this in two batches; keep the first batch warm on an ovenproof plate in the oven, on its lowest temperature setting.) Serve.

Yield: 4 servings, each with 2 grams of carbohydrate and 1 gram of fibre, for a total of 1 gram of usable carbs and 30 grams of protein.

☺ Stewed Chicken with Moroccan Seasonings

This is almost a Moroccan 'tagine', but all the recipes I've seen call for some sort of starch. So I got rid of the starch and just kept the seasonings, which are exotic and delicious.

> 75 ml olive oil
> 1 1/2 to 2 kg chicken, cut into pieces
> 1 medium onion, thinly sliced
> 2 cloves garlic, crushed
> 200 ml chicken stock
> 1/2 tsp ground coriander
> 1/2 tsp ground cinnamon

$1/2$ tsp paprika

$1/2$ tsp ground cumin

1 tsp ground ginger

$1/2$ tsp freshly ground black pepper

$1/4$ tsp cayenne

1 Tbsp Splenda

1 Tbsp tomato purée

1 tsp salt

1. Heat the oil in a Dutch oven over a medium heat and brown the chicken in the oil.
2. When the chicken is golden all over, remove it from the Dutch oven and pour off the fat. Put the chicken back in the Dutch oven and scatter the onion and garlic over it.
3. Combine the garlic, stock, coriander, cinnamon, paprika, cumin, ginger, pepper, cayenne, Splenda, tomato purée and salt, and whisk together well. Pour over the chicken, cover the Dutch oven and turn the heat down to low. Let the whole thing simmer for a good 45 minutes.
4. Uncover the chicken and let it simmer for another 15 minutes or so, to let the juices concentrate a bit. Serve each piece of chicken with some of the onion and juices spooned over it.

Yield: 4 generous servings, each with 6 grams of carbohydrate and 1 gram of fibre, for a total of 5 grams of usable carbs and 58 grams of protein.

☉ Greek Roasted Chicken

Many take-away places do a brisk business in chickens roasted Greek-style and it's no wonder – they're delicious. But the best-kept secret about these is that they're as easy as can be to make at home.

> 1 1/2 to 2 kg chicken (whole, halved, quartered
>   or cut up as you prefer)
> Juice of 1/4 lemon
> 125 ml olive oil
> 1/2 tsp salt
> 1/4 tsp freshly ground black pepper

1. Wash the chicken and pat it dry with kitchen paper.
2. Combine the lemon juice, olive oil, salt and pepper and stir them together well. If you're using a whole chicken, rub it all over with some of this mixture, making sure to rub plenty inside the body cavity as well. If you're using chicken pieces, put them in a large freezer bag, pour the marinade over and seal the bag.
3. Let the chicken marinate for at least an hour, or as long as a day.
4. At least 1 hour before you want to serve the chicken, take it out of the bag. You can either grill your chicken or you can roast it in a 190ºC/Gas Mark 5 oven for about 1 hour. Either way, cook it until the juices run clear when it's pierced to the bone.

Yield: 5 servings, each with less than 1 gram of carbohydrate, a bare trace of fibre and 52 grams of protein.

> 🍓 If you have a rotisserie, this is a marvellous dish to cook in it. Follow the instructions that come with your unit for cooking times.

↻ Chicken Liver and 'Rice' Casserole

I'm a big fan of chicken livers and they're highly nutritious.

110 g butter

1 small onion, chopped

1 stick celery, including leaves, diced

1 bay leaf, crumbled fine

1/2 tsp dried thyme

1/2 tsp salt

1/2 tsp seasoned salt

450 g chicken livers, cut into bite-sized pieces

750 g Cauliflower Rice Deluxe (see page 161)

30 g grated Parmesan cheese

1. Preheat oven to 190°C/Gas Mark 5.
2. Melt the butter in a heavy frying pan over a medium heat and sauté the onion, celery, bay leaf, thyme, salt and seasoned salt.
3. When the onion is golden, add the chicken livers and cook for another 5 minutes, stirring frequently. Toss the vegetables and livers together with the Cauliflower Rice Deluxe.
4. Spray a good-sized casserole (around 2 1/2 litres) with nonstick cooking spray and put the liver and 'rice' mixture into the casserole. Sprinkle the top with the Parmesan and bake the whole thing, uncovered, for 15 minutes.

Yield: 5 servings, each with 16 grams of carbohydrate and 3 grams of fibre, for a total of 13 grams usable carbs and 21 grams of protein.

↺ Chicken with Camembert and Almonds

4 boneless, skinless chicken breasts
6 Tbsp butter
225 g Camembert
30 g slivered almonds
4 spring onions, thinly sliced

1. Place a chicken breast in a large, heavy, freezer bag and, using a rolling pin, pound it to a depth of 5 mm. Repeat with the remaining chicken breasts.
2. Melt 4 tablespoons of the butter in a heavy frying pan over a medium heat. Sauté the chicken until it's golden on the first side.
3. While the first side of the chicken is cooking, divide the cheese into four equal portions, peel off the white rind and thinly slice each portion.
4. Turn the chicken over and lay a portion of cheese over each chicken breast.
5. Melt the remaining 2 tablespoons of butter in a small frying pan, add the almonds and stir until they're lightly golden.
6. When the second side of the chicken is golden and the cheese is melted, place each breast on a serving plate and divide the almonds evenly over them. Scatter a sliced spring onion over each breast and serve.

Yield: 4 servings, each with 4 grams of carbohydrate and 2 grams of fibre, for a total of 2 grams of usable carbs and 43 grams of protein.

🍓 If you are good at doing several things at the same time, this recipe is for you. If you can slice and peel the cheese while the first side of the chicken cooks and get the almonds toasting, you should be able to get the almonds done just in time to move hot almonds on to just-done chicken breasts.

CHAPTER EIGHT

Fish

Of all the good things that can be said about fish, this is the one that is likely to appeal to the greatest number of people: fish is very quick to cook. Unlike the poultry, beef, and lamb and pork chapters, this is a chapter where the vast majority of the recipes take no more than 15 minutes to get on the table. With today's busy schedules, that's a good thing to keep in mind. The tighter your time is, the better the idea of eating fish becomes.

Of course, it's a good idea for another excellent reason: fish is really, really good for you. In particular, if you're in the minority whose total cholesterol levels have gone up since starting your low-carb diet, you'll want to eat fish frequently, especially salmon, with its heart-healthy EPA oils.

You'll see it noted again and again in this chapter, and I'll say it here, too: most mild, white fishes are interchangeable in recipes. They'll taste a bit different and have slightly different textures, but the same recipes that work for tilapia will work for sole; the same recipes that work for orange roughy will work for cod. By the way, if you haven't tried tilapia, you ought to check it out. It's a mild, white fish that is being farmed more and more widely. Because tilapia is farmed, it tends to be less expensive than fish that has to be caught, so look for it.

More and more varieties of fish from around the world are becoming available everywhere, and some are used in the following recipes. But, as I've said, if you cannot find a particular fish, really almost any white fish will substitute well.

◌ The Simplest Fish

Not only is this simple, it's lightning-quick, too.

> 170 g mild white fish
> 1 Tbsp butter
> 1 Tbsp finely chopped fresh parsley
> Wedge of lemon

1. Melt the butter in a heavy-bottomed frying pan over a low heat. Add the fish fillets and sauté for 5 minutes on each side, or until the fish is opaque and flakes easily, turning carefully.
2. Transfer to a serving plate, top with the parsley and serve with a wedge of lemon.

    Yield: 1 serving, with a trace of carbohydrate, no fibre and 31 grams of protein.

◌ Unbelievably Easy Prawns

Want cold, cooked prawns for dipping? Here's how to get them perfect, every time.

> 2 litres water
> 1 Tbsp salt
> 450 g shelled, deveined raw prawns

1. Put the water in a large saucepan, put the salt in the water and put the saucepan over a high heat. When the water is boiling, throw in the prawns.

2. Bring the water just back up to the boil and turn off the heat. Leave this for another minute if the prawns are tiny, or 2 to 3 minutes if they're big.

3. Drain them in a colander and run them under some cold water. Chill them and serve with cocktail sauce, aioli or mustard-mayonnaise.

Yield: 4 generous servings, each with 1 gram of carbohydrate, no fibre and 23 grams of protein.

⌒ Scampi!

75 ml olive oil

100 g butter

3 cloves garlic, crushed

450 g raw prawns in the shell

75 ml dry white wine

1 1/2 Tbsp finely chopped fresh parsley

1. Melt the butter with the olive oil in a heavy frying pan over a medium-low heat. Add the garlic and stir it around.

2. Add the prawns to the pan. If they're at room temperature, they'll take 2 to 3 minutes per side; frozen prawns will take 4 to 5 minutes per side. Be careful not to overcook them.

3. Add the wine and simmer for another 1 to 2 minutes. Serve garnished with the parsley and put out plenty of napkins!

Yield: 3 servings, each with 3 grams of carbohydrate, a trace of fibre and 31 grams of protein.

🍓 Feel free to increase this recipe to however much your frying pan can hold. It makes a great fast-and-easy dinner party; just add a salad and some crusty bread for the carb-eaters.

☾ Obscenely Rich Prawns

This is a bit of trouble and it's not cheap, so you'll probably only want to make it for company – but it is well worth it.

600 g frozen chopped spinach

3 Tbsp butter

450 g mushrooms, sliced

1 small onion, diced

400 g frozen, cooked, shelled prawns (the little ones are best)

2 tsp liquid beef stock concentrate

350 ml double cream

225 ml soured cream

150 g grated Parmesan cheese

100 g unsweetened desiccated coconut

1. Preheat the oven to 180°C/Gas Mark 4.

2. Cook the spinach; I put mine in an ovenproof glass casserole, cover it and microwave it on High for 7 minutes.

3. Melt the butter in a heavy frying pan over a medium heat and start sautéing the mushrooms and onions. When they're starting to get limp, break up your frozen prawns a bit and add them to the frying pan.

4. When the prawns are thawed and the onions are quite limp and translucent, scoop out the vegetables and prawns with a slotted spoon and put them aside in a bowl. Turn up the heat, medium to high. A fair amount of liquid will have accumulated in the bottom of the frying pan; add the beef stock concentrate to it and boil the liquid until it's reduced to about one-third of its original volume.

5. Turn the heat back down to low, stir in the double cream, soured cream and Parmesan, and just heat it through (don't let it boil). Stir the prawns and vegetables back into this sauce.

6. Rescue your spinach from the microwave and drain it well by putting it in a strainer and pressing it with the back of a spoon, to make sure all the liquid is removed.

7. Spray a 2 1/2-litre casserole with nonstick cooking spray and spread half of the spinach in the bottom of it. Put half of the prawns mixture

over that. Repeat the layers with the rest of the spinach and the rest of the sauce.

8. Top with the coconut and bake for 1 1/2 hours.

Yield: 6 servings, each with 15 grams of carbohydrate and 5 grams of fibre, for a total of 10 grams of usable carbs and 26 grams of protein. (Not to mention outrageous amounts of fat, but that doesn't bother us!)

Scallops on Spinach with Walnut Sauce

From the kitchen of Tanya Rachfal.

Walnut Sauce

500 ml water

30 g chopped walnuts

2 Tbsp lemon juice

1 tsp grated lemon peel

4 Tbsp extra-virgin olive oil

1/2 tsp salt

1/2 tsp freshly ground black pepper

Remaining ingredients

450 g turkey or pork bacon

350 g large sea scallops (16 to 20)

Peanut oil

450 g spinach

1. Bring the water to the boil in a small saucepan. Add the walnuts and boil for 30 seconds, then drain. Put the walnuts in a bowl and combine with the lemon juice, lemon peel, olive oil, salt and pepper. Mix well and set aside.

2. Cut the slices of turkey bacon in half. Wrap a piece of bacon around a scallop and slip on to a skewer. Baste the scallops with the peanut oil.

3. Wash the spinach leaves thoroughly and cook over high heat until done. Grill the scallops for 5 minutes, turn, baste and grill the other side for 5 minutes. Serve the scallops over the spinach and top with the sauce.

Yield: 4 servings, each with 10 grams of carbohydrate and 4 grams of fibre, for a total of 6 grams of usable carbs and 37 grams of protein.

◯ Baked Orange Roughy

650 g orange roughy fillets, cut into serving-sized pieces

1 tsp salt

Freshly ground black pepper

1/4 medium onion, very thinly sliced

Juice of 1 lemon, or 2 Tbsp bottled lemon juice

50 g butter, melted

Paprika

Finely chopped fresh parsley (optional)

1. Preheat the oven to 170°C/Gas Mark 3. Spray a shallow baking dish with nonstick cooking spray.
2. Arrange the fish in the prepared dish and sprinkle with salt and pepper to taste. Scatter the onion over the fish.
3. In a small bowl, combine the lemon juice and butter and pour over the fish and onions. Sprinkle with paprika.
4. Bake, uncovered, for 30 minutes. Sprinkle with parsley (if using) and serve.

Yield: 4 servings, each with 2 grams of carbohydrate, a trace of fibre and 25 grams of protein.

↻ Fish Baked in a Bed of Rock Salt

Maureen Bernardis sent me this recipe all the way from Trieste, Italy, saying, 'I have never been a fish eater, unless it was not fishy fish. After discovering this recipe I am a total convert and we now have fresh fish at least once a week.'

> 1 kg fresh whole fish
> Rock salt (enough to cover the fish)
> Salt and freshly ground black pepper
> Olive oil

1. Preheat the oven to 180ºC/Gas Mark 4.
2. Clean fish, leaving the scales and heads on. (Your fishmonger might do this for you, if you ask.)
3. Line the bottom of a baking dish with a layer of rock salt, place the fish on the salt and cover it completely with more rock salt. Bake for 40 minutes.
4. Remove from the oven and break away the salt. Open the fish and season with salt, pepper and olive oil to taste. Serve hot.

Yield: 4 generous servings, each with no carbohydrates, no fibre and 35 to 40 grams of protein.

> 🍓 You can also put a lemon slice, a bay leaf, sage or rosemary inside the fish before you cook it, for a different-flavoured dish every time you cook. Don't be afraid to experiment.

ꙮ Orange Roughy Bonne Femme

This is my favourite fish recipe and it's very, very simple to make. Kids will probably like it, too.

> 30 g low-carb bake mix
> Pinch of salt
> 3 to 4 Tbsp butter
> 650 g orange roughy fillets

1. Mix the bake mix with the pinch of salt. Dip the fillets in the bake mix, covering them lightly all over.
2. Melt the butter in a heavy frying pan over medium heat. Sauté the 'floured' fillets in the butter for 5 to 7 minutes per side, or until golden brown. Serve just as it is, or with a squeeze of lemon juice.

Yield: 4 servings, each with 1 gram of carbohydrate, no fibre and 25 grams of protein.

☾ Wine and Herb Tilapia Packets

A simple company fish dish.

> 650 g tilapia fillets (4 portions)
> 4 Tbsp butter
> 125 ml dry white wine
> 2 Tbsp finely chopped fresh herbs
>   (chives, basil, oregano, thyme, or a combination)
> Salt

1. Preheat the oven to 180°C/Gas Mark 4.
2. Tear a piece of foil about 45 cm square for each fillet. Place a fillet in the centre of the foil square and curl the edges up a little. Put 1 tablespoon of butter, 2 tablespoons of wine, a tablespoon of chopped herbs and just a little salt on the fillet.
3. Fold the foil up around the fish, rolling the edges down in the middle and at the ends, so the packet won't leak in the oven. Repeat for all 4 servings.
4. Place the packets direct on the oven shelf – there's no need for a dish – and bake for 35 minutes.

Yield: 4 servings, each with 2 grams of carbohydrate and 1 gram of fibre, for a total of 1 gram of usable carbs and 31 grams of protein.

> ☙ When it's time to serve dinner, simply place a foil packet on each plate and let diners open their own. That way, no one loses a drop of the yummy butter, wine and herb sauce the fish has cooked in.

◌ Tilapia on a Nest of Vegetables

Quite beautiful to look at and a fast one-dish dinner. You could substitute green pepper for either the red or the yellow, if you like.

3 Tbsp olive oil

50 g red pepper, cut into thin strips

50 g yellow pepper, cut into thin strips

75 g courgette, cut in matchstick strips

75 g yellow squash, cut in matchstick strips

100 g sweet red onion, thinly sliced

1 clove garlic, crushed

450 g tilapia fillets

Salt and freshly ground black pepper

1/4 tsp guar or xanthan

Lemon wedges (optional)

1. Heat the olive oil in a heavy frying pan over a medium to high heat and sauté the peppers, courgette, squash, onion and garlic for just 2 to 3 minutes, stirring frequently.

2. Sprinkle the tilapia fillets lightly on either side with the salt and pepper and lay them over the vegetables in the frying pan. Cover, turn the heat to medium-low and let the fish steam in the moisture from the vegetables for 10 minutes, or until it flakes easily.

3. With a fish slice, carefully transfer the fish to a serving platter and use a slotted spoon to pile the vegetables on top of the fish. Pour the liquid that has accumulated in the frying pan into a blender and add the guar. Run the blender for a few seconds, then pour the thickened juices over the fish and vegetables. To serve, spoon a mound of the vegetables on to each diner's plate and place a piece of the fish on top. A few lemon wedges are nice with this, but not essential.

Yield: 4 servings, each with 11 grams of carbohydrate and 2 grams of fibre, for a total of 8 grams of usable carbs and 22 grams of protein.

↻ Ranch Fish

Karen Andrews sent me this easy and delicious recipe.

> 1 kg white fish fillets
>
> 30-g sachet purchased Ranch Dressing mix, dry
>
> 75 ml lemon juice
>
> 2 Tbsp. olive oil
>
> 3 Tbsp white wine

1. Spray a baking tray with nonstick cooking spray. Arrange the fillets on the tray.

2. Combine the dressing mix, lemon juice, oil and wine, and pour over fish. Grill for 9 to 12 minutes, or until done.

   Yield: 4 servings, each with 2 grams of carbohydrate, a trace of fibre and 41 grams of protein.

↻ Tuna Melt Casserole

Tuna casserole was always on our table when I was growing up. Here's one with no noodles, for the low-carb grown-ups we've become.

> 1 tsp oil
>
> 170 g tinned tuna, drained and mashed
>
> 100 g grated Cheddar cheese
>
> 40 g processed cheese
>
> 3 eggs
>
> 3 Tbsp low-carbohydrate bake mix (see page 28)
>
> 1 tsp garlic powder
>
> 1/2 to 1 tsp salt

1. Preheat the oven to 200°C/Gas Mark 6 and grease a 25-cm pie plate with the oil.
2. In a large bowl, combine the tuna, cheeses, eggs, bake mix, garlic and salt. Mix well.
3. Pour the tuna mixture into the prepared pie plate, pat down firmly and bake for approximately 30 minutes, or until browned and bubbly.

   Yield: 3 servings, each with 5 grams of carbohydrate and 3 grams of fibre, for a total of 2 grams of usable carbs and 38 grams of protein.

Crispy Parmesan Fish

This comes from Dona Crawford, who says she first tried it on a retreat in Sun Valley, Idaho, USA.

450 g cod fillets

2 1/2 Tbsp mayonnaise

1 tsp Dijon Mustard

1 tsp Worcestershire sauce

1 Tbsp finely chopped onion

30 g grated Parmesan cheese

1. Preheat the oven to 180ºC/Gas Mark 4 and spray a shallow baking dish with nonstick cooking spray. Place the fish in the prepared dish.
2. In a small bowl, combine the mayonnaise, mustard, Worcestershire sauce and onion, and spread evenly over fillets.
3. Sprinkle the fillets with the Parmesan and bake uncovered for 30 minutes, or until crispy.

Yield: 3 servings, each with 1 gram of carbohydrate, a trace of fibre and 31 grams of protein.

🍓 This combination of seasonings tastes great on chicken, too.

Grilled Marinated Whiting

With a big salad, and some crusty bread for the carb-eaters, this makes a nice, simple supper.

> 125 ml olive oil
> 3 Tbsp wine vinegar
> 1 Tbsp lemon juice
> 1 tsp Dijon mustard
> 1 clove garlic, crushed
> 1/2 tsp dried basil
> 1/4 tsp salt
> 1/4 tsp freshly ground black pepper
> 6 whiting fillets

1. Combine the oil, vinegar, lemon juice, mustard, garlic, basil, salt and pepper, and mix well.

2. Place the fillets in a large freezer bag and pour in the oil mixture. Refrigerate for several hours, turning the bag over from time to time.

3. Remove the fish from the marinade. Grill about 20 cm from the heat, for 4 to 5 minutes per side, or cook on a cooker-top grill pan.

4. While the fish is cooking, put the left-over marinade in a saucepan and boil it briefly, then served it as a sauce.

Yield: 3 servings, each with just over 1 gram of carbohydrate, no fibre and 34 grams of protein.

🍓 If you're in a hurry or you just don't have all the ingredients to make this dish, use 200 ml of purchased vinaigrette dressing instead.

ᢒ Salsa Fish

>1 fillet (about 170 g) firm-fleshed white fish,
  such as cod or sole
>
>2 Tbsp salsa

1. Preheat the oven to 180°C/Gas Mark 4.
2. Place the fish in a shallow baking dish, cover with the salsa and bake for 30 to 40 minutes, or until the fish flakes easily.

Yield: 1 serving, with 2 grams of carbohydrate and 1 gram of fibre, for a total of 1 gram of usable carbs and 31 grams of protein.

ᢒ Salmon with Lemon-Dill Butter

A classic flavour combination and, after you make this, you'll understand why.

>4 Tbsp butter, softened
>
>1 Tbsp lemon juice
>
>1 tsp dry dill (or 1 Tbsp snipped fresh)
>
>4 salmon steaks, each 2.5 cm thick
>
>Olive oil

1. Put the butter, lemon juice and dill in a food processor with the S-blade in place. Pulse until well combined, scraping down the sides once or twice if necessary. (If you don't have a food processor, you can simply beat these things together by hand.) Chill.
2. About 15 minutes before you will serve the meal, rub each salmon steak on both sides with olive oil. Arrange the steaks on the grill rack and grill 20 cm from high heat for 5 to 6 minutes per side, or until the salmon flakes easily.
3. Place on the serving plates, top each steak with a tablespoon of the lemon-dill butter and serve.

Yield: 4 very generous servings, each with only a trace of carbohydrate, a trace of fibre and about 34 grams of protein.

◯ Feta-Spinach Salmon Roast

I saw something like this being sold for an outrageous amount of money on the fish counter at my local supermarket and I thought, 'I can do that!'

> 75 g cream cheese, beaten to soften
>
> 75 g crumbled feta cheese
>
> 2 spring onions, thinly sliced, including the crisp green part
>
> 30 g g fresh spinach, chopped
>
> 2 skinless salmon fillets of roughly equal size and shape, 170 g each
>
> Olive oil

1. Preheat the oven to 180°C/Gas Mark 4.

2. Combine the cream cheese and feta, mashing and stirring with a fork until well blended. Add the spring onions and spinach, and combine well.

3. Spread the mixture evenly over one salmon fillet. (The filling will be about 2 cm thick.) Top with the second salmon fillet. Brush both sides with olive oil, turning the whole thing over carefully with a fish slice.

4. Place the 'loaf' on a shallow baking dish and bake for 20 minutes. Slice carefully with a sharp, serrated knife.

Yield: 2 servings, each with 5 grams of carbohydrate, a trace of fibre and 45 grams of protein.

⑨ Orange Salmon Packets

75 ml plain yoghurt

2 Tbsp mayonnaise

$1/4$ tsp orange extract

1 Tbsp Splenda

1 Tbsp lemon juice

2 spring onions, finely chopped

1 Tbsp parsley, finely chopped

450 g salmon fillets

1. Preheat the oven to 220°C/Gas Mark 7.
2. Combine the yoghurt, mayonnaise, orange extract, Splenda, lemon juice, spring onions and parsley. Set aside.
3. If your salmon fillets have skin on them, remove it and cut the fish into 4 serving-size pieces.
4. Tear 4 large squares of heavy-duty kitchen foil. Place each piece of salmon in the centre of a square of foil and spoon 2 tablespoons of the sauce over it. Fold the foil up over the salmon, bringing the edges together and roll the edges to make a tight seal. Roll up each end, as well.
5. When all your salmon fillets are snug in their own little packets, bake them for 15 minutes.
6. Place on individual serving plates, cut open and serve. If you have a little sauce left over, serve it on the side.

> 🍓 You can put your salmon packets in a roasting tin, if you're afraid they'll spring a leak, but I just put mine right on the oven rack.

Yield: 4 servings, each with less than 2 grams of carbohydrate, a trace of fibre and 24 grams of protein.

☾ Mustard-Glazed Salmon

>1 salmon fillet (150 g)
>1 Tbsp Mellow 'Honey' Mustard Dressing (see page 239)
>1 spring onion, finely chopped
>1/2 tsp dried thyme

1. Preheat the oven to 180°C/Gas Mark 4.
2. If there's skin on your salmon, remove it. Place the fillet on a baking tray.
3. In a small bowl, mix together the dressing, spring onion and thyme; spread it evenly over the fish. Bake for 12 to 15 minutes, or until the fish flakes easily.

Yield: 1 serving, with 4 grams of carbohydrate and 1 gram of fibre, for a total of 3 grams of usable carbs and 29 grams of protein.

🍓 Don't be too worried about buying salmon with skin on it. It actually peels off quite easily and it adds almost no time to the preparation process.

☾ Aioli Fish Bake

>1 fillet (about 170 g) mild, white fish
>2 Tbsp Aioli (see page 424)
>1 Tbsp grated Parmesan cheese

1. Preheat the oven to 180°C/Gas Mark 4.
2. Spray a shallow baking dish (a Swiss roll tin is ideal) with nonstick cooking spray.
3. Working directly on the baking tin, spread a fillet thickly with Aioli and sprinkle 1/2 tablespoon of Parmesan over that. Turn carefully and spread Aioli and sprinkle Parmesan on other side. Bake for 20 minutes and serve.

Yield: 1 serving, with 1 gram of carbohydrate, a trace of fibre and 32 grams of protein.

☽ Panned Swordfish Steaks with Garlic and Vermouth

Simple, fast and elegant. You'd pay a fortune for this at a restaurant!

450 g swordfish steaks
Salt and freshly ground black pepper
1 Tbsp olive oil
75 ml water
75 ml dry vermouth
2 or 3 cloves garlic, crushed
3 to 4 Tbsp finely chopped parsley

1. Sprinkle the swordfish steaks lightly on both sides with salt and pepper.
2. Place a heavy frying pan over high heat and add the olive oil. When the oil is hot, add the swordfish and sear on both sides (about 1 to 1 1/2 minutes per side). Then add the water, vermouth and garlic and turn down the heat to medium. Cover and let the fish simmer for 10 minutes.
3. Remove to a serving platter or individual serving plates and keep warm. Turn the heat under the frying pan to high and boil the pan juices hard for a minute or two, until they're reduced to 75 ml or so. Pour over the fish and top with parsley.

Yield: 3 servings, each with 2 grams of carbohydrate, no fibre and 32 grams of protein.

ᘯ Noodleless Prawn Pad Thai

This isn't terribly low in carbs – it's a maintenance dish, really – but I know that there are a lot of Thai food fans out there and that Pad Thai is the most popular Thai dish. So this is a lot lower-carb than Pad Thai with noodles, and it's fast and incredibly tasty.

2 Tbsp Thai fish sauce (nam pla)

1 Tbsp Splenda

2 Tbsp peanut oil or other bland oil

2 cloves garlic, crushed

12 cooked peeled prawns

2 eggs, beaten slightly

700 g cooked spaghetti squash

75 g beansprouts

2 Tbsp dry-roasted peanuts, chopped

4 spring onions, sliced

2 Tbsp fresh coriander leaves, chopped

1 lime, cut into wedges

1. Mix the fish sauce and Splenda and set the mixture aside.
2. Put the oil in a heavy frying pan over a medium to high heat and sauté the garlic for a minute. Add the prawns and sauté for another minute. Add the fish sauce mixture.
3. Pour the beaten eggs into the frying pan, let them set for 15 to 30 seconds and then scramble. Stir in the spaghetti squash and beansprouts, mixing with the prawns and egg mixture. Cook until just heated through.
4. Place on serving plates. Top each serving with chopped peanuts, spring onions and fresh coriander, and serve with a wedge of lime on the side.

Yield: 3 servings, each with 19 grams of carbohydrate and 2 grams of fibre, for a total of 17 grams of usable carbs and 13 grams of protein.

If this carb count sounds way too high to you, keep in mind that regular Pad Thai usually has over 60 grams of carbohydrate per serving, making this dish quite a bargain, carb-wise.

Sautéed Seafood and Red Pepper

This outstanding recipe comes from Alix Sudlow, who says that the left-overs are delicious for lunch the next day.

> 2 Tbsp olive oil
>
> 2 salmon fillets (about 170 g each)
>
> 1 red pepper, deseeded and thickly sliced
>
> 225 g large fresh prawns, shelled and deveined
>
> 225 g sea scallops, rinsed and patted dry
>
> 4 cloves of garlic, peeled and chopped
>
> 1 Tbsp fresh lemon or lime juice (optional)
>
> 1/2 tsp ground red pepper, or dried hot chilli flakes, or a dash of Tabasco sauce
>
> Salt and freshly ground black pepper
>
> 2 Tbsp fresh coriander and/or parsley, finely chopped

1. Heat the olive oil in a large frying pan – do not crowd the ingredients – over medium heat. Put the salmon fillets in the frying pan, skin side down. Scatter the red pepper slices around. Cook for about 6 minutes on a medium heat, turning once halfway through.

2. Add the prawns, scallops, garlic, lemon juice (if using), red pepper, salt and pepper. Fry for 2 to 3 minutes more, until the prawns and scallops are opaque.

3. Move to serving dishes. Scatter the coriander over, and serve.

Yield: 4 servings, each with 5 grams of carbohydrate and 1 gram of fibre, for a total of 4 grams of usable carbs and 38 grams of protein.

↻ Prawn and Andouille Jambalaya

If you can't find andouille sausage, just substitute the lowest-carb smoked sausage you can find.

350 g andouille, sliced 1 cm thick

75 ml olive oil

150 g chopped onion

2 cloves garlic, crushed

1 large green pepper, diced

400 g tinned diced tomatoes, including liquid

225 ml chicken stock

1 tsp dried thyme

800 g Cauliflower Rice (about one good-size cauliflower; see page 161)

225 g shelled, deveined, medium-size prawns

Salt and freshly ground black pepper

Tabasco sauce

1. In a Dutch oven, start browning the andouille in the olive oil. When it's lightly golden on both sides, add the onion, garlic and green pepper. Sauté the vegetables until the onion is becoming translucent.

2. Add the tomatoes, chicken stock and thyme, and bring to a simmer. Let it simmer for 20 minutes or so, uncovered, to blend the flavours.

3. Add the 'rice' and simmer for another 15 minutes, or until the cauliflower is starting to get tender.

4. Add the prawns and simmer for another 5 minutes or so – just long enough to cook the prawns. Season and add Tabasco to taste, and serve.

Yield: 6 servings, each with 12 grams of carbohydrate and 4 grams of fibre, for a total of 8 grams of usable carbs and 32 grams of protein.

◯ Salmon Patties

These are quick, easy and convenient. If you don't have spring onions in the refrigerator, use a tablespoon or so of finely chopped onion.

> 400 g tinned salmon
>
> 30 g oat bran
>
> 1 egg
>
> 2 spring onions, finely sliced
>
> 3 Tbsp butter

1. Drain the salmon, place it in a mixing bowl and mash it well. (Don't worry about any skin that may be in there, just mash it right in.)

2. Add the oat bran, egg and spring onions, and mix everything well. Form into 4 patties.

3. Melt the butter in a heavy frying pan over medium heat. Sauté the patties in the butter, turning carefully, until they're quite golden on both sides (7 to 10 minutes per side).

Yield: 2 servings, each with 9 grams of carbohydrate and 2 grams of fibre, for a total of 7 grams usable carbs and 47 grams of protein.

🍓 Not only do these patties have lots of healthy fish oils, they also contain half your day's requirement of calcium.

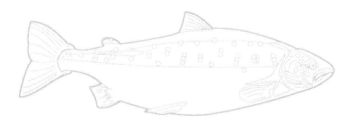

⌒ Tequila Lime Grilled Prawns

Tired of burgers and chicken at your barbecues? Try this instead.

> 1 kg really large raw prawns in their shells (about 30 prawns)
> 1 batch Tequila Lime Marinade (see page 426)

1. Put your prawns in a big freezer bag, pour the marinade over them, squeeze out the air and seal the bag. Put the bag in the refrigerator and let the prawns marinate for at least a few hours, turning the bag now and then.

2. When it's time for dinner, drain off the marinade into a saucepan and barbecue or grill your prawns (3 to 4 minutes per side should do it; you want them pink all the way through, of course).

3. While the prawns are cooking, boil the marinade hard for a few minutes. This kills any bacteria so you can serve it as a dipping sauce.

Yield: It should be 6 servings (but you know how appetites can be at barbecues), each with 3 grams of carbohydrate, a trace of fibre and 31 grams of protein.

Teriyaki Prawns: most people only use teriyaki on steak or chicken, but it's just as good on prawns. Just follow the directions for the Tequila Lime Grilled Prawns, but use Teriyaki Sauce (see page 426) instead of Tequila Lime Marinade.

Yield: 6 servings, each with 4 grams of carbohydrate, a trace of fibre and 32 grams of protein.

ᗡ Instant Prawn Stir-Fry

75 ml peanut oil

15 medium-size, frozen, cooked, peeled prawns

100 g frozen 'stir-fry' mixed vegetables

1 1/2 Tbsp Stir-Fry Sauce (see page 416)

1. Heat the oil in a frying pan or wok over a high heat. Put the prawns and vegetables, both still frozen, in the pan. Stir-fry for 3 to 5 minutes, or until the prawns are heated through and the vegetables are tender-crisp.

2. Stir in the stir-fry sauce and serve. If you want to make 2 servings, double everything but the oil.

Yield: 1 serving, with 9 grams of carbohydrate and 3 grams of fibre, for a total of 6 grams of usable carbs and 21 grams of protein.

ᗡ Cajun Pan-Fry Prawns

I threw this together when my husband brought a friend home for a quick lunch. It took no more than 10 minutes and was a big hit.

3 Tbsp olive oil

225 g shelled, deveined prawns (cooked or uncooked)

1 clove garlic, crushed

1 small onion, sliced

1/2 green pepper

1/2 yellow pepper

1 tsp Cajun seasoning

1. Heat the oil in a heavy frying pan over medium-high heat. If your prawns are uncooked, throw them in now, along with the garlic, onion and peppers and stir-fry the lot together until the prawns are pink clear through and the vegetables are just tender-crisp. If you're using cooked prawns, sauté the vegetables first, then add the prawns and cook just

long enough to heat them through. (I threw mine in still frozen and they were thawed and hot in just 4 or 5 minutes.)

2. Sprinkle the Cajun seasoning over everything. Stir it in and serve.

Yield: 2 servings, each with 11 grams of carbohydrate and 2 grams of fibre, for a total of 9 grams of usable carbs and 28 grams of protein.

◌ Prawns Alfredo

I invented this for my Alfredo-obsessed husband and he loves it.

> 450 g frozen broccoli florets
>
> 3 Tbsp butter
>
> 3 cloves garlic, crushed
>
> 225 g thawed small, frozen prawns, cooked, shelled
>   and deveined
>
> 200 ml double cream
>
> 1/4 tsp guar or xanthan
>
> 150 g grated Parmesan cheese

1. Steam or microwave the broccoli until tender-crisp.
2. Melt the butter in a heavy frying pan over medium heat and stir in the garlic. Add the broccoli, drained, and the prawns, and stir to coat with garlic butter.
3. While the prawns are heating through, put the cream in the blender, turn it to a low speed and add the guar. Turn the blender off quickly, so you don't make butter.
4. Pour the cream into the frying pan and stir in the Parmesan. Heat to a simmer and serve.

Yield: 3 servings, each with 11 grams of carbohydrate and 4 grams of fibre, for a total of 7 grams of usable carbs and 30 grams of protein.

☉ Parmesan Prawns

This recipe came from reader Karen Nichols, who said: 'This is a beautiful dish served with steamed asparagus alongside and it's also good presented over baked fish fillets. The prawns can go further this way and serve more people.'

2 Tbsp butter

1 Tbsp finely chopped onion

1 clove garlic, crushed

1/4 tsp salt

1/4 tsp ground red pepper

1/4 tsp white pepper

350 ml double cream

3 Tbsp grated Parmesan cheese

3 Tbsp low-carb ketchup (see page 422)

450 g cooked prawns, peeled and deveined

Fresh chopped chives for garnish (optional)

1. Melt the butter in a medium saucepan and sauté the onion in it until tender, but not browned. Add the garlic, salt and red and white peppers. Stir in the cream, Parmesan cheese and low-carb ketchup.
2. Bring to the boil, then reduce heat and simmer, uncovered, stirring occasionally, until the sauce thickens (15 to 20 minutes).
3. Stir in the cooked prawns. Move to a serving plate and garnish with chopped chives, if using.

Yield: 4 servings, each with 4.5 grams of carbohydrate, a trace of fibre and 27 grams of protein.

↻ Low-Carb Prawns and 'Grits'

Here's one for you Southerners, from Adele Hite of Durham, North Carolina, USA. My recipe tester – Kay, an Alabaman – loved this and said the 'grits' were great all by themselves, too.

'Grits'

1 recipe Fauxtatoes Deluxe (see page 160)

100 g cream cheese

100 g grated white Cheddar cheese

150 g grated Parmesan cheese

1 tsp freshly ground black pepper

Prawns

2 Tbsp butter

50 g chopped bacon

75 g sliced mushrooms

50 g very thinly sliced oil-packed sun-dried tomatoes (about 4 tomatoes)

2 tsp lemon juice

1 tsp crushed garlic

125 ml dry white wine

225 g peeled, cleaned prawns

75 g chopped spring onion

1. Combine the Fauxtatoes, cream cheese, Cheddar, Parmesan and black pepper in a saucepan. Stir over low heat until smooth.

2. Put 2 tablespoons of butter in a frying pan and add the chopped bacon. Brown the bacon slightly and add the mushrooms, tomatoes, lemon juice, garlic and wine. Simmer until the mushrooms are cooked.

3. Add the prawns and cook until they're just done. Toss with spring onions and serve over the 'grits'.

Yield: 5 servings, each with about 18 grams of carbohydrate and 5 grams of fibre, for a total of 13 grams of usable carbs and 33 grams of protein.

🍓 If you want to follow Kay's suggestion and serve the 'cheese grits' by themselves as a side dish, calculate as for 6 servings, each with 7 grams of carbohydrate and 2 grams of fibre, for a total of 5 grams of usable carbs and 15 grams of protein.

↻ Fried Catfish

I admit that without cornmeal this is somewhat inauthentic, but my catfish-loving spouse thought it was great.

30 g finely ground almonds

30 g finely ground hazelnuts

2 Tbsp rice protein powder

1 1/2 tsp seasoned salt

1 egg

1 Tbsp water

450 g catfish fillets

Oil for frying (peanut, rapeseed or sunflower)

Lemon wedges

1. On a plate, combine the almonds, hazelnuts, protein powder and seasoned salt, stirring well.
2. In a shallow bowl, beat the egg with the water.
3. Wash and dry the catfish fillets. Dip each one in the egg, then in the nut mixture, pressing it well into the fish.
4. If you have a deep fryer, by all means use it to fry your fish until it's a deep gold colour (7 to 10 minutes). If you don't, use a large, heavy frying pan. Pour 2.5 cm of oil into the frying pan and put it over a medium to high heat. Let it heat for at least 5 minutes; you don't want to put your fish in until the oil is up to temperature.
5. When the oil is hot, put in your fish and fry it until it's deep gold in colour. If the oil doesn't completely cover the fish, you'll have to turn it carefully after about 5 minutes. (Calculate 7 to 10 minutes' total frying time.) Serve with lemon wedges.

🍓 To test the oil, carefully put in one drop – no more – of water. It should sizzle, but not make the oil spit. If the oil spits, it's too hot. Turn the heat down and wait for it to cool a bit.

Yield: Serves 3, unless one of them is my husband, in which case it may only serve 2. Assuming my husband isn't at your house (and if he is, I'd like to hear about it), each serving has 4 grams of carbohydrate and 1 gram of fibre, for a total of 3 grams of usable carbs and 30 grams of protein.

CHAPTER NINE

Beef

There seems to be no end to the ways we can use beef – by itself, in casseroles and in sandwiches, sauces and pizzas, beef is a delicious way to get plenty of protein for no carbs at all. This chapter gives you some low-carb editions of high-carb favourites, as well as showing you some ways to use beef that you may never have even considered before. So read on.

Hamburgers

Let's talk about hamburgers for a moment. There is much to be said in favour of the humble hamburger – it's cheap, it's quick, it's easy and just about everybody likes it. Rarely will you hear the kids complain, 'Oh, no – not hamburgers again!' Furthermore, it's a food that is easy to make for both the 'normal' eaters and the low-carbers: just leave the bun off yours!

On the other hand, plain hamburgers, without a bun, can become just a wee bit boring to the adult palate over time. What follows are some recipes to help you vary your burgers. All the carb and protein analyses are based on burgers that weigh 150 g before cooking.

⟳ Blue Burger

1 hamburger patty

1 Tbsp crumbled blue cheese

1 tsp finely chopped sweet red onion

Cook your burger by your preferred method. When it's almost done to your liking, top with the blue cheese and let it melt. Remove from the heat, put it on plate and top with onion.

Yield: 1 serving, with only a trace of carbohydrate, no fibre and 27 grams of protein.

Smothered Burgers

Mmmmushrooms and onions!

4 hamburger patties

2 Tbsp butter or olive oil

50 g sliced onion

30 g sliced mushrooms

Dash of Worcestershire sauce

Cook your burgers by your preferred method. While the burgers are cooking, melt the butter or heat the oil in a small, heavy frying pan over medium-high heat. Add the onion and mushrooms, and sauté until the onions are translucent. Add a dash of Worcestershire sauce, stir and spoon over burgers.

Yield: 4 servings, each with just 2 grams of carbohydrate, at least a trace of fibre and 27 grams of protein.

⟲ Mexiburgers

    1 hamburger patty

    30 g Monterey Jack cheese, chilli-flavoured or plain

    1 Tbsp salsa

Cook your burger by your preferred method. When it's almost done to your liking, melt the cheese over the burger. Top with salsa and serve.

Yield: 1 serving, with 2 grams of carbohydrate, a trace of fibre and 27 grams of protein.

⟲ Poor Man's Poivrade

A real peppery bite – not for the timid!

    1 hamburger patty

    1 Tbsp coarse cracked black pepper

    1 Tbsp butter

    2 Tbsp dry white wine, dry sherry, or dry vermouth

1. Roll your raw hamburger patty in the pepper until it's coated all over.
2. Fry the burger in the butter over medium heat, until it's done to your liking.
3. Remove the burger to a plate. Add the wine to the frying pan and stir it around for a minute or two, until all the nice brown crusty bits are scraped up. Pour this over the hamburger and serve.

Yield: 1 serving, with between 4 and 6 grams of carbohydrate per serving (depending on whether you use wine, sherry, or vermouth – wine is lowest, vermouth is highest) and 2 grams of fibre, for a total of 2 to 4 grams of usable carbs and 27 grams of protein.

ꙷ Pizza Burger

>　1 hamburger patty
>
>　1 Tbsp purchased sugar-free pizza sauce
>
>　2 Tbsp grated mozzarella cheese

Cook the burger by your preferred method. When it's almost done to your liking, top with pizza sauce, then mozzarella. Cook until the cheese is melted and serve.

Yield: 1 serving, with (depending on your brand of pizza sauce), no more than 2 grams of carbohydrate, no fibre and 28 grams of protein.

>🍓 Some of the lowest-carb commercial brands of spaghetti sauce can be as low as 7.5 grams of carbs per 100 ml serving, of which 4 g is fibre, for an effective carb count of just 3.5 grams.

ꙷ Ellen's Noodleless Lasagne

Ellen Radke sent this recipe for people who miss lasagne! My dear friend Maria, who tested it on her husband and five kids, was asked if she would make this again. Her answer? An enthusiastic 'Yes!'

>　450 g minced beef
>
>　225 ml low-carb spaghetti sauce
>
>　100 g tinned sliced mushrooms
>
>　225 g ricotta cheese
>
>　1 egg, beaten
>
>　150 g grated mozzarella cheese
>
>　1/2 Tbsp Italian seasoning
>
>　20 to 25 slices pepperoni

1. Preheat the oven to 180°C/Gas Mark 4.
2. Brown the minced beef in a frying pan and drain off the oil. Add the spaghetti sauce and mushrooms, and simmer for 10 minutes.

3. In a small bowl, mix the ricotta, egg, 30 g of the mozzarella and the Italian seasoning. Beat well with a fork.

4. Grease a 20 x 20-cm ovenproof glass baking dish with nonstick cooking spray. Spread the beef mixture in the bottom of the dish. Spread the ricotta mixture on top of the mixture. Lay half the pepperoni slices on top of the ricotta mixture. Put the remaining grated mozzarella over the pepperoni slices and lay the remaining pepperoni on top of the cheese. Bake until bubbly (about 20 minutes).

Yield: 4 servings, each with 9 grams of carbohydrate and 3 grams of fibre, for a total of 6 grams of usable carbs and 43 grams of protein.

🍓 Recipe-tester Ellen adds: 'Next time, I'll try mixing in some Parmesan cheese with the ricotta and maybe adding a layer of spinach.'

⟳ Ultra Meat Sauce

Spaghetti without the spaghetti, as it were.

650 g minced beef

1 small onion, diced

1 clove garlic crushed

1 green pepper, diced

100 g tinned mushrooms, drained

500 ml low-carb spaghetti sauce

1. Brown and crumble the minced beef in a large, heavy frying pan. As the grease starts to collect in the pan, add the onion, garlic, green pepper and mushrooms. Continue cooking until pepper and onion are soft.

2. Pour off the excess grease. Stir in the spaghetti sauce and serve.

Yield: 5 servings, with (if you use the lowest-carbohydrate spaghetti sauce) 11 grams of carbohydrate and 4.6 grams of fibre, for a total of 6.4 grams of usable carbs and 25 grams of protein.

🍓 This is a good supper for the family, because, again, it's easy to add carbs for those who want them – you eat your very meaty meat sauce with a good sprinkling of Parmesan and you let the carb-eaters have theirs over spaghetti. Serve a big salad with it, and there's dinner.

↻ Pan-Fried Stroganoff

450 g minced beef

1 medium onion, diced

1 clove garlic, crushed

100 g tinned mushrooms, drained

1 tsp liquid beef stock concentrate

2 Tbsp Worcestershire sauce

1 tsp paprika

200 ml soured cream

Salt and freshly ground black pepper, to taste

1. Brown and crumble the minced beef in a heavy frying pan over medium heat. Add the onion and garlic as soon as there's a little grease in the bottom of the pan and cook until all pinkness is gone from the beef.

2. Drain the excess grease. Add the mushrooms, stock concentrate, Worcestershire sauce and paprika. Stir in the soured cream, then add salt and pepper to taste. Heat through, but don't let it boil. This is great as it is, but you may certainly serve it over noodles for the non-low-carb set.

Yield: 3 servings, each with 9 grams of carbohydrate and 2 grams of fibre, for a total of 7 grams of usable carbs and 28 grams of protein.

☾ Minced Beef 'Helper'

When your family starts agitating for the 'normal' food of yore, whip up this recipe.

450 g lean minced beef or turkey

50 g chopped green pepper

50 g chopped onion

50 g diced celery

500 g tinned tomato sauce

2 cloves garlic, crushed

1/2 tsp Italian seasoning

225 g grated Cheddar or Monterey Jack cheese

45 g low-carb pasta

75 ml water

Salt and freshly ground black pepper, to taste

1. In a large, oven-safe frying pan, brown the meat with the pepper, onion and celery. Drain off the grease.
2. Add the tomato sauce, garlic, seasoning, 100 g of the cheese, pasta, water, salt and pepper to taste. Cover and simmer over low heat for 10 minutes. Turn on the grill to preheat during last the few minutes of cooking time.
3. Stir well. Spread the remaining cheese over the top and grill until the cheese starts to brown.

Yield: 6 servings, each with 11 grams of carbohydrate and 2 grams of fibre, for a total of 9 grams of usable carbs and 36 grams of protein.

↺ Mexican Meatballs

Marilee Wellersdick sent me this easy, South-of-the-Border frying pan meal.

450 g minced beef or turkey

2 eggs

1 medium onion, finely chopped

3 cloves garlic, crushed

2 tsp ground coriander

1/2 tsp salt

2 Tbsp oil

400 g tinned chopped tomatoes

225 ml tinned tomato sauce

1 Tbsp chilli powder

1/2 tsp ground cumin

1. Mix together the minced beef, eggs, half the onion, two-thirds of the garlic, the coriander and the salt. Shape the mixture into 5-cm balls.
2. Heat the oil in a large frying pan. Add the meatballs and brown them. Add the tomatoes, tomato sauce, the remaining onion, the remaining garlic, chilli powder and cumin to the frying pan. Cover and simmer over medium-low heat for 45 minutes.

Yield: 4 servings, each with 15 grams of carbohydrate and 3 grams of fibre, for a total of 12 grams of usable carbs and 24 grams of protein.

↺ Minced Beef Stir-Fry

This looks like a lot of instructions, but it actually goes together rather quickly. It's good when you're missing Chinese food, which often has high amounts of added sugar and starch.

2 Tbsp soy sauce

3 Tbsp dry sherry

1 or 2 cloves garlic, crushed

450 g minced beef

Peanut oil or other bland oil for stir-frying

50 g coarsely chopped walnuts

225 g frozen sliced green beans, thawed,
  or 350 g frozen broccoli florets, thawed

1 medium onion, sliced

1 1/2 tsp grated fresh ginger

🍓 Remember the Law of Stir-Frying: have everything chopped, thawed, sliced and prepared before you start cooking!

1. In a bowl, combine 1 tablespoon soy sauce, 4 1/2 teaspoons sherry and the garlic. Add the minced beef and, with clean hands, mix the flavourings into the meat.

2. Heat 2 to 3 tablespoons of oil in a wok or large, heavy frying pan over a high heat. Put the walnuts in the pan and fry for a few minutes, until crispy. Drain and put aside.

3. Using the same oil, stir-fry bite-sized chunks of the minced beef mixture until cooked through. Lift out the beef and drain.

4. Pour the oil and fat out of the frying pan and put a few tablespoons of fresh oil in. Heat it up over high heat and add the green beans, onion and ginger. Stir-fry until the vegetables are tender-crisp.

5. Add the beef back to the pan and stir everything up. Stir in the remaining soy sauce and sherry and another clove of crushed garlic if you like.

6. Serve without rice for you and on top of rice for the carb-eaters in the family. Sprinkle the toasted walnuts on top of each serving and pass around the soy sauce at the table for those who like more.

Yield: 3 servings, each with 19 grams of carbohydrate and 6 grams of fibre, for a total of 13 grams of usable carbs and 34 grams of protein.

⟲ Burger Scramble Florentine

The only name I have to attribute this to is 'Dottie', which is a pity, because my sister, who tested this recipe, says it's great.

650 g lean minced beef

50 g onion, finely diced

300 g frozen spinach, thawed and drained

225 g cream cheese, beaten to soften

125 ml double cream

75 g grated Parmesan cheese

Salt and freshly ground black pepper

1. Preheat the oven to 180°C/Gas Mark 4. Spray a large casserole with nonstick cooking spray.

2. In a large frying pan, brown the minced beef and onion. Add the spinach and cook until the meat is done.

3. In a bowl, combine the cream cheese, double cream, Parmesan, salt and pepper to taste. Mix well.

4. Combine the cream cheese mixture and the meat mixture and spoon into the prepared casserole. Bake, uncovered, for 30 minutes or until bubbly and browned on top.

Yield: 6 servings, each with 5 grams of carbohydrate and 2 grams of fibre, for a total of 3 grams of usable carbs and 28 grams of protein.

⟳ Green Bean Spaghetti

This recipe comes from *Lowcarbezine!* reader Marcia McCance and it's a great dish if you're craving Italian food. If you use French beans, they'll remind you more of spaghetti.

> 350 g frozen green beans
>
> 1 small onion, chopped
>
> 1 green pepper, diced
>
> 4 or 5 medium mushrooms, sliced
>
> 2 to 3 Tbsp olive oil
>
> 450 g minced beef, turkey or chicken
>
> Salt
>
> 100 ml tinned tomato sauce
>
> 1 Tbsp Italian seasoning
>
> Parmesan cheese

1. Cook the green beans according to package directions.
2. While the beans are cooking, put the olive oil in a large, heavy frying pan over medium heat and sauté the onion, green pepper and mushrooms until the onion is translucent.
3. Add the minced beef, cook and stir, crumbling the meat until all pinkness is gone. Salt to taste.
4. Add the tomato sauce and the Italian seasoning. Bring to the boil, reduce to a simmer and cook for about 5 minutes. Do not overcook.
5. Drain your green beans, pour the meat sauce over them, top with Parmesan and serve.

Yield: 4 servings, each with 19 grams of carbohydrate and 5 grams of fibre, for a total of 14 grams of usable carbs and 26 grams of protein.

↻ Meatza!

Here's a dish for all you pizza-lovers and I know you are legion. Just add a salad and you have a supper that will please the whole family.

> 700 g minced beef, or 350 g minced beef mixed with 350 g Italian-style sausage
>
> 1 small onion, finely chopped
>
> 1 clove garlic, crushed
>
> 1 tsp dried oregano or Italian seasoning (optional)
>
> 225 g sugar-free pizza sauce
>
> Parmesan or Romano cheese (optional)
>
> 225 g grated mozzarella
>
> Toppings (peppers, onions, mushrooms, or whatever you like)
>
> Olive oil (optional)

1. Preheat the oven to 180ºC/Gas Mark 4.
2. In a large bowl and with clean hands, combine the meat with the onion and garlic and a teaspoon of oregano or Italian seasoning (if using). Mix well.
3. Pat the meat mixture out in an even layer in a 25 x 30-cm baking dish. Bake for 20 minutes.
4. When the meat comes out, it will have shrunk a fair amount, because of the grease cooking off. Pour off the grease and spread the pizza sauce over the meat. Sprinkle the Parmesan on the sauce (if using) and then distribute the grated mozzarella evenly over the sauce.
5. Top with whatever you like: green peppers, mushrooms, olives, anchovies. I love broccoli on pizza and thawed frozen broccoli florets work perfectly. You could also use meat toppings, such as sausage and pepperoni, but they seem a little redundant, since the whole bottom layer is meat.
6. Drizzle the whole thing with a little olive oil (if using; it's really not absolutely necessary).
7. Put your Meatza! 10 cm below a grill set on a high heat. Grill for about 5 minutes, or until the cheese is melted and starting to brown.

Yield: 6 servings, each with about 5 grams of carbohydrate per serving, only a trace of fibre and 27 grams of protein. (Based on using sugar-free pizza sauce and only cheese, no vegetables.)

🍓 If you haven't been able to find a pizza sauce that doesn't have sugar, you might combine 225 g tinned tomato sauce with a crushed clove of garlic and some oregano.

⌒ Joe

Our favourite one-dish frying-pan supper. It's flexible, too; don't worry if you use a little less or a little more burger, or one more or one fewer egg. It'll still come out great.

> 650 g minced beef
> 300 g frozen chopped spinach
> 1 medium onion, chopped
> 1 or 2 cloves garlic, crushed
> 5 eggs
> Salt and freshly ground black pepper

1. In a heavy frying pan over a medium flame, begin browning the minced beef.
2. While the beef is cooking, cook the spinach according to the package directions (or 5 to 7 minutes on high in the microwave should do it).
3. When the beef is half done, add the onion and garlic and cook until the beef is completely done. Pour off the extra fat.
4. Drain the spinach well – I put mine in a strainer and press it with the back of a spoon – and stir it into the minced beef.
5. Mix up the eggs well with a fork and stir them in with the beef and spinach. Continue cooking and stirring over low heat for a few more minutes, until the eggs are set. Salt and pepper to taste and serve.

Yield: 6 servings, each with 4 grams of carbohydrate and 2 grams of fibre, for a total of 2 grams of usable carbs and 25 grams of protein.

My sister likes a little Parmesan cheese sprinkled over her "Joe" and I surely wouldn't argue about a little thing like that!

↻ Sloppy José

So easy it's almost embarrassing and the kids will probably like it. Different brands of salsa vary a lot in their carb contents, so read labels carefully.

> 450 g minced beef
> 225 ml salsa (mild, medium or hot, as you prefer)
> 100 g grated Mexican-style cheese

1. In a large frying pan, crumble and brown the minced beef and drain off the fat.
2. Stir in the salsa and cheese, and heat until the cheese is melted.

Yield: About 4 servings, each with 4 grams of carbohydrate and 1 gram of fibre, for a total of 3 grams of usable carbs and 27 grams of protein.

Mega Sloppy José: try adding another 100 ml salsa and another 50 g cheese.

Yield: 4 servings, each with 6 grams of carbohydrate and 2 grams of fibre, for a total of 4 grams of usable carbs and 30 grams of protein.

🍓 This is good with a salad, or even on a salad. Of course, if you have carb-eaters around, they'll love the stuff on some corn tortillas.

All-Meat Chilli

Some people consider tomatoes in chilli to be anathema, but I like it this way. Don't worry about that cocoa powder, by the way – it's the secret ingredient!

1 kg minced beef

100 g chopped onion

3 cloves garlic, crushed

400 g tinned tomatoes with green chillies

100 ml tinned tomato sauce

4 tsp ground cumin

2 tsp dried oregano

2 tsp unsweetened cocoa powder

1 tsp paprika

1. Brown and crumble the beef in a heavy frying pan over medium-high heat. Pour off the grease and add the onion, garlic, tomatoes, tomato sauce, cumin, oregano, cocoa and paprika. Stir to combine.

2. Turn the heat down to low, cover and simmer for 30 minutes. Uncover and simmer for another 15 to 20 minutes, or until the chilli thickens a little. Serve with grated cheese, soured cream, chopped raw onion or other low-carb toppings.

Yield: 6 servings, each with 7 grams of carbohydrate and 2 grams of fibre, for a total of 5 grams of usable carbs and 27 grams of protein.

It's easy to vary this recipe to the tastes of different family members. If some people like beans in their chilli, just heat up a tin of kidney or pinto beans and let them spoon their beans into their own serving. If you like beans in your chilli, buy a tin of black soya beans at a health food shop; there's only a couple of grams of usable carbs in a couple of table-spoons. And of course, if you like your chilli hotter than this, just add crushed red pepper, cayenne or hot sauce to take things up a notch.

⑤ Mexicali Meat Loaf

450 g minced beef

450 g mild pork sausage

1 cup crushed plain pork rinds

150 g tinned mild green chillies, diced

1 medium onion, finely chopped

225 g Monterey Jack cheese, cut into small cubes or grated

200 ml salsa (mild, medium or hot, as desired)

1 egg

2 or 3 cloves garlic, crushed

2 tsp dried oregano

2 tsp ground cumin

1 tsp salt

1. Preheat the oven to 180°C/Gas Mark 4.
2. Combine all the ingredients in a really big bowl and then, with clean hands, knead it all until it's thoroughly blended.
3. Put it in a clean baking dish and form into a loaf – it'll be a big loaf – about 8 cm thick. Bake for 1 1/2 hours.

> 🍓 Chop the onion quite finely for your meat loaves. If it's in pieces that are too big, it tends to make the loaf fall apart when you cut it. The Mexicali Meat Loaf may crumble a bit anyway, because it's quite tender.

Yield: 8 servings, each with 5 grams of carbohydrate and 1 gram of fibre, for a total of 4 grams of usable carbs and 28 grams of protein.

⌒ Low-Carb Swiss Loaf

I adapted this from a recipe that contained breadcrumbs and milk. I simply left them out and I've never missed them.

> 1 kg minced beef
>
> 150 g Swiss cheese, diced small or grated
>
> 2 eggs, beaten
>
> 1 medium onion, chopped
>
> 1 green pepper, chopped
>
> 1 small stick celery, chopped
>
> 1 tsp salt
>
> 1/2 tsp freshly ground black pepper
>
> 1/2 tsp paprika

1. Preheat the oven to 180°C/Gas Mark 4.
2. With clean hands, combine all the ingredients in a large bowl, until the mixture is well blended.
3. Pack the meat into one large loaf tin or two small ones. Bake a large loaf for 1 1/2 to 1 3/4 hours. Bake two small loaves for 1 1/4 hours.

> 🍓 I turn the loaf out of the tin and on to a rack in a baking dish so the excess fat runs off – not because I'm afraid of fat, but because I like it better that way. If you like, though, you could bake yours throughout in the tin and it would probably be a bit more tender.

Yield: 8 servings, each with 3 grams of carbohydrate and 1 gram of fibre, for a total of 2 grams of usable carbs and 30 grams of protein.

↷ Courgette Meat Loaf Italiano

The inspiration for this meat loaf was a recipe in an Italian cookbook but the original recipe had mostly courgette in it, and only a tiny bit of meat. I thought to myself, 'How could adding more minced beef be a problem here?' And I was right; it's very moist and flavourful.

3 Tbsp olive oil

2 medium courgettes, chopped

1 medium onion, chopped

2 or 3 cloves garlic, crushed

650 g minced beef

2 Tbsp snipped fresh parsley

1 egg

100 g grated Parmesan cheese

1 tsp salt

1/2 tsp freshly ground black pepper

1. Preheat the oven to 180°C/Gas Mark 4.
2. Heat the olive oil in a frying pan and sauté the courgette, onion and garlic in it for 7 to 8 minutes.
3. Let the vegetables cool a little, then put them in a big bowl with the beef, parsley, egg, cheese, salt and pepper. Using clean hands, mix thoroughly.
4. Take the rather soft meat mixture and put it in a big loaf tin, if you like, or form the loaf on a rack in a baking dish so the grease will drip off. (Keep in mind if you do it this way, your loaf won't stand very high, it'll be about 5 cm thick.)
5. Bake for 75 to 90 minutes, or until the juices run clear but the loaf is not dried out.

Yield: 5 servings, each with 3 grams of carbohydrate and 1 gram of fibre, for total of 2 grams of usable carbs and 29 grams of protein.

⌒ My Grandma's Standby Casserole

My grandma used egg noodles instead of spaghetti squash, but it tastes good this way, too. This is handy for pot-luck suppers and such.

> 450 g minced beef
>
> 2 Tbsp butter
>
> 1 clove garlic, crushed
>
> 1 tsp salt
>
> Dash of freshly ground black pepper
>
> 500 ml tinned tomato sauce
>
> 6 spring onions
>
> 80 g cream cheese
>
> 225 ml soured cream
>
> 700 g cooked spaghetti squash
>
> 50 g grated Cheddar cheese

1. Preheat the oven to 180°C/Gas Mark 4.
2. Brown the minced beef in the butter. Pour off the grease and stir in the garlic, salt, pepper and tomato sauce.
3. Cover, turn the heat down to low and simmer for 20 minutes.
4. While the meat's simmering, slice the spring onions, including the crisp green part, and combine with the cream cheese and soured cream. Blend well.
5. In the bottom of a 1 1/2-litre casserole, layer half the spaghetti squash, half the spring onion mixture and half the tomato-beef mixture; repeat the layers. Top with the Cheddar and bake for 20 minutes.

Yield: 5 servings, each with 15 grams of carbohydrate and 2 grams of fibre, for a total of 13 grams of usable carbs and 23 grams of protein.

↺ Beef Taco Filling

450 g minced beef

2 Tbsp Taco Seasoning (see page 418)

75 ml water

1. Brown and crumble the minced beef in a heavy frying pan over medium-high heat.

2. When the meat's cooked through, drain the grease and stir in the seasoning and water. Let it simmer for about 5 minutes and serve.

Yield: 4 servings, each with less than 1 gram of carbohydrate, no fibre and 19 grams of protein.

🍓 Use in taco omelettes, taco salads or to fill taco shells made from cheese (see page 80) or low-carb tortillas.

☌ Reuben Casserole

Another great recipe from Vicki Cash. Thanks, Vicki!

> 4 small summer squash or courgettes
>
> 2 Tbsp water
>
> 800 g tinned sauerkraut, drained
>
> 1 Tbsp caraway seeds
>
> 2 Tbsp Dijon mustard
>
> 225 g chopped beef brisket or pastrami
>
> 100 g grated Swiss cheese

1. Slice the squash into bite-sized pieces. Place the pieces in a 2-litre microwave-safe casserole and add the water. Cover and microwave on High for 3 minutes.

2. Add the sauerkraut, caraway seeds, mustard and meat, mixing well. Cover and microwave on High for 6 minutes, stirring halfway through.

3. Stir in the cheese and microwave for 3 to 5 more minutes, or until the cheese is melted.

Yield: 4 servings, each with 16 grams of carbohydrate and 8 grams of fibre, for a total of 8 grams of usable carbs and 21 grams of protein.

☉ Beef Fajitas

This is my take on a recipe sent to me by Carol Vandiver. You can serve these with low-carb tortillas, if you like, but I just pile mine on a plate, top them with salsa, soured cream and guacamole, and eat 'em with a fork.

125 ml lite beer

125 ml oil

2 Tbsp lime juice

1/2 small onion, thinly sliced

1 tsp chilli flakes

1/4 tsp ground cumin

1/4 tsp freshly ground black pepper

650 g chuck steak

1 medium onion, thickly sliced

1 green pepper, cut into strips

1 Tbsp oil

Low-carb tortillas, purchased or home-made

Guacamole (see page 53)

Salsa

Soured cream

1. Mix together the beer, oil, lime juice, onion, pepper flakes, cumin and pepper; this is your marinade.

2. Place the steak in a large freezer bag and pour the marinade over it. Seal the bag, pressing out the air and put it in the fridge. Let your steak marinate for a minimum of several hours.

3. When you're ready to cook, remove your steak from the bag, reserving a couple of tablespoons of the marinade. Slice your steak quite thinly, across the grain.

4. Add the oil to a large, heavy frying pan over high heat and tilt to coat the bottom. When the pan is good and hot, add the steak slices, onion and pepper. Stir-fry them until the meat is done through and the vegetables are crisp-tender.

5. Stir in the reserved marinade and serve, with or without low-carb tortillas, topped with guacamole, salsa and soured cream.

   Yield: 4 servings, each with about 5 grams of carbohydrate and 1 gram of fibre, for a total of 4 grams of usable carbs and 34 grams of protein. (Analysis does not include guacamole, soured cream, salsa or low-carb tortillas).

◠ Steakhouse Steak

Ever wonder why steak is better at a steak restaurant than it is at home? Part of it is that the best grades of meat are reserved for the restaurants, but it's also the method: quick grilling, at very high heat, very close to the flame. Try it at home, with this recipe.

> Olive oil
>
> 750 g to 1 kg well-marbled steak (such as sirloin),
>   2.5 to 4 cm thick

1. Rub a couple of teaspoons of olive oil on either side of the steak.
2. Arrange your grill so you can get the steak so close that it's almost, but not quite, touching the heat source. (I have to put my grill pan on top of a frying pan turned upside down to do this.) Turn the heat to high. For a 2.5-cm-thick steak, give this 5 to 5 1/2 minutes; for a 4-cm-thick steak, you can go up to 6 minutes.
3. At the end of this time, quickly turn the steak over and start to time it again. If you like your steak a lot rarer or more well-done than I do, you may need to adjust how long you grill the second side.
4. When the steak is done to your liking, put it quickly on a serving plate and season it any way you like.

   Yield: The number of servings will depend on the size of your steak, but what you really need to know is that there are no carbs here at all.

☾ Southwestern Steak

I adore steak, I adore guacamole, and the combination of the two is fantastic.

> Olive oil
>
> 750 g to 1 kg well-marbled steak (such as sirloin),
>   2.5 to 4 cm thick
>
> Guacamole (see page 53)
>
> Salt and freshly ground black pepper

Cook the Steakhouse Steak (see page 331) to your liking. Spread each serving with a heaped tablespoon of guacamole and salt and pepper to taste.

Yield: The number of servings will depend on the size of the steak, but the guacamole will add 4 grams of carbohydrate and 1 gram of fibre, for a total of 3 grams of usable carbs. You'll also get 275 milligrams of potassium.

☾ Cajun Steak

> 2 to 3 tsp Cajun Seasoning
>
> 450 g sirloin steak, 2.5 cm thick

Simply sprinkle Cajun seasoning over both sides of your steak. Then either pan-grill it (cook it on a very hot, ungreased, heavy frying pan) or cook it on a cooker-top grill pan over maximum heat. Either way, cook it just 6 1/2 minutes per side.

Yield: 3 or 4 servings; the Cajun seasoning adds a bare trace of carbohydrate to each.

◯ Steak Vinaigrette

You don't have to make a batch of home-made vinaigrette every time you want a steak; purchased will work just as well here.

> Steak, in your preferred cut and quantity
> 125 ml vinaigrette dressing for each 450 g of steak

1. Put your steak in a large freezer bag and pour the vinaigrette dressing over it. Let the steak marinate for at least 15 minutes, or leave it all day, if you have the time.
2. When you're ready to cook your steak, remove it from the bag, discard the marinade and grill (see page 331) or barbecue it, as you prefer.

Yield: Assume 450 g of steak is 2 servings, each with about 1 gram of carbohydrate, maximum, no fibre and 33 grams of protein.

◯ Blue Cheese Steak Butter

This is one of those recipes that would have horrified me back in my low-fat days – and it's so good! If you don't have a food processor, you can make this by hand; it will just take some vigorous mixing.

> 225 g blue cheese, crumbled
> 170 g softened butter
> 1 or 2 cloves garlic, crushed
> 1 Tbsp Dijon mustard
> 2 or 3 drops Tabasco sauce

1. Put all the ingredients in your food processor and run it until it's all well blended and smooth. Taste it to see if it needs a little extra mustard or Tabasco.
2. Put it in a pretty dish and chill it. Then drop a tablespoonful over each serving of freshly barbecued or grilled steak.

Yield: Roughly 12 tablespoons, each with 1 gram of carbohydrate, only a trace of fibre and 4 grams of protein.

🍓 If you have some steak-loving people on your Christmas list, a ball of Blue Cheese Steak Butter wrapped in foil makes a nice present.

◌ Platter Sauce for Steak

Make this with the drippings when you're pan-grilling a steak (cooking it in a hot, dry frying pan).

> 2 Tbsp butter
> 1 tsp dry mustard
> 1/2 tsp Worcestershire sauce
> 1/2 tsp salt
> 1/2 tsp freshly ground black pepper

1. After pan-grilling a steak, pour off most of the grease. Melt the butter in the pan, then stir in the mustard, Worcestershire sauce, salt and pepper, stirring it around so you scrape up the nice brown bits from the pan.
2. Let it bubble a minute, pour it over the hot steak and serve.

   Yield: This is about enough for a 450-g steak and will add only 1 gram of carbohydrate, no fibre and no protein.

◌ Garlic Butter Steak

And you thought garlic butter was only good on bread.

> 4 Tbsp butter, softened
> 1 or 2 cloves garlic, crushed
> 700 g steak

1. Blend the butter with the garlic. (A food processor is good for this, but not essential.)
2. Grilll (see page 331) or barbecue your steak, as you prefer. Melt a tablespoon of garlic butter over each serving.

   Yield: 4 servings, each with less than 1 gram of carbohydrate, no fibre and 25 grams of protein.

◯ Marinated Sirloin

225 ml water

125 ml soy sauce

3 Tbsp Worcestershire sauce

1/2 medium onion, finely chopped

1 1/2 Tbsp balsamic vinegar

1/2 Tbsp wine vinegar

1 1/2 Tbsp lemon juice

1 Tbsp Dijon mustard

2 cloves garlic, crushed

750 g to 1 kg sirloin steak, 2.5 cm thick

1. Combine the water, soy sauce, Worcestershire sauce, onion, balsamic vinegar, wine vinegar, lemon juice, mustard and garlic in a large measuring jug or bowl with a pouring lip. This is your marinade.

2. Place the steak in a large freezer bag, pour in the marinade and seal the bag. Place it in a flat dish (in case the bag springs a leak) and put in the fridge for at least several hours, or overnight if you have the time.

3. About 15 minutes before you're ready to cook, remove the steak from the bag and grill (see page 331) or barbecue to your liking.

Yield: Calculate at least 4 servings from a 750-g steak and 5 or 6 servings from 1 kg. There are a few grams of carbs in the marinade, but since you discard most of it, there's less than 1 gram of carbohydrate added to each serving, no fibre and no protein. Each serving of steak has no carbohydrates, no fibre and about 25 grams of protein.

◯ Teriyaki Steak

1 kg thinly cut, lean, boneless steak

1 batch Teriyaki Sauce (see page 426)

1. Put your steak in a large freezer bag and pour the sauce over it. Squeeze out the extra air, seal the bag and let the steak marinate for at least a half an hour, or overnight if you have the time.

2. When you're ready to cook the steak, pour the marinade into a small saucepan. Barbecue or grill (see page 331) the steak quickly with high heat.

3. While the steak is cooking, boil the marinade hard for a few minutes.

4. When the steak is done, slice it thinly, across the grain. Serve with the boiled marinade.

Yield: 6 servings. The marinade has 3 grams of carbohydrate per Tbsp; however, if you don't spoon any over your steak, you'll get only a fraction of a gram, no fibre and no protein. Each serving of steak has no carbohydrates, no fibre and 23 grams of protein.

☺ Steak Au Poivre with Brandy Cream

For black pepper lovers only!

> 350 g tender, well-marbled steak (such as sirloin),
>   1 to 2 cm thick
> 4 tsp coarse cracked black pepper
> 1 Tbsp butter
> 1 Tbsp olive oil
> 2 Tbsp brandy
> 2 Tbsp double cream
> Salt

1. Place your steak on a plate and sprinkle 2 teaspoons of the pepper evenly over it. Using your hands or the back of a spoon, press the pepper firmly into the steak's surface. Turn the steak over and do the same thing to the other side.

2. Add the butter and oil to a large, heavy frying pan over high heat. When the pan is hot, add the steak. For a 1-cm-thick steak, 4 1/2 minutes per side is about right; go maybe to 5 1/2 minutes for a 2-cm-inch-thick steak.

3. When the steak is done on both sides, turn off the heat, pour the brandy over it and set it alight.

4. When the flames die down, remove the steak to a serving platter and pour the cream into the frying pan. Stir it around, dissolving the meat juices and brandy into it. Salt lightly and pour it over the steak.

Yield: 2 servings, each with 3 grams of carbohydrate and 1 gram of fibre, for a total of 2 grams of usable carbs and 25 grams of protein.

☺ Basil Beef Stir-Fry

Basil in stir-fries is a Thai touch, but this isn't hot, as most Thai food is.

450 g boneless chuck steak

6 spring onions, including the crisp green part, cut into 2.5-cm lengths

75 ml peanut oil, or other bland oil

2 tsp dried basil (or 2 Tbsp chopped fresh)

1 Tbsp soy sauce

1/4 tsp Splenda

Freshly ground black pepper

1. Thinly slice the beef across the grain.
2. Put the oil in a wok or heavy frying pan over a high heat. When it's hot, add the beef and stir-fry for a minute or two. Add the spring onions and stir-fry for another 3 to 4 minutes, or until all the pink is gone from the beef.
3. Add the basil, soy sauce, Splenda and pepper to taste, and toss with the beef, cooking just another minute or so.

Yield: 3 servings, each with 3 grams of carbohydrate and 1 gram of fibre, for a total of 2 grams of usable carbs and 25 grams of protein.

ᔕ Beef Burgundy

A handy one-dish dinner-party meal. Put it together on a
Saturday morning and it will cook happily by itself all afternoon.

  75 ml olive oil

  1 kg boneless chuck steak, cut into 5-cm cubes

  225 ml dry red wine

  3/4 tsp guar or xanthan

  1 1/2 tsp salt

  1 tsp paprika

  1 tsp dried oregano

  1 large onion, sliced

  225 g mushrooms, wiped clean with a damp cloth

  2 green peppers, cut into chunks

1. Preheat the oven to 130ºC/Gas Mark 1/2.
2. Put the oil in a heavy frying pan over medium-high heat and brown the
   beef in the oil.
3. Put the browned beef in a 2 1/2-litre casserole with a lid.
4. Combine the wine and guar in the blender, blending for 10 seconds or
   so, and then pour the mixture over the beef.
5. Add the salt, paprika, oregano, onion, mushroom and green peppers to
   the casserole and give it a quick stir. Cover and put it in the oven for 5
   hours. When it comes out, you can boil down the liquid in a saucepan
   to make it thicker, if you like, but it's quite nice just like this.

Yield: 6 generous servings, each with 8 grams of carbohydrate and
3 grams of fibre, for a total of 5 grams of usable carbs and 25 grams
of protein.

Regarding Slow Cookers

Slow cookers are tremendously useful for people who are out all day, but it can be hard to find the time to assemble everything before you get out of the house in the morning. Here's the solution: put together your slow-cooker recipe the night before. If your slow cooker is like mine, it has a removable crockery liner. Just put all of your ingredients into this, cover it and put it in the refrigerator. When you get up in the morning, slip that crockery liner into your microwave – I have to turn the lid upside down to make mine fit – and zap it on half-power for about 10 minutes to take off the chill. Slip the crockery liner back into the base unit, set the slow cooker and you're ready to go.

If you can't fit your crockery liner in your microwave, calculate an extra hour of slow cooking to make up for the chill. And you know not to take the lid off the slow cooker while it's cooking – every time you do this, you slow down the cooking by about half an hour!

Good Low-Carb Slow-Cooked Beef Rib

225 ml tinned tomato sauce

200 ml water

2 Tbsp wine or cider vinegar

4 Tbsp soy sauce

2 tsp Splenda

1 1/4 to 1 3/4 kg short beef ribs

1 large onion

1. In a bowl, mix together the tomato sauce, water, vinegar, soy sauce and Splenda.

2. Put the beef ribs in the slow cooker. (You can cook from frozen, you don't have to bother thawing.) Slice the onion and place it on top of the ribs. Pour the sauce over the onion and ribs.

3. Set the slow cooker on Low and cook for 8 to 9 hours. (If you put the ribs in thawed, cut about 1 hour off the cooking time.)

Yield: 5 servings from 1 1/4 kg of ribs, 7 servings from 1 3/4 kg, each with about 7 grams of carbohydrate and 1 gram of fibre, for a total of 6 grams of usable carbs and 41 grams of protein. (Total carbs will vary with how much of the sauce you eat, since most of the carbs are in there.)

This recipe gives you a tremendously tasty rib of beef in a rather thin but flavourful sauce – it's more like a broth. If you'd like, you could put about 225 ml of the sauce through the blender with 3/4 tsp or so of guar or xanthan to thicken it, but I rather like it as is.

◌ New England Boiled Dinner

This is the American traditional St Patrick's Day dinner, but it's a simple, satisfying one-pot meal on any chilly night. If you have carb-eaters in the family, you can add a few little red boiling potatoes, still in their jackets, to this.

6 small turnips (golf-ball to tennis-ball size)

2 big sticks celery, cut into chunks

2 medium onions, cut into chunks

1 corned beef for simmering (about 1 1/3 kg)

1/2 cabbage

Dijon mustard

Horseradish

Butter

🍓 This is easy, but it takes a long time to cook. Do yourself a favour and assemble it ahead of time.

1. Peel the turnips and put them into the slow cooker, along with the celery and the onions. Set your beef on top and add water to cover.

2. Season, then put the lid on the slow cooker, set it on Low and leave it alone for 10 to 12 hours. (You can cut the cooking time down to 6 to 8 hours if you set the slow cooker on High, but the Low setting yields the most tender results.)

3. When you come home all those hours later, remove the beef from the cooker with a fork or some tongs, put the lid back on the slow cooker to retain heat, put the beef on a platter and keep it warm. Cut the cabbage into big wedges and drop it into the slow cooker with the other vegetables.

4. Re-cover the slow cooker and turn it up to High. Leave it to cook for half an hour.

5. With a slotted spoon, remove all the vegetables and pile them around the beef on a platter. Serve with the mustard and horseradish as condiments for the beef and butter for the vegetables.

Yield: 8 servings (and of course, you don't need a thing with it), each with 9 grams of carbohydrate and 2 grams of fibre, for a total of 7 grams of usable carbs and 26 grams of protein.

↷ Beef in Beer

The tea, the beer and the long, slow cooking make this as tender as can be.

> 30 g soya powder or low-carb bake mix
>
> Salt and freshly ground black pepper
>
> 1 kg boneless roasting beef
>
> Olive oil
>
> 1 medium onion, sliced
>
> 225 ml tinned tomato sauce
>
> 1 can (350 ml) lite beer
>
> 1 tsp instant tea powder
>
> 100 g tinned mushrooms, drained
>
> 2 cloves garlic, crushed

1. Combine the soya powder with a little salt and pepper and dredge the beef in it.
2. Heat a few tablespoons of oil in a heavy frying pan over medium-high heat and sear the meat until it's brown all over. Place the meat in a slow cooker.
3. In the oil left in the frying pan, fry the onion for a few minutes and add that to the slow cooker, too.
4. Now pour the tomato sauce and beer over the beef. Sprinkle the instant tea over it and throw in the mushrooms and garlic. Put the lid on the slow cooker, set it on Low and let it cook for 8 to 9 hours. Good served with puréed cauliflower.

Yield: 6 servings, each with 8 grams of carbohydrate and 1 gram of fibre, for a total of 7 grams of usable carbs and 31 grams of protein.

🍓 To keep the carbs super-low, use the lowest-carb lite beer available: Miller Lite is a good choice.

◠ Peking Slow-Cooker Pot Roast

This sounds rather odd, but tastes great! You'll need to prepare well ahead of time, but it's not a lot of work.

1 1/4 to 2 1/4 kg brisket of beef

5 or 6 cloves garlic

225 g cider vinegar

225 g water

1 small onion, sliced

350 ml strong coffee (instant works fine)

1 tsp guar or xanthan

1. At least 24 to 36 hours before you want to actually cook your roast, stick holes in the meat with a thin-bladed knife, cut your garlic cloves into slices and insert a slice into each hole. Put your garlicked roast in a big bowl and pour the vinegar and the water over it. Put it in the fridge and let it sit there for a day or so, turning it over occasionally, so the whole thing marinates.

2. On the morning of the day you want to serve your roast, pour off the marinade and put the meat in your slow cooker. Thinly slice the onion and put it on top of the roast. Pour the coffee over the roast and onion, put on the lid, set the cooker on Low and leave it alone for 8 hours for a smaller roast or up to 10 hours for a larger one.

3. When you're ready to eat, remove your roast from the cooker carefully, because it will now be so tender it's likely to fall apart.

4. Scoop out 500 ml of the liquid and some of the onions, and put them in the blender with the guar. Blend for few seconds, then pour into a saucepan set over a high heat. Boil this sauce hard for about 5 minutes, to reduce it a little. Salt and pepper the sauce to taste (it's amazing the difference the salt and pepper make, here; I didn't like the flavour of this sauce until I added the salt and pepper and then I liked it a lot) and slice and serve your roast with this sauce.

Yield: If you use a 1 3/4-kg boneless roast, you'll get 12 servings, each with 3 grams of carbohydrate, a trace of fibre and 34 grams of protein.

🍓 Don't try to make this with a tender cut of beef! This recipe will tenderise the toughest cut; a tender one will practically dissolve. Use inexpensive, tough cuts and prepare to be amazed at how fork-tender they get.

↻ Ruben Beef Casserole

This recipe comes from my pal Diana Lee, of *Baking Low Carb* fame.

225 g fresh beef, finely chopped

2 eggs

125 ml mayonnaise

125 ml double cream

1 tsp dried onion

1/2 tsp dry mustard

2 tsp caraway seeds

150 g sauerkraut

225 g grated Swiss cheese

1. Preheat the oven to 190°C/Gas Mark 5.
2. Grease a 1 1/2-litre casserole and place the beef in the bottom of it.
3. In a bowl, combine the eggs, mayonnaise, cream, onion, dry mustard and caraway seed. Drain and rinse the sauerkraut and add it to the mayonnaise mixture.
4. Pour the mayonnaise mixture over the beef and sprinkle the cheese on top. Bake covered for 30 minutes, then uncover for an additional 15 minutes.

Yield: 4 servings, each with 6 grams of carbohydrate and 1 gram of fibre, for a total of 5 grams of usable carbs and 29 grams of protein.

Anglo-Saxon Soul Food, aka Roast Beef and Yorkshire Pudding

This is the typical taste of the British Sunday dinner. Your family and friends will love these dishes.

◯ The Noble Beef

From the price of prime rib these days, I suspect they're feeding the cattle pure gold. Still, this will cost you little more than buying one slice in a restaurant.

> 1 3/4 kg beef rib roast
>
> 75 ml oil

1. Preheat the oven to its highest setting.
2. Have the beef at room temperature and rub it all over with the oil. Put it on a rack in a roasting tin, fatty side up. Push a meat thermometer in it, deep in the centre, but not touching a bone.
3. Put the roast in the oven and immediately turn the heat down to 180°C/Gas Mark 4. Beef generally takes about 20 minutes per 450 g to come out medium-rare, so calculate about 1 hour and 20 minutes to cook this roast. Check that meat thermometer, though; I've had a roast surprise me more than once. When the thermometer reads between 60°C (rare) and 70°C (almost well-done), take it out, put it on a platter in a warm place and let it stand while you bake the Yorkshire Pudding.

Yield: Enough to serve 6 people quite handsomely and of course, there are no carbohydrates here.

⟳ Yorkshire Pudding

Have the wet and dry ingredients assembled and ready to go when your beef comes out of the oven, or your roast will cool too much while you're making this.

75 ml beef drippings (both the fat
  and the nice brown juice, mixed)

75 g low-carb bake mix

30 g rice protein powder

1 tsp salt

4 eggs

2 tsp oil

225 ml half milk and half cream, mixed

🍓 It is essential that the oven be really hot before you put in your Yorkshire pudding, or it won't puff up the way it should, so turn up the oven when you're taking out the roast.

1. Preheat the oven to 220°C/Gas Mark 7.

2. Spray a large, cast-iron frying pan or a 25-cm pie dish with nonstick cooking spray, then put the beef drippings in it and tilt the tin to cover the whole bottom. Set aside.

3. In a bowl, combine the bake mix, protein powder and salt, stirring them together.

4. In a separate bowl, combine the eggs, oil and half-milk, half-cream mixture.

5. When the oven is up to temperature, whisk the liquid ingredients well for 1 to 2 minutes. Add the dry ingredients and whisk until everything is well combined.

6. Pour the mixture into the prepared tin and bake for 20 minutes. Turn the oven down to 180°C/Gas Mark 4 and give it another 5 minutes or so. Cut into wedges and serve with Beef Gravy (see overleaf).

Yield: 8 servings, each with 3 grams of carbohydrate and 1 gram of fibre, for a total of 2 grams of usable carbs and 9.5 grams of protein.

↺ Beef Gravy

Faced with left-over roast beef and no gravy, I came up with this and it's as good as any beef gravy I've ever had. If you have any nice, brown beef juices from your roast, they can only improve it further, but be sure to skim off the fat before adding them, as it will ruin the texture.

> 400 ml tinned beef stock
>
> 2 Tbsp dry red wine
>
> 1 tsp liquid beef stock concentrate
>
> 1 Tbsp finely chopped onion
>
> 1 small clove garlic, crushed
>
> 3/4 tsp guar or xanthan
>
> 150 ml double cream
>
> 1/4 tsp gravy seasoning/browning liquid
>
> Salt and freshly ground black pepper

1. In a heavy saucepan, combine the stock, wine, stock concentrate, onion and garlic. Bring this to the boil over a medium heat and let it boil until reduced to one-third the original volume. (This will take at least 15 to 20 minutes.)

2. When the mixture is reduced, pour it into a blender (if you're not sure your blender will take the heat, let it cool for 5 to 10 minutes first), turn it on and add the guar. Blend for 15 seconds or so. Pour it back into the saucepan, turn the heat back on to low and whisk in the cream and the gravy seasoning liquid. Salt and pepper to taste, heat through and serve.

Yield: Makes 8 servings of 2 Tbsp, each with less than 2 grams of carbohydrate and 1 gram of fibre, for a total of just under 1 gram of usable carbs and 3 grams of protein.

↻ Ginger Beef

This is my favourite thing to do with a pot roast. It has a bright flavour full of tomato, fruit and ginger.

> 3 Tbsp olive oil
>
> 1 1/4 to 1 3/4 kg roasting joint of beef, about 5 cm thick
>
> 1 small onion
>
> 1 clove garlic, crushed
>
> 400 g tinned chopped tomatoes
>
> 1 Tbsp Splenda
>
> 1 tsp ground ginger
>
> 75 ml cider vinegar

1. Place the oil in a large, heavy frying pan and brown the roast in it over medium-high heat. When both sides are well-seared, add the onion, garlic and tomatoes.

2. In a bowl, stir the Splenda and ginger into the vinegar and add that mixture to the frying pan, stirring to combine.

3. Cover the frying pan, turn the heat down to low and let the whole thing simmer for about 1 1/4 hours. Serve with the vegetables piled on top.

Yield: A 1 1/4-kg roast should yield at least 6 servings, each with 6 grams of carbohydrate and 1 gram of fibre, for a total of 5 grams of usable carbs and 47 grams of protein.

↻ Yankee Pot Roast

For Americans, this is a great old-time favourite.

> 75 ml olive oil
>
> 1 to 1 1/4 kg boneless roasting joint of beef
>
> 400 ml water
>
> 1 medium onion, sliced
>
> 1 large stick celery, sliced
>
> 2 small turnips, cut into chunks

1 medium carrot, sliced

30 g chopped fresh parsley

100 g mushrooms, thickly sliced

1 tsp liquid beef stock concentrate

1/2 tsp guar or xanthan gum

1. Put the oil in a Dutch oven over medium heat and sear the roast in the oil until it's dark brown all over. Remove the roast from the Dutch oven.

2. Put 75 ml of the water and the sliced onions in the Dutch oven and place the roast directly on top of the onions. Cover the Dutch oven, set the heat to low and forget about it for 1 1/2 to 2 hours.

3. Remove the roast again – it'll be very tender and may break a bit – and add 225 ml of the water and the celery, turnips, carrot, parsley and mushrooms. Put the roast back in, on top of the vegetables and re-cover the Dutch oven. Let it simmer for another 30 to 45 minutes, or until the turnip and carrot are soft.

4. Remove the roast to a serving platter and use a slotted spoon to pile the vegetables over the roast or in a separate bowl, as you prefer.

5. Put the remaining water in your blender with the stock and guar, and blend for 15 seconds or so, or until all the thickener is dissolved. Scrape the mixture into the Dutch oven and stir it around to thicken the gravy. Pour the gravy over the roast, or put it in a gravy boat or table jug and serve.

Yield: 6 to 8 servings, depending on the size of your roast. A 1 1/4-kg roast gives 8 servings, each with 5 grams of carbohydrate and 1 gram of fibre, for a total of 4 grams of usable carbs and 28 grams of protein.

CHAPTER TEN

Pork and Lamb

Pork is popular and with good reason: it's tasty and inexpensive. If you still think of pork as being very fatty, think again. The low-fat craze has dramatically affected pork breeding and feeding and most pork is now very lean. This means you'll want to take care not to overcook your pork, or it may well end up dry. It also means that most pork is less flavourful than the pork of yore, so you'll want to season it well. This chapter will show you how.

Lamb is quite expensive, so I usually wait until my supermarket is selling it on special offer, and then I stock up my freezer on lamb joints, chops and steaks.

☉ Pork Chops with Mustard Cream Sauce

Something good to do with pork chops, now that you're not breading them.

> 1 pork chop, 2.5 cm thick
> Salt
> Freshly ground black pepper
> 1 Tbsp olive oil
> 1 Tbsp dry white wine
> 1 Tbsp double cream
> 1 Tbsp Dijon mustard

1. Salt and pepper the chops on both sides.
2. Heat the oil in a heavy frying pan over medium heat. Sauté the chops until they're browned on both sides and cooked through (depending on the size of your frying pan, this may take a couple of batches). Put the chops on a serving platter and keep them warm.
3. Put the wine in the pan and stir it around, scraping all the tasty brown bits off the pan as you stir. Stir in the cream and mustard, blend well and cook for a minute or two. Pour over the chops and serve.

Yield: 1 serving, with 2 grams of carbohydrate, a trace of fibre and about 20 grams of protein.

↺ Italian Herb Pork Chops

1 clove garlic, crushed

1 pork chop, 2.5 cm thick

1/2 tsp dried, powdered sage

1/2 tsp dried, powdered rosemary

Salt

2 Tbsp dry white wine

1. Rub the crushed garlic into both sides of each pork chop.
2. In a bowl, mix the sage and rosemary together and sprinkle this evenly over both sides of each chop, as well. Sprinkle lightly with the salt.
3. Place the chops in a heavy frying pan (if you're feeding several people, you may well need two frying pans) and add water just up to the top edge of the pork chops. Cover the frying pan, turn the heat down to low and let the chops simmer for about 1 hour, or until the water has all evaporated.
4. Once the water is gone, the chops will start to brown. Turn them once or twice to get them browned on both sides. (The chops will be very tender, so use a spatula and be careful, but if they break a little, they'll still taste great.)
5. Remove the chops to a serving platter and pour the wine into the frying pan. Turn up the heat to medium-high and stir the wine around, scraping up the stuck-on brown bits from the pan. Bring this to the boil and let it boil hard for a minute or two to reduce it just a little. Pour this sauce over the chops and serve.

Yield: 1 chop per serving, each with 2 grams of carbohydrate, a trace of fibre and about 23 grams of protein.

⟳ Pork Chops and Sauerkraut

3 rashers bacon

3 pork chops, 2.5 cm thick

1 small onion, chopped

400 g sauerkraut, drained

2 Tbsp Splenda

1/4 tsp dry mustard

2 Tbsp dry white wine

1/4 tsp black treacle

1. Fry the bacon until just barely crisp in a heavy frying pan over medium heat. Drain and set aside.

2. Pour off all but about 2 tablespoons of the grease and brown the chops in it over medium heat. (You want them to have just a little colour on each side.) Remove from the frying pan and set aside.

3. Put the onion, sauerkraut, Splenda, mustard, wine and treacle in the frying pan and stir for a moment to blend. Crumble in the bacon and stir again, just for a moment. Place the chops on top of the sauerkraut mixture, turn the heat down to low and cover the pan. Simmer for 45 minutes.

Yield: 3 servings, each with 11 grams of carbohydrate and 4 grams of fibre, for a total of 7 grams of usable carbs and 27 grams of protein.

↻ Apple-Glazed Pork Chops

Pork and apples are a great combination. Ever since I stopped eating apple sauce, I've been looking for a way to have this combination of flavours again!

2 pork chops, 2.5 cm thick (about 225 g each)

2 Tbsp olive oil

75 ml cider vinegar

1 1/2 Tbsp Splenda

1/2 tsp soy sauce

1 small onion, thinly sliced

1. Put the oil in a heavy frying pan and brown the pork chops in the oil.

2. When both sides are brown, stir together the vinegar, Splenda and soy sauce and pour the mixture over the chops. Scatter the onion on top.

3. Cover and turn the heat down to low. Let the chops simmer, turning at least once, for 45 minutes or until the pan is almost dry. Serve the chops with the onions and scrape all the nice, syrupy pan liquid over them.

Yield: 2 servings, each with 8 grams of carbohydrate and 1 gram of fibre, for a total of 7 grams of usable carbs and 36 grams of protein.

◌ Pork Chops with Garlic and Balsamic Vinegar

The balsamic vinegar gives these a tangy-sweet flavour.

2 Tbsp olive oil
2 or 3 pork rib chops, 5 cm thick
200 ml chicken stock
3 Tbsp balsamic vinegar
3 cloves garlic, crushed
1/4 tsp guar or xanthan

1. Put the oil in a large, heavy frying pan over medium-high heat and sear the chops in the oil until well-browned on both sides. Add the stock, vinegar and garlic.

2. Cover the frying pan, turn the heat down to low and let the chops simmer for 1 hour. Remove the chops to a serving platter or serving plates and put the liquid from the pan into a blender. Add the guar or xanthan, run the blender for a few moments and pour the thickened sauce over the chops.

Yield: 2 or 3 servings, each with 2 grams of carbohydrate, a trace of fibre and 36 grams of protein.

◌ Artichoke-Mushroom Pork

This is wonderful and it cooks quite quickly because you pound the pork thin.

650 g boneless pork loin, cut into 4 slices across the grain
4 Tbsp butter
1 small onion
1 clove garlic
225 g sliced mushrooms

1 can quartered artichoke hearts, drained

125 ml chicken stock

2 tsp Dijon mustard

1. Put a piece of pork into a heavy freezer bag and pound until it is 5 mm thick. Repeat for the remaining pieces of pork.

2. Melt 2 tablespoons of the butter in a large, heavy frying pan over medium heat and brown the meat on both sides, (about 4 minutes per side). You'll have to do them one or two at a time. Set the browned pork on a plate and keep it warm.

3. Add the rest of the butter to the frying pan and add the onion, garlic and mushrooms. Sauté until the mushrooms and onion are limp. Add the artichokes, chicken stock and mustard and stir around to dissolve the tasty brown bits on the bottom of the frying pan.

4. Put the pork back into the frying pan (you'll have to stack it a bit), cover and leave to simmer for about 5 minutes. Serve the pork with the vegetables spooned over the top.

Yield: 4 servings, each with 6 grams of carbohydrate and 2 grams of fibre, for a total of 4 grams of usable carbs and 25 grams of protein.

🍓 If you prefer, you can make this out of 4 pork chops with the bones taken out.

◯ Looed Pork

This is a great way to add a lot of flavour to the usually bland boneless pork loin.

650 g boneless pork loin, sliced about 2 cm thick

1 batch Chinese Looing Sauce (see page 428)

Spring onions, sliced

Toasted sesame oil

1. Put the pork in a slow cooker, pour the looing sauce over it, cover the cooker and set it to Low. Forget about it for 8 to 9 hours.
2. At dinnertime, remove the pieces of pork from the looing sauce. Put each piece on a serving plate, scatter a few sliced spring onions over each serving and top with a few drops of toasted sesame oil.

Yield: 4 generous servings with no more than 1 gram of carbohydrate, no fibre and 35 grams of protein.

◯ Mu Shu Pork

I hear from lots of people that they miss Chinese food, so here's a Chinese restaurant favourite, de-carbed. Low-carb tortillas stand in here for mu shu pancakes and they work fine. If you want to de-carb this even further, eat it with a fork and forget the tortillas.

3 eggs, beaten

Peanut oil

30 g mushrooms, sliced and then cut into slivers

225 g boneless pork loin, sliced across the grain and then cut into matchsticks

75 g finely chopped Chinese napa cabbage

3 spring onions, sliced

50 g beansprouts

3 Tbsp soy sauce

2 Tbsp dry sherry

4 low-carb tortillas

Hoisin Sauce (see page 418)

🍓 Make sure you have everything cut up and ready to go before you start, and this recipe will be a breeze.

1. First, in a wok or heavy frying pan over high heat, scramble the eggs in a few tablespoons of the peanut oil until they're set but still moist. Remove and set aside.

2. Wipe the wok out if there's much egg clinging to it. Add another 75 ml or so of peanut oil and heat. Add the pork and stir-fry until it's mostly done. Add the cabbage, spring onions and sprouts, and stir-fry for 3 to 4 minutes. Put the eggs back into the wok and stir them in, breaking them into small pieces. Now add the soy sauce and sherry and stir.

3. To serve, take a warmed, low-carb tortilla and smear about 2 teaspoons of hoisin sauce on it. Put about a quarter of the stir-fry mixture on the tortilla and wrap it up.

Yield: 2 servings, each with 11 grams of carbohydrate and 3 grams of fibre, for a total of 8 grams of usable carbs and 27 grams of protein. (Analysis does not include low-carb tortillas or hoisin sauce.)

☉ Robinsky's Cabbage and Sausage

Robin Wilkins says this makes a great one-plate meal. Just make sure you read the label on the low-carb sausage carefully, as these can vary widely in carb count.

> 1 medium onion, chopped
> 450 g low-carb sausage, sliced
> 1 cabbage, chopped
> 2 to 3 Tbsp butter

1. Divide the butter between two frying pans. Sauté the onion and sausage in one and sauté the cabbage in the other. The cabbage will overwhelm your frying pan at first, but it will reduce in volume as it fries.

2. When cooked to the texture you like (I like mine tender-crisp), combine the contents of both frying pans and toss.

Yield: 3 servings. The carb content of this depends completely on the sausage used. Using a low-carb sausage, each serving has 8 grams of carbohydrate and 1 gram of fibre, for a total of 7 grams of usable carbs and 21 grams of protein.

↻ Country Sausage Pan-Fried Supper

450 g pork sausagemeat, hot or mild

1 small onion, chopped

100 g grated Cheddar cheese

1. Crumble the sausage in a heavy frying pan over medium heat. As the grease starts to cook out of it, add the onion.

2. Cook until the sausage is no longer pink and the onion is translucent. Pour off the grease, spread the sausage mixture evenly in the pan and scatter the Cheddar over the top. Cover and return to the heat for a minute or two, until the cheese is melted and serve.

Yield: 3 servings, each with 5 grams of carbohydrate and 1 gram of fibre, for a total of 4 grams of usable carbs and 25 grams of protein.

🍓 Feel free to substitute turkey sausagemeat, if you prefer it.

↻ Low-Carb Sausage and Brussels Sprouts

My sister, who tested this recipe, just loved it. Sadly, this is the one recipe sent in by a *Lowcarbezine!* reader that I can't credit – the original e-mail was lost. My apologies to the inventor and my thanks.

450 g frozen Brussels sprouts

450 g low-carb sausage, sliced into 2.5-cm pieces

1. Preheat the oven to 180°C/Gas Mark 4. Spray a 20 x 20-cm ovenproof glass baking dish with nonstick cooking spray.

2. Place the frozen sprouts on the bottom of the prepared baking dish. Arrange the low-carb sausage over the sprouts, to let the juices flow over them. Cover with foil and bake for 40 minutes Remove the cover and bake for 15 additional minutes, if you like your low-carb sausage browned.

Yield: 3 servings, each with 15 grams of carbohydrate and 5 of fibre, for a total of 10 grams of usable carbs and 25 grams of protein. (This was analysed for the average low-carb sausage, so you could knock off a few extra grams by choosing the lowest-carb sausage available.)

☺ Polynesian Pork

4 or 5 large pork chops, 2.5 to 3.5 cm thick
125 ml soy sauce
4 cloves garlic, crushed
30 g Splenda
1/2 tsp black treacle
1 1/2 tsp grated fresh ginger

1. Preheat the oven to 170°C/Gas Mark 3.
2. Put the pork chops in a large freezer bag.
3. Combine the soy sauce, garlic, Splenda, treacle and ginger, mixing them in a blender for a second or two, if possible.
4. Pour the mixture into the bag with the pork. Seal the bag and let it sit for 20 minutes or so, turning once.
5. Remove the pork from the marinade, reserving the marinade in a small bowl. Place the chops in a shallow roasting tin and bake for 60 to 90 minutes, or until done through. Brush once or twice with the left-over marinade while cooking.

Yield: 4 or 5 servings. If you were to eat all the marinade, each serving would have 7 grams of carbohydrate, but you don't, so figure 2 or 3 grams of carbohydrate, a trace of fibre and 25 grams of protein.

🍓 This marinade works well with a pork roast, too, but of course it will take longer to roast.

⌒ Sausage Frypan Mix-Up

450 g pork sausagemeat, hot or mild

1 small onion, chopped

2 sticks celery, chopped

1 green pepper, chopped

225 ml chicken stock

2 tsp chicken stock powder

2 Tbsp Worcestershire sauce

1/2 tsp freshly ground black pepper

500 g Cauliflower Rice (see page 161)

1. Brown and crumble the sausage in a heavy frying pan over a medium to high heat. When the sausage is no longer pink, pour off the grease, add the remaining ingredients and give the mixture a stir.

2. Turn the heat down to low, cover the frying pan and let it simmer for 15 to 20 minutes, or until the cauliflower is tender.

Yield: 3 servings, each with 16 grams of carbohydrate and 4 grams of fibre, for a total of 12 grams of usable carbs and 22 grams of protein.

ᕲ Cocido de Puerco

This Mexican-style pork stew is simply marvellous. Do use bony cuts of meat, as they're more flavourful – and cheaper, too.

1 1/4 kg bony cuts of pork
2 Tbsp olive oil
1 clove garlic, crushed
1 large onion, sliced
1 large green pepper, diced
2 medium courgettes, cut into chunks
400 g tinned chopped tomatoes
2 tsp cumin
2 tsp dried oregano
1/2 tsp chilli flakes (optional)

1. In a heavy frying pan over medium-high heat, sear the pork bones in the oil until they're brown all over.

2. Turn the heat to Low and add the garlic onion, pepper, courgette, tomatoes, cumin, oregano and pepper flakes. Cover the frying pan and let it simmer for 1 hour.

Yield: About 6 servings, depending on how meaty your bones are, each with 13 grams of carbohydrate and 4 grams of fibre, for a total of 9 grams of usable carbs and about 35 grams of protein.

☽ Ham Slice with Mustard Sauce

2 to 3 Tbsp oil

Ham slice, about 1 kg

125 ml water

3 Tbsp prepared mustard

3 Tbsp Splenda

1/4 tsp black treacle

Salt and freshly ground black pepper

1. Put the oil in a heavy frying pan over medium heat and fry the ham steak until it is golden on both sides. Remove the ham from the frying pan, set it on a platter and keep it warm.

2. Pour the water into the frying pan and stir it around, scraping up all the brown bits from the ham. Stir in the mustard, Splenda, treacle and salt and pepper to taste. Pour over the ham and serve.

Yield: 5 servings, each with 2 grams of carbohydrate, a trace of fibre and 36 grams of protein.

☽ Jerk Pork

1 recipe Jerk Marinade (see page 427)

6 pork chops, 2.5 cm thick (about 225 g each)

1. Smear jerk marinade all over the chops, put the chops in a large freezer bag and refrigerate. Now wash your hands – that marinade is hot! Let the chops marinate for at least several hours, or overnight.

2. When you're ready to cook, do these chops slowly, well above a low charcoal fire or a gas barbecue set on Low. Cook them under the grill only if you must.

Yield: 6 servings, each with 3 grams of carbohydrate and 1 gram of fibre, for a usable carb count of 2 grams (that's assuming you eat all the marinade, but of course some will fall off in the cooking process) and 42 grams of protein.

❍ Winter Night Lamb Stew

On a raw winter's night, sometimes you just want stew. Here's one with no potatoes and you can make it in your big frying pan.

    3 Tbsp olive oil
    650 g lean stewing lamb, cut into chunks
    100 g chopped onion
    250 g diced turnip
    250 g diced swede
    200 ml beef stock
    1/2 tsp guar or xanthan
    1/2 tsp salt
    1/4 tsp freshly ground black pepper
    1 bay leaf
    3 cloves garlic, crushed

1. Put the oil in a heavy frying pan over medium-high heat and brown the lamb in the oil. Add the onion, turnip and swede.

2. Put the beef stock and guar in a blender and blend for a few moments. Pour the mixture into the frying pan. (If you choose not to use a thickener, just add the stock directly to the pan.) Add the salt, pepper, bay leaf and garlic, and stir.

3. Cover, turn the heat down to low and let simmer for 1 hour.

Yield: 4 servings, each with 12 grams of carbohydrate and 3 grams of fibre, for a total of 9 grams of usable carbs and 38 grams of protein.

⌒ Quick Curried Lamb

I invented this for a quick lunch for my husband one day when there just happened to be a joint of lamb in the fridge that needed to be used. It was so good, I decided it was worth repeating.

> 3 Tbsp butter
>
> 1 Tbsp curry powder
>
> 1 clove garlic
>
> 1 large onion
>
> 450 g lean lamb, cut in 1-cm cubes
>
> Salt and freshly ground black pepper

1. Melt the butter in a heavy frying pan over medium heat. Add the curry powder and stir for a minute or so.
2. Add the garlic, onion and lamb. Sauté, stirring frequently, for 7 minutes or so, or until the lamb is done through. Salt and pepper to taste and serve.

Yield: 3 servings, each with 5 grams of carbohydrate and 1 gram of fibre, for a total of 4 grams of usable carbs and 31 grams of protein.

Lamb Kebabs

Very simple and very Greek. Add a Greek salad and there's dinner.

> 1 kg lean lamb, cut into 2.5-cm cubes
>
> 125 ml olive oil
>
> 75 ml lemon juice
>
> 1 clove garlic, crushed
>
> 1/2 tsp dried oregano
>
> 2 small onions, quartered

1. Put the lamb cubes into a large freezer bag.
2. Mix together the olive oil, lemon juice, garlic and oregano. Pour it over the lamb cubes in the bag and refrigerate it for an hour or two (or overnight, if possible).
3. When it's time to cook dinner, pour off the marinade into a bowl and set it aside. Thread your lamb chunks on skewers, alternating the pieces of meat with a 'layer' or two of the onion. You can barbecue these, if you like, or grill them 20 cm or so from the heat. Turn the kebabs while they're cooking and brush once or twice with the reserved marinade, but only towards the beginning of the cooking time; you don't want to reintroduce raw meat bacteria to your cooked kebabs. Check by cutting into a chunk of meat after 10 minutes; they should be done within 15 minutes.

Yield: I get 6 skewers from this, each with 4 grams of carbohydrate and 1 gram of fibre, for a total of 3 grams of usable carbs and 31 grams of protein.

⟲ Thyme-Perfumed Lamb Steaks

>1 lamb steak (170 to 225 g)
>2 tsp olive oil
>2 tsp lemon juice
>1 Tbsp fresh thyme leaves, stripped from their stems

1. Rub each lamb steak with the olive oil and then the lemon. Cover the lamb with the thyme leaves, letting them stand for at least a couple of hours, so the thyme flavour permeates the lamb.
2. Grill close to the heat for 4 to 5 minutes per side, or barbecue.

Yield: 1 serving, with 1 gram of carbohydrate, a trace of fibre and 30 grams or so of protein.

⟲ Mediterranean Leg of Lamb

Lamb makes a wonderful Sunday dinner roast. If you don't want to roast a whole leg of lamb at once because it's a lot of meat, ask the butcher to cut one leg into two roasts. Make half now and freeze the other half for another day.

>Leg of lamb, with or without the bone in
>225 ml dry red wine
>225 ml olive oil
>5 cloves garlic, crushed
>3 Tbsp lemon juice
>1 Tbsp dried rosemary
>1 Tbsp dried oregano

1. Place your leg of lamb in a bowl or pan large enough to hold it.
2. Combine the wine, 125 ml of the olive oil, 3 cloves of the garlic and the lemon juice, rosemary and oregano. Pour this marinade over the lamb and let the lamb sit in it for at least 5 to 6 hours, turning it from time to time.

3. When the time comes to cook your lamb, preheat the oven to 220°C/Gas Mark 7. Remove the meat from the marinade and place it on a rack in a roasting tin. Leave the rosemary needles and bits of oregano clinging to it.

4. Combine the remaining olive oil and cloves of garlic, and spoon this mixture over the lamb, coating the whole leg. Position the leg with the fat side up and insert a meat thermometer deep into the centre of the thickest part of the meat, but don't let it touch the bone.

5. When the oven is up to temperature, put your roast in and set the timer for 10 minutes. After 10 minutes, turn the oven down to 180°C/Gas Mark 4 and roast for about 30 minutes per 450 g of meat, or until the meat thermometer registers 75°C to 82°C. Remove the lamb from the oven and let it stand for 15 to 20 minutes before carving.

Yield: 3 servings per 450 g, each with no carbohydrates or fibre to speak of and about 21 grams of protein. (This sounds low, I know, but remember: part of that weight is bone.)

🍓 Make Lamb Gravy (see below) to go with your roast lamb and serve it with some Cauliflower Rice (see page 161).

☌ Lamb Gravy

Drippings from Mediterranean Leg of Lamb

225 ml chicken stock

3/4 tsp guar or xanthan

Salt and freshly ground black pepper, to taste

1. Skim the fat off of the drippings from the roast. (Fat will ruin the texture of your gravy.)

2. Pour 125 ml of the chicken stock into the roasting tin with the skimmed drippings and stir it around, scraping up the tasty browned bits from the rack and the bottom of the pan. When most of the stuck-on stuff is dissolved into the stock, put the roasting tin over a medium to high heat.

3. Put the rest of the chicken stock in a blender with the guar or xanthan and run the blender for a few seconds to dissolve all of the thickener. Pour the thickened stock into the roasting tin and stir until all the gravy is thickened. (If it gets too thick, add a little more chicken stock; if it's not quite thick enough, let it simmer for a few minutes to cook down.)

4. Season the gravy to taste and serve with the leg of lamb.

Yield: The only carbohydrates in this gravy will be some fibre from the guar or xanthan, plus maybe 1 gram per serving from the herbs and wine.

The easiest way to skim drippings is to pour them into a large, heavy freezer bag. Seal the bag and tip it so one corner points down over the roasting tin. Let it hang this way for a minute or so, until you see the fat float to the top and the good, flavourful, dark-coloured pan juices at the bottom. Snip a tiny triangle off the bottom corner of the bag and let the juices run out. Grab the corner of the bag to stop the flow before the fat runs into the pan and throw the bag and the grease away.

CHAPTER ELEVEN

Main Dish Salads

I think main dish salads are one of the very best things for a low-carber to eat, because they offer infinite variety. Of course, they contain enough vegetables so that you probably won't want to eat much else in the way of carbohydrates at that particular meal, but with all the flavour and eye appeal these salads offer, who needs anything else?

☉ Chicken Waldorf Salad

Measure your apple carefully, as it's the main source of carbs here.

> 170 g diced cooked chicken
> 75 g diced apple
> 2 big sticks celery, diced
> 50 g chopped walnuts
> 75 ml mayonnaise

Combine all the ingredients, mix well and serve.

Yield: 2 servings, each with 9 grams of carbohydrate and 3 grams of fibre, for a total of 6 grams of usable carbs and 40 grams of protein.

↻ Cajun Chicken Salad

2 boneless, skinless chicken breasts

1 tsp Cajun Seasoning (purchased,
  or home-made – see page 420)

1 red pepper, cut into small strips

1 green pepper, cut into small strips

1/4 sweet red onion, thinly sliced

3 Tbsp tarragon vinegar

1 tsp Dijon mustard

1 clove garlic, crushed

75 ml olive oil

1 tsp dried tarragon

Salt and freshly ground black pepper, to taste

1. Place a chicken breast in a large, heavy freezer bag and pound with a rolling pin, until it's 5 mm thick. Repeat with the second breast.

2. Sprinkle both sides of each pounded chicken breast with the Cajun Seasoning. Barbecue or sauté until cooked through.

3. Cut both chicken breasts in strips about 5 mm wide. Combine with the peppers and onion.

4. In a small bowl, combine the tarragon vinegar, mustard, garlic, oil, dried tarragon, salt and pepper to taste; mix well. Pour over the chicken and vegetables and toss. Serve right away, or let it stand for several hours for the flavours to blend.

Yield: 2 servings, each with 11 grams of carbohydrate and 3 grams of fibre, for a total of 8 grams of usable carbs and 29 grams of protein.

ꙩ Dana's Tuna Salad

This is my lunchtime standby. With so many vegetables, this really is a tuna salad.

>   2 large sticks celery, or 3 small ones
>   1/2 green pepper
>   1/4 medium-sized sweet red onion
>   1 can light tuna chunk
>   75 ml mayonnaise

1. Dice up the vegetables. I like them fairly chunky, so I get lots of crunchy texture. This should come to 150 to 200 g of vegetables.
2. Add the tuna and mayonnaise, and mix it up. Sometimes I eat this with fibre crackers, or stuff it into a tomato, but it's awfully good just eaten with a fork, right out of the mixing bowl (now you know my secrets!).

Yield: This could feed 2, but most of the time I treat it as 1 serving. If you're nice enough to share, each serving will have 5 grams of carbohydrate and 1 gram of fibre, for a total of 4 grams of usable carbs and 21 grams of protein.

ꙩ Classic Egg Salad

Here's your lunch for the week after Easter.

>   4 hard-boiled eggs, chopped
>   1 stick celery, diced
>   5 or 6 spring onions, sliced
>   1/2 green pepper, diced
>   75 ml mayonnaise
>   1/2 tsp prepared mustard

Combine all the ingredients and serve on lettuce.

Yield: 2 servings, each with 7 grams of carbohydrate and 2 grams of fibre, for a total of 5 grams of usable carbs and 14 grams of protein.

Not Quite So Classic Egg Salad: My mother has always liked olives in her egg salad, so I tried it and it's surprisingly good. Just make Classic Egg Salad, but substitute 4 or 5 chopped green olives for the green pepper and leave out the mustard.

Yield: 2 servings, each with 6 grams of carbohydrate and 2 grams of fibre, for a total of 4 grams of usable carbs and 14 grams of protein.

☾ Chicken Pecan Salad

A good reason to cook an extra couple of pieces of chicken every time you're roasting some. This will keep you full for hours.

170 g cooked chicken, diced

2 big sticks celery, diced

1/4 medium-sized sweet red onion, diced

30 g chopped pecans

75 ml mayonnaise

Salt

Toss the chicken, celery, onion, pecans and mayonnaise together. Salt to taste and serve.

Yield: 2 servings, each with 5 grams of carbohydrate and 2 grams of fibre, for a total of 3 grams of usable carbs and 24 grams of protein.

↻ Dilled Chicken Salad

170 g cooked chicken, diced

1 large stick celery, diced

1/2 green pepper, diced

1/4 medium-sized sweet red onion, diced

3 Tbsp mayonnaise

3 Tbsp soured cream

1 tsp dried dill

Salt

1. Combine the chicken, celery, pepper and onion in a bowl.
2. In a separate bowl, mix together the mayonnaise, soured cream and dill. Pour the mixture over the chicken and vegetables, toss, salt to taste, and serve.

Yield: 2 servings, each with 5 grams of carbohydrate and 1 gram of fibre, for a total of 4 grams of usable carbs and 24 grams of protein.

🍓 This is wonderful when made with left-over turkey, too.

Ꭷ Chef's Salad

250 g romaine, iceberg, English round, or any other
favourite lettuce

100 g deli turkey breast

100 g deli ham

100 g deli roast beef

100 g Swiss cheese

1 green pepper, cut into strips or rings

1/2 sweet red onion, cut into rings

4 hard-boiled eggs, halved or quartered

2 ripe tomatoes, cut vertically into 8 wedges each

Salad dressing

1. Make beds of the lettuce on 4 serving plates.
2. Cut the turkey, ham, roast beef and Swiss cheese into strips. (It's nice, by the way, to get fairly thickly sliced meat and cheese for this.) Arrange all of this artistically on the beds of lettuce and garnish with the pepper, onion, eggs and tomatoes. Let each diner add his or her own dressing.

Yield: 4 servings, each with 13 grams of carbohydrate and 4 grams of fibre, for a total of 9 grams of usable carbs and 37 grams of protein. (Analysis does not include salad dressing.)

🍓 This salad is infinitely variable, of course; if you don't eat ham, hate roast beef, or love Swiss cheese, feel free to play around with these instructions. I only put down amounts so we could analyse the carb count and give you a guide to work from.

◯ Chicken Caesar Salad

1 boneless, skinless chicken breast

50 to 75 g romaine lettuce, washed, dried and broken up

2 Tbsp Caesar Dressing (purchased, or see page 243)

2 Tbsp Parmesan cheese, shaved or grated

1. Grill the chicken breast. (I do mine in an electric tabletop grill for about 5 minutes, but you could sauté it, if you prefer.)
2. While the chicken cooks, put the lettuce in a bowl, pour the dressing over it and toss well. Pile it on your serving plate.
3. Slice the cooked chicken breast into thin strips and pile it on top of the lettuce. Scatter the Parmesan on top and serve.

Yield: 1 serving, with 5 grams of carbohydrate and 2 grams of fibre, for a total of 3 grams of usable carbs and 26 grams of protein.

Prawn Caesar Salad: Make this just like Chicken Caesar Salad, but substitute 10 to 12 good-sized cooked prawns for the chicken breast. Frozen, precooked, shelled prawns are handy for this because they thaw quickly, especially if you put them in a freezer bag and set them in warm tap water for a few minutes.

Yield: 5 grams of carbohydrate and 2 grams of fibre, for a total of 3 grams of usable carbs and 30 grams of protein.

ᔑ Souvlaki Salad

This skewered lamb is usually served as a sandwich in pitta bread, but it makes a fabulous salad for a lot fewer carbs.

> 1 kg lean lamb, cut into 2.5-cm cubes
>
> 125 ml olive oil
>
> 225 ml dry red wine
>
> 1 tsp salt
>
> 1/4 tsp pepper
>
> 1 tsp oregano
>
> 3 cloves garlic, crushed
>
> 1 romaine lettuce
>
> 1/4 sweet red onion, sliced paper-thin
>
> 24 cherry tomatoes, halved
>
> 150 ml Greek Lemon Dressing (see page 237)
>
> 6 Tbsp plain yoghurt or soured cream
>   (the yoghurt is more authentic)

🍓 If you don't have any skewers, you can always just lay the lamb cubes on the grill pan. They're a lot easier to turn over if they're on skewers, however.

1. Put the lamb cubes in a large freezer bag.

2. Combine the oil, wine, salt, pepper, oregano and garlic. Pour the mixture over the lamb cubes in the bag. Let this marinate for at least a few hours.

3. When you're ready to cook the lamb, pour off the marinade and thread the cubes on to skewers. You can barbecue these, or grill them 20 cm or so from the heat. Turn the kebabs while they're cooking and check by cutting into a chunk of meat after 10 minutes. They should be thoroughly cooked in 15 minutes.

4. While the meat is cooking, wash and dry the lettuce, and arrange it on serving plates.

5. Push the cooked meat off the skewers and on to the prepared beds of lettuce. Scatter some red onion over each plate and arrange 8 cherry tomato halves on each. Drizzle each plate with a couple of tablespoons of dressing and top each with a tablespoon of yoghurt.

Yield: 6 servings, each with 11 grams of carbohydrate and 4 grams of fibre, for a total of 7 grams of usable carbs and 34 grams of protein.

↻ Sirloin Salad

I admit it: I copied this directly from a salad I had at a rather smart restaurant which shall remain nameless. It was so good and so easy, I just had to tell you about it.

> 225 g sirloin steak, 2.5 cm thick
>
> 50 g romaine lettuce, washed, dried and broken up
>
> 1/2 medium-sized ripe tomato, cut into thin wedges
>
> 1/8 sweet red onion, thinly sliced
>
> Salad dressing of your choice
> (vinaigrette and blue cheese dressing are both good with this)

1. Barbecue or grill the steak to your liking. While the steak's cooking, arrange the lettuce on a serving plate.
2. Cut the cooked steak into thin slices across the grain and pile it on top of the lettuce. Arrange the tomato wedges around the edge and scatter the onion over the top. Serve with the dressing of your choice.

Yield: 1 serving, with 7 grams of carbohydrate and 3 grams of fibre, for a total of 4 grams of usable carbs and 44 grams of protein. (Analysis does not include dressing.)

⟲ Asian Chicken Salad

This is a wonderful salad, different from any I've ever tried. Do use rice vinegar instead of another kind and Chinese napa cabbage instead of regular. They may seem like small distinctions, but they make all the difference.

50 g walnuts, chopped

2 Tbsp oil

4 boneless, skinless chicken breasts

225 g thinly sliced Chinese leaves

225 g thinly sliced Chinese napa cabbage

2 Tbsp grated carrots

1 cucumber, thinly sliced

50 g sliced spring onions

2 Tbsp chopped fresh coriander

75 ml soy sauce

75 ml rice vinegar

1 Tbsp lime juice

2 Tbsp Splenda

3 cloves garlic, crushed

1/2 tsp chilli flakes (or to taste)

1. Put the oil in a heavy frying pan over medium heat and toast the walnuts, stirring for about 4 to 5 minutes or until they're brown and crisp. Set aside.

2. Grill your chicken breasts and slice them into strips; I use my electric tabletop grill, but you can use whatever method you prefer.

3. Combine the Chinese leaves, napa cabbage, carrots, cucumber, spring onions and coriander in a big bowl.

4. In a separate bowl, combine the soy sauce, rice vinegar, lime juice, Splenda, garlic and chilli flakes. Pour about two-thirds of this dressing over the salad and toss well, coating all the vegetables.

5. Heap the salad onto four serving plates, top each with a sliced chicken breast and drizzle the rest of the dressing over them. Sprinkle with chopped walnuts and serve.

Yield: 4 generous servings, each with 15 grams of carbohydrate and 4 grams of fibre, for a total of 11 grams of usable carbs and 36 grams of protein.

🍓 We generally only have 2 people to eat all this salad, so I set half of the vegetable mixture aside in a container in the refrigerator. Don't put dressing on the half you plan to reserve, just put the dry, prepared vegetables in a container in the fridge, save half of your dressing to go with it and reserve some of the walnuts, as well. This is wonderful to have on hand for a quick, gourmet lunch – just grill a chicken breast, toss the salad with the dressing and presto, lunch is served.

⟲ Nicer Niçoise

Salad Niçoise is traditionally made with green beans and cold, boiled potatoes, but of course, we're not going to be eating those potatoes. I thought I'd try it with cauliflower and sure enough, it worked great!

1/3 cauliflower

450 g frozen, sliced green beans, thawed but not cooked

1 clove garlic, crushed

2 to 3 Tbsp fresh parsley, chopped

1/4 medium-sized red onion, diced

8 to 10 olives (stuffed or unstuffed), sliced

150 to 200 ml vinaigrette dressing (home-made or bottled)

Lettuce (to line plate)

500 g tinned tuna, drained

6 hard-boiled eggs, sliced

3 tomatoes, sliced

1. Slice your cauliflower quite thinly. Put it in a microwave-safe bowl with about 1 tablespoon of water, cover and cook it for 4 to 5 minutes (it should be just tender).

2. Combine the green beans, garlic, parsley, onion and olives in a good-size bowl. When the cauliflower is done, add that as well and pour 125 ml of dressing over the whole thing.
3. Stir well and put it in the fridge. Let it marinate for several hours to a day, stirring now and then.
4. When you're ready to eat the salad, put a few lettuce leaves on each plate and spoon a mound of the marinated mixture on top. Put the tuna on top and in the middle – use as much as you like – and surround it with slices of hard-boiled egg and tomato. Garnish it with more olives and drizzle more dressing on top, if you like and serve.

Yield: 6 servings, each with 12 grams of carbohydrate and 3 grams of fibre, for a total of 9 grams of usable carbs and 30 grams of protein.

⟳ Dinner Salad Italiano

1 head romaine lettuce, washed, dried and broken up

75 g sliced fresh mushrooms

1/2 cucumber, sliced

1/4 sweet red onion, thinly sliced

225 g sliced salami, cut into strips

225 g sliced provolone, cut into strips

Italian vinaigrette dressing (bottled, or see page 236)

2 ripe tomatoes, cut into wedges

Make a big tossed salad from the lettuce, mushrooms, cucumber, onion, salami and provolone. Toss with bottled Italian or vinaigrette dressing, then add the sliced tomatoes and serve.

Yield: 3 servings, each with 17 grams of carbohydrate and 6 grams of fibre, for a total of 11 grams of usable carbs and 36 grams of protein.

◯ Taco Salad

A great summer supper. The wild card in this recipe is the ranch dressing – different brands vary tremendously in carb count. Choose a really, really low-carb one and you'll drop the carb count below what's listed here. Better still, check out the recipe in this book (page 239).

2 heads romaine or iceberg lettuce, washed, dried
and broken up

100 g diced green pepper

1/2 medium cucumber, sliced

1 medium tomato, sliced into thin wedges,
or 15 cherry tomatoes, halved

50 g diced sweet red onion

1/2 ripe avocado, peeled, stoned, and cut into small chunks

2 Tbsp fresh coriander, chopped (optional)

100 g sliced black olives, drained (optional)

150 ml salsa, plus additional for topping

125 ml Ranch Dressing (see page 239)

1 batch Chicken or Beef Taco Filling (see pages 269 and 328)

100 g grated Cheddar or Monterey Jack cheese

Soured cream

1. Put the lettuce, pepper, cucumber, tomato, onion, avocado, coriander (if using) and olives (if using) in a large salad bowl.

2. Stir together the salsa and the Ranch Dressing, pour it over the salad and toss.

3. Divide the salad among the serving plates and top each one with the taco filling and grated cheese. Put the salsa and soured cream on the table, so people can add their own.

Yield: 6 servings, each with 12 grams of carbohydrate and 4 grams of fibre, for a total of 8 grams of usable carbs and 22 grams of protein.

↻ Sweet 'n' Nutty Tuna Salad

Here's something a little different for when you get tired of your usual tuna salad. That's actually how I invented this recipe.

> 1 stick celery, diced
> 2 Tbsp chopped pecans, walnuts or almonds
> 10 red, seedless grapes, quartered
> 2 Tbsp diced red onion
> 170 g tinned tuna
> 75 ml mayonnaise

Combine all the ingredients and enjoy!

Yield: I eat the whole thing by myself, but then, I'm a glutton. This could easily be 2 servings, each with 7 grams of carbohydrate and 1 gram of fibre, for a total of 6 grams of usable carbs and 23 grams of protein.

↻ Mozzarella Salad

This is rich and filling. The texture is quite different, depending on whether you use grated or cubed cheese, but they're both good.

> 170 g grated or diced mozzarella
> 30 g sliced spring onions
> 50 g diced celery
> 75 ml mayonnaise
> 2 Tbsp wine vinegar
> 1/2 tsp oregano
> 1/2 tsp basil

1. Combine the mozzarella, spring onions and celery in a mixing bowl.
2. In a separate bowl, combine the mayonnaise, vinegar, oregano and basil. Pour the mixture over the salad, stir to combine and serve.

Yield: 2 servings, each with 6 grams of carbohydrate and 2 grams of fibre, for a total of 4 grams of usable carbs and 20 grams of protein.

⟲ Mediterranean Chicken and 'Rice' Salad

300 g Cauliflower Rice (see page 161)

1 clove garlic, crushed

3 Tbsp wine vinegar

2 Tbsp olive oil

1 Tbsp mayonnaise

1/4 tsp salt

1/4 tsp freshly ground black pepper

100 g diced cooked chicken

40 g diced sweet red onion

50 g diced celery

50 g diced green pepper

2 Tbsp chopped fresh parsley

🍓 Use the time while you wait for the cauliflower to cool to do all the dicing and chopping for the rest of the recipe.

1. Steam your cauliflower 'rice' until just tender; for this small amount, I put it in a bowl, add about 1 tablespoon of water, cover it and microwave it on High for 5 minutes. Put it in the refrigerator to cool.

2. Mix together the garlic, vinegar, oil, mayonnaise, salt and pepper, and blend well.

3. Toss the chicken, onion, celery, pepper and parsley with the cooled cauliflower. Pour the dressing on the mixture and toss. This is good served right away, but even better the next day.

Yield: 2 servings, each with 14 grams of carbohydrate and 5 grams of fibre, for a total of 9 grams of usable carbs and 24 grams of protein.

⟲ Summer Tuna Salad

1 medium cucumber, cut into chunks

40 g sweet red onion, sliced

2 Tbsp chopped fresh parsley

1/2 large green pepper, cut into small strips

15 cherry tomatoes, quartered

170 g tinned tuna, drained

75 ml extra-virgin olive oil

2 Tbsp wine vinegar

1 clove garlic, crushed

1/4 tsp salt

1/8 tsp freshly ground black pepper

1. Put the cucumber, onion, parsley, pepper, tomatoes and tuna in a salad bowl.

2. In a separate bowl, combine the oil, vinegar, garlic, salt and pepper. Pour the mixture over the salad, toss and serve.

Yield: 2 servings, each with 16 grams of carbohydrate and 4 grams of fibre, for a total of 12 grams of usable carbs and 25 grams of protein.

◌ Cottage Cheese Salad

This makes a nice light lunch that would carry well in a snap-top container.

1 spring onion, sliced, including the crisp green part
2 radishes, thinly sliced
50 g cucumber, quartered lengthways and thinly sliced
100 g cottage cheese
2 Tbsp soured cream
A few lettuce leaves

Mix together the spring onion, radishes, cucumber, cottage cheese and soured cream. Place a few leaves of lettuce on a serving dish and scoop the cottage cheese mixture on to it. Serve.

Yield: 1 serving, with 8 grams of carbohydrate and 1 gram of fibre, for a total of 7 grams of usable carbs and 17 grams of protein.

◌ Tuna Egg Waldorf

2 large sticks celery, diced
50 g diced red onion
50 g diced red apple
50 g chopped pecans
170 g tinned tuna, drained
3 hard-boiled eggs, chopped
200 ml mayonnaise
Salt
Lettuce

Put the celery, onion, apple, pecans, tuna and hard-boiled eggs in a big bowl. Toss with the mayonnaise until it's all coated. Salt to taste and serve on a lettuce-lined plate. (Or not; if you want just to eat it by itself, I won't tell.)

Yield: 3 servings, each with 10 grams of carbohydrate and 3 grams of fibre, for a total of 7 grams of usable carbs and 23 grams of protein.

CHAPTER TWELVE

Soups

Everybody loves soup. Unfortunately, far too many people think of soup as something that comes out of a can or a packet and the vast majority of packaged soups have added carbohydrate in the form of sugar or cornflour, plus, of course, things like rice, noodles, potatoes, beans and other ingredients we simply can't have.

So make some soup yourself. Most of these soups are quite simple to make and many of them are filling, nutritious, one-dish meals. Making a big batch (or even a double batch) of soup over the weekend is one of the greatest things you can do to save cooking time all week long.

If you want to make a soup to use as a starter or snack, choose one of the soups with lowest carb counts. On the other hand, if you want a lunch or supper, keep an eye on the protein content and calculate that the vegetables in the soup will be all your carbs for that meal.

⟲ California Soup

A quick and elegant first course.

> 1 large or two small very ripe avocados, stoned, peeled
> and cut into chunks
>
> 1 litre chicken stock, heated

Put the avocados through the blender with the stock, purée until very smooth and serve.

Yield: 6 servings (as a first course), each with 3 grams of carbohydrate and 1 gram of fibre, for a total of 2 grams of usable carbs and 4 grams of protein.

> 🍓 If you like curry, you've got to try this: melt a tablespoon of butter and add 1/2 tsp or so of curry powder. Cook for just a minute and add the mixture to the blender with the stock and avocados.

⟲ Corner-Filling Consommé

> 2 Tbsp butter
>
> 100 g sliced mushrooms
>
> 1 small onion, sliced paper-thin
>
> 1 litre beef stock
>
> 2 Tbsp dry sherry
>
> 1/4 tsp freshly ground black pepper

Melt the butter in a frying pan and sauté the mushrooms and onions in the butter until they're limp. Add the beef stock, sherry and pepper. Let it simmer for 5 minutes or so, just to blend the flavours, and serve.

Yield: 6 starter-size servings, each with 5 grams of carbohydrate and 1 gram of fibre, for a total of 4 grams of usable carbs and 8 grams of protein.

☉ Crock-Pot Tomato Soup

Delicious tomato soup from *Splendid Low Carbing*, by Jennifer Eloff of sweety.com. So easy!

550 ml mixed vegetable juice

550 ml boiling water

225 ml tinned tomato sauce

1 small onion, thinly sliced

1 bay leaf

3 Tbsp Splenda

1 Tbsp beef stock granules or liquid beef-stock concentrate

1/2 tsp freshly ground black pepper

1/4 tsp dried basil

Combine all ingredients in a slow cooker and stir. Cover and cook on Low for 4 hours. Strain and serve.

Yield: 6 servings, each with 10 grams of carbohydrate and 2 grams of fibre, for a total or 8 grams of usable carbs and 2 grams of protein.

⟡ Mulligatawny

This is a curried soup that came out of the British Colonial times in India. It's also wonderful made with stock made from a turkey carcass, or, for that matter, from the remains of a leg of lamb.

2 litres chicken stock

225 g or more diced cooked chicken
  or diced boneless, skinless chicken breast

3 Tbsp butter

1 medium onion, chopped

1 clove garlic, crushed

1 small carrot, grated

2 sticks celery, diced

2 tsp to 1 1/2 heaped Tbsp curry powder
  (I like it with lots of curry!)

1 bay leaf

1/2 sharp apple, finely chopped

1 to 2 tsp salt

1/2 tsp freshly ground black pepper

1/2 tsp dried thyme

Grated peel of 1 fresh lemon

225 ml double cream

1. Put the stock and diced chicken in a large stockpot and set over a low heat.
2. Melt the butter in a heavy frying pan and add the onion, garlic, carrot, celery and curry powder. Sauté until the vegetables are limp and add them to the pot.
3. Add the bay leaf, apple, salt, pepper, thyme and lemon and simmer for half an hour. Just before serving, stir in the cream.

Yield: 6 servings, each with 8 grams of carbohydrate and 2 grams of fibre, for a total of 6 grams of usable carbs and 18 grams of protein.

☌ Sopa Azteca

That's soup made by Aztecs, not soup made from Aztecs!

3 litres chicken stock

225 g diced cooked chicken or boneless, skinless chicken breast

75 ml olive oil

1 medium onion, chopped

4 or 5 cloves garlic, crushed

2 or 3 sticks celery, diced

1 green pepper, diced

1 small carrot, grated

1 small courgette, diced

800 g tinned chopped tomatoes, including juice

1 package frozen chopped spinach

2 Tbsp dried oregano

2 Tbsp dried basil

2 tsp freshly ground black pepper

225 g Mexican Queso Quesadilla or Monterey Jack cheese, grated

Chipotle peppers in adobo sauce (these come tinned)

1/2 ripe Haas avocado per serving

1. Heat the stock and the chicken in a large pot over low heat.

2. Heat the olive oil in a frying pan over medium heat and sauté the onion, garlic, celery, pepper, carrot and courgette together until they're limp. Add them to the soup, along with the tomatoes and spinach. Let the whole thing simmer for 1/2 to 1 hour, to let the flavours blend.

3. When you're ready to serve the Sopa Azteca, put the cheese in the bottom of each bowl and anywhere from 1 to 3 chipotles, depending on how spicy you like your food. (If you don't like spicy food at all, leave the chipotles out entirely.) Ladle the hot soup over the cheese and peppers.

4. Use a spoon to scoop chunks of avocado on to the top of each bowl of soup.

Yield: 10 servings. Each serving of soup alone has 21 grams of carbohydrate and 6 grams of fibre, for a total of 15 grams of usable carbs and 25 grams of protein. 50 g of grated cheese adds only a gram or so of carbohydrates and 14 grams of protein. Each chipotle pepper adds no more than 1 gram or so of carbs and half a Haas avocado has about 6 grams of carbohydrate and 2.5 grams of fibre, for a total of 3.5 grams of usable carbs per serving.

> The totals on this soup may sound like a lot when you add them all up, but don't forget that this is a whole meal in a bowl: meat, vegetables, melted cheese and lovely ripe avocado in each bite! You don't need to serve another thing with it, although you could serve tortillas or quesadillas for the carb-eaters in the crowd.

Hot-and-Sour Soup

Really authentic Hot-and-Sour Soup uses Chinese mushrooms, but this is mighty good with any variety – especially when you have a cold!

> 2 litres chicken stock
> 1 piece of fresh ginger about the size of a walnut, peeled and thinly sliced
> 225 g lean pork (I use boneless loin)
> 3 Tbsp soy sauce
> 1 to 1 1/2 tsp freshly ground black pepper
> 125 ml white vinegar
> 400 g tinned mushrooms
> 300 g firm tofu
> 225 g tinned bamboo shoots
> 5 eggs

1. Put the stock in a saucepan and set it over medium heat. Add the ginger to the stock and let it simmer for a few minutes.

2. While the stock simmers, slice the pork into small cubes or strips (I like strips). Stir the soy sauce, pork, pepper, vinegar and mushrooms (you don't need to drain them) into the stock. Let it simmer for 10 minutes or so, until the pork is done through.

3. Cut the tofu into small cubes. If you like, you can also cut the tinned bamboo shoots into thinner strips. (I like them better that way, but sometimes I don't feel like doing the extra work.) Stir the tofu and bamboo shoots into the soup and let it simmer another few minutes. Taste the soup; it won't be very hot – spicy-hot, that is, not tempera-ture-hot – so if you like it hotter, add more pepper and some hot sauce. If you like, you can also add a little extra vinegar.

4. Beat the eggs in a bowl and then pour them in a thin stream over the surface of the soup. Stir them in and you'll get a billion little shreds of cooked egg in your soup. Who needs noodles?

   🍓 This is good served with a few finely sliced spring onions on top (include some of the green part) and a few drops of toasted sesame oil. Since I like my soup hotter than my husband does, I use hot toasted sesame oil, rather than putting hot sauce in the whole batch.

   Yield: 6 servings, each with 10 grams of carbohydrate and 2 grams of fibre, for a total of 8 grams of usable carbs and 25 grams of protein.

ᏩPeanut Soup

If you miss split pea or bean soup, try this. Try it even if you don't miss other soups – you may find you have a new favourite.

3 Tbsp butter

2 or 3 sticks celery, finely chopped

1 medium onion, finely chopped

2 litres chicken stock

1/2 tsp salt

275 g natural peanut butter (I use smooth)

1 tsp guar gum (optional)

500 ml half milk and half cream, or double cream

Salted peanuts, chopped

🍓 If your slow cooker will hold this quantity of ingredients (mine will), it's ideal for cooking this soup. Set it on high, cover it and leave it for 2 to 3 hours.

1. Melt the butter in a large sauce pan and sauté the celery and onion in the butter. Add the stock, salt and peanut butter, and stir. Cover and simmer on the lowest temperature for at least 1 hour, stirring now and then.

2. If you're using guar gum (it makes the soup thicker without adding carbs; most peanut soup is thickened with flour), scoop 225 ml of the soup out of the pot about 15 minutes before you want to serve it. Add the guar gum to this, run the mixture through the blender for a few seconds and whisk it back into the soup.

3. Stir in the milk and cream mixture, and simmer for another 15 minutes. Garnish with the peanuts.

Yield: 5 servings, The carb count will depend on what brand of natural peanut butter you use (they have varying amounts of fibre) and whether you use a milk and cream mixture or double cream. Calculate each serving has about 19 grams of carbohydrate and 3 grams of fibre, for a total of 16 grams of usable carbs and 29 grams of protein.

⟳ Spring Chicken Soup

This soup is a great way to use up left-overs – just substitute 100 g of left-over chicken for the chicken breast listed with the ingredients.

1 1/2 litres chicken stock

200 g tinned mushrooms

200 g tinned cut asparagus

1 boneless, skinless chicken breast, diced into small cubes

75 ml dry sherry

1 Tbsp soy sauce

Freshly ground black pepper

Sliced spring onions

Combine the stock, mushrooms, asparagus, chicken, sherry and soy sauce in a pot and heat. If you're using raw chicken, let it cook for 5 to 10 minutes (that's all it should take to cook small cubes of chicken through). Add pepper to taste and serve with a scattering of spring onions on top.

🍓 If you're feeling ambitious, there's no reason you couldn't make this with fresh mushrooms and fresh asparagus; you'll just have to simmer it a little longer. As it is, though, this soup is practically instantaneous!

Yield: 4 servings. Depending on the stock you use, this should have no more than about 17 grams of usable carbs in the whole pot, plus about 0.5 gram for the little bit of spring onion you put on top of each bowl. Figure each serving has 6 grams of carbohydrate and 2 grams of fibre, for a total of 4 grams of usable carbs and 23 grams of protein.

☾ Judie's Chicken 'Noodle' Soup

Judie Edwards created this when she was craving chicken noodle soup and it's so easy to make.

> 500 ml chicken stock
> 1 tin Chinese vegetables, drained

Simply combine, heat and serve.

Yield: 1 serving, with 7 grams of carbohydrate and 2.5 grams of fibre, for a total of 4.5 grams of usable carbs and 7 grams of protein.

☾ Easy Tomato-Beef Soup

> 100 to 225 g minced beef
> 800 ml tinned beef stock
> 400 g tinned chopped tomatoes

In a frying pan, brown the minced beef. Pour off the grease and add the stock and tomatoes. Heat through and serve.

Yield: 4 servings, each with 9 grams of carbohydrate, a trace of fibre and 19 grams of protein.

↻ Italian Tuna Soup

I admit it's not authentically Italian, but it's a lot like minestrone. It's easy, too.

1 litre chicken stock

400 g tinned chopped tomatoes

400 g tinned Italian green beans (or 300 g frozen)

100 g frozen broccoli florets

100 g frozen cauliflower florets

100 g thinly sliced courgette, frozen or fresh

3 Tbsp tomato purée

1 tsp Italian seasoning

350 g tinned tuna

Tabasco sauce

Combine the stock, tomatoes, beans, broccoli, cauliflower, courgette, tomato purée, seasoning and tuna. Add a few drops of Tabasco (more if you like it hotter, less if you just want a little zip) and simmer until the vegetables are tender.

Yield: 5 servings, each with 14 grams of carbohydrate and 3 grams of fibre, for a total of 11 grams of usable carbs and 23 grams of protein.

⟡ Zesty Seafood Soup

Marilee Wellersdick came up with this. Just make sure you use real crab, not the high-carb fake crab that's widely available these days, when you make this soup.

2 Tbsp olive oil
1 medium onion, chopped
2 cloves garlic, crushed
100 g chopped celery
2 Tbsp fresh or dried parsley, chopped
1 tsp dried basil
1/2 tsp dried rosemary
1/2 tsp dried thyme
Dash of cayenne pepper
700 ml tinned tomato sauce
225 g clam juice
400 ml tinned chicken stock
450 g firm fish (such as cod, halibut or snapper), cut into 2.5-cm cubes
130 g small tinned, fresh or frozen prawns
225 g tinned crab meat, or 1 fresh crab
Salt

1. Heat the oil in a Dutch oven. Add the onion, garlic and celery, and sauté until the onion is limp.
2. Stir in the parsley, basil, rosemary, thyme, cayenne, tomato sauce, clam juice and chicken stock. Cover and simmer for about 10 minutes.
3. Add the fish; cover and simmer until the fish flakes (about 7 minutes). Stir in the prawns and crab. Cover and cook for a few minutes, until everything is thoroughly heated. Salt to taste.

Yield: About 8 servings, each with 12 grams of carbohydrate and 2 grams of fibre, for a total of 10 grams of usable carbs and 12 grams of protein.

↷ Cream of Cauliflower

You'll be surprised by how much this tastes like Cream of Potato!

3 Tbsp butter

75 g diced onion

75 g diced celery

1 litre chicken stock

300 g frozen cauliflower

1/2 tsp guar or xanthan (optional)

125 ml double cream

Salt and freshly ground black pepper

1. Melt the butter over low heat and sauté the onion and celery in it until they're limp. Combine with the chicken stock and cauliflower in a large saucepan and simmer until the cauliflower is tender.

2. Use a slotted spoon to transfer the vegetables into a blender and then pour in as much of the stock as will fit. Add the guar or xanthan (if using) and purée the ingredients.

3. Pour the mixture back into the saucepan. Stir in the cream and salt and pepper to taste.

Yield: 4 servings, each with 9 grams of carbohydrate and 3 grams of fibre, for a total of 6 grams of usable carbs and 7 grams of protein.

⟲ Skydancer's Courgette Soup

Jo Pagliassotti, an artist who works under the name Skydancer, came up with this savoury and versatile soup.

> 500 g courgette, cut into chunks
>
> 225 g chopped Spanish onion
>
> 1 litre chicken stock, home-made or tinned
> (if home-made, salt to taste)
>
> 1 to 2 tsp dry summer savory
> or 2 Tbsp fresh summer savory leaves, chopped
>
> 1 Tbsp dry basil or 2 Tbsp fresh leaves, lightly packed
>
> 225 g cream cheese, at room temperature

🍓 It won't hurt this soup a bit if you turn the heat down to low, cover the pan and forget it for a couple of hours. You want it to be squashy (pun intended!)

1. Place the courgette, onion, stock, summer savory and basil into a pan. Cook over low heat until the vegetables are soft (30 minutes minimum).

2. Put the cream cheese and a small quantity of the cooked mixture into a blender and blend until smooth. (Add more liquid if needed to get the cheese smooth.) Pour that into another pan. Add more of the cooked courgette and onion mixture to the blender and blend until smooth (or as smooth as you like it). Blend the rest of the cooked mixture, pouring each blended batch into the soup and cheese mixture as you go.

3. Once everything is puréed, stir it well to mix in the initial cheese and cauliflower blend and rewarm over low heat if necessary.

Yield: 9 servings, each with 6 grams of carbohydrate and 2 grams of fibre, for a total of 4 grams of usable carbs and 3 grams of protein.

Try making this with a mixture of yellow squash and courgette, but note that yellow squash has more carbs than courgette. You can also use spring onion or leeks instead of the Spanish onion. Keep in mind that 225 g of spring onion will give you 9.6 grams of carbs instead of 22, and 225 g of leeks will give you 61.6 grams of carbs (why are they so high?) instead of 22.

Want even more variety and some more protein, along with it? Left-over flaked salmon and chunks of cold left-over chicken are both great in this. You can garnish the soup with some sliced spring onions or shallots and that's also wonderful. This soup lends itself to many variations – be creative. Oh, and it freezes well! The cream cheese seems to hold up to this just fine.

⟲ Jodee's Courgette Soup

Here's another take on courgette soup, from reader Jodee Rushton. She says this is satisfying as a quick between-meals snack, not to mention versatile: 'In the summer, pour it into a mug and drink it cold. In the winter, you might microwave it.'

> 50 g butter
> 1 medium onion, chopped
> 650 g courgette, washed and sliced
> 800 ml chicken stock
> 1/8 tsp salt
> 1/8 tsp freshly ground black pepper
> 1/2 tsp ground nutmeg
> 125 ml half milk and half cream, mixed

1. Melt the butter and sauté the onion in it until golden. Add the cour-gette and sauté over medium-high heat until limp (10 to 15 minutes).
2. Add the chicken stock, salt, pepper and nutmeg. Simmer for 15 minutes, add the milk-cream mixture and let it all cool.
3. Purée the stock mixture in a blender. (Do this in batches, if necessary.)

Refrigerate for a minimum of 4 hours, to allow the flavours to blend. Serve hot or cold.

Yield: 8 servings, each with 5 grams of carbohydrate and 1 gram of fibre, for a total of 4 grams of usable carbs and 2 grams of protein.

☉ Jamaican Pepperpot Soup

Unbelievably hearty, almost like a stew and very tasty!

225 g bacon, diced

1 kg braising steak, cut into 2.5-cm cubes

1 large onion, chopped

1 litre water

225 ml tinned beef stock

600 g frozen chopped spinach

1/2 tsp dried thyme

1 green pepper, diced

400 g tinned chopped tomatoes

1 bay leaf

2 tsp salt

1/2 tsp freshly ground black pepper

1 tsp Tabasco sauce (or to taste)

300 g frozen sliced okra, thawed

3 Tbsp butter

125 ml double cream

Paprika

1. Place the bacon, braising steak, onion, water and beef stock in a large, heavy soup pan. Bring to the boil, turn the heat down to low and let the mixture simmer for 1 hour.

2. Add the spinach, thyme, green pepper, tomatoes, bay leaf, salt, pepper and Tabasco. Let it simmer for another 30 minutes.

3. Sauté the okra in the butter over the lowest heat for about 5 minutes, then add to the soup and simmer just 10 minutes more.

4. Just before serving, stir in the cream and sprinkle just a touch of papri-ka on each serving.

Yield: 6 servings, each with 16 grams of carbohydrate and 5 grams of fibre, for a total of 11 grams of usable carbs and 49 grams of protein.

⌒ Eggdrop Soup

Quick and easy, but filling and it can practically save your life when you've got a cold. You don't have to use the guar, but it gives the stock the same rich quality that the cornflour-thickened Chinese broths have.

> 1/4 tsp guar (optional)
> 1 litre chicken stock
> 1 Tbsp soy sauce
> 1 Tbsp rice vinegar
> 1/2 tsp grated fresh ginger
> 1 spring onion, sliced
> 2 eggs

1. Put 225 ml or so of the chicken stock in your blender, turn it on Low and add the guar (if using). Let it blend for a second, then put it in a large saucepan with the rest of the stock. (If you're not using the guar, just put the stock directly in a saucepan.)
2. Add the soy sauce, rice vinegar, ginger and spring onion. Heat over medium-high heat and let it simmer for 5 minutes or so to let the flavours blend.
3. Beat your eggs in a glass measuring jug or a small bowl with a pouring lip. Use a fork to stir the surface of the soup in a slow circle and pour in about 1/4 of the eggs, stirring as they cook and turn into shreds (which will happen almost instantaneously). Repeat three more times, using up all the egg, then serve!

Yield: 3 biggish servings, or 4 to 5 small ones (but this recipe is easy to double). In 4 servings, each will have 2 grams of carbohydrate, a trace of fibre and 8 grams of protein.

☾ Stracciatella

This is the Italian take on eggdrop soup and it's delightful.

1 litre chicken stock

2 eggs

75 g grated Parmesan cheese

1/2 tsp lemon juice

Pinch of nutmeg

1/2 tsp dried marjoram

🍓 Don't expect this to form long shreds like Chinese eggdrop soup; because of the Parmesan, it makes small, fluffy particles, instead.

1. Put 75 ml of the stock in a glass measuring jug. Pour the rest into a large saucepan over medium heat.

2. Add the eggs to the stock in the measuring jug and beat with a fork. Then add the Parmesan, lemon juice and nutmeg, and beat with a fork until well blended.

3. When the stock in the saucepan is simmering, stir it with a fork as you add small amounts of the egg and cheese mixture, until it's all stirred in.

4. Add the marjoram, crushing it between your fingers, and simmer the soup for another minute or so before serving.

Yield: 4 servings, each with 2 grams of carbohydrate, a trace of fibre and 12 grams of protein.

Manhattan Clam Chowder

4 rashers bacon, diced

1 large onion, chopped

2 sticks celery, diced

1 green pepper, chopped

450 g diced white turnip

1 grated carrot

400 g tinned chopped tomatoes

700 ml water

1 tsp dried thyme

800 g tinned minced clams, including liquid

Tabasco sauce

1 tsp salt

1 tsp freshly ground black pepper

1. In a large, heavy-bottomed stock pot, start the bacon cooking. As the fat cooks out of it, add the onion, celery and green pepper, and sauté them in the bacon fat for 4 to 5 minutes.

2. Add the turnip, carrot, tomatoes, water and thyme, and let the whole thing simmer for 30 minutes to 1 hour.

3. Add the clams, including the liquid, a dash of Tabasco, and the salt and pepper. Simmer for another 15 minutes and serve.

Yield: 10 servings, each with 11 grams of carbohydrate and 1 gram of fibre, for a total of 10 grams of usable carbs and 21 grams of protein.

☉ Lo-Carb Clam Chowder

Clam Chowder fans will want to try this recipe from reader
Tricia Hudgins.

> 8 rashers bacon
>
> 50 g finely chopped onion
>
> 50 g finely chopped celery
>
> 400 g tinned clams, drained and with the juice reserved
>
> 225 ml chicken stock
>
> 2 large turnips, peeled and chopped into small cubes
>
> 1/2 tsp freshly ground black pepper
>
> 1/2 tsp dried thyme
>
> Salt
>
> 225 ml double cream

1. Fry the bacon and set it aside, reserving the bacon fat. Sauté the
   onion and celery in 3 tablespoons of the bacon fat until they're soft.

2. Remove the onion and celery from the heat and add the clam juice,
   chicken stock, turnips, pepper, thyme and salt. Cover and cook over
   medium heat, stirring occasionally, until the turnips are soft (about
   15 minutes).

3. Remove from the heat and stir in the double cream and clams. Crumble
   the bacon and add it to the soup. Reheat over a low heat and serve.

Yield: 4 servings, each with 13 grams of carbohydrate and 2 grams of
fibre, for a total of 11 grams of usable carbs and 31 grams of protein.

> 🍓 The sharp or bitter part of the turnip is the outside layer near
> the skin. Peel your turnips with a paring knife, being careful
> to get all the outer layer.

☉ Quick Green Chowder

300 g frozen chopped spinach, thawed

400 g tinned minced clams, including the liquid

225 ml milk and cream, mixed

225 ml double cream

225 ml water

Salt and freshly ground black pepper

1. Put the spinach, clams, milk and cream mixture, cream and water in a blender or food processor and purée.

2. Pour the mixture into a saucepan and bring to a simmer (use very low heat and don't boil!) Simmer for 5 minutes, and season to taste.

🍓 If you prefer, you can purée everything but the clams, adding them later so they stay in chunks.

Yield: 4 servings, each with 12 grams of carbohydrate and 2 grams of fibre, for a total of 10 grams of usable carbs and 29 grams of protein.

⟲ Artichoke Soup

3 to 4 Tbsp butter
1 small onion, finely chopped
2 stalks celery, finely chopped
1 clove garlic, crushed
400 g tinned artichoke hearts, drained and quartered
1 litre chicken stock
1/2 tsp guar or xanthan
225 ml milk and cream, mixed
Juice of 1/2 lemon
Salt
Freshly ground black pepper

1. In a heavy frying pan, melt the butter and sauté the onion, celery and garlic over a low to medium heat. Stir from time to time.

2. Drain the artichoke hearts and trim off any tough bits of leaf. Put the artichoke hearts in a food processor with the S-blade in position. Add 125 ml of the chicken stock and the guar gum, and process until the artichokes are a fine purée.

3. Scrape the artichoke mixture into a saucepan, add the remaining chicken stock and set over a medium-high heat to simmer.

4. When the onion and celery are soft, stir them into the artichoke mixture. When it comes to a simmer, whisk in the milk-cream mixture. Bring it back to a simmer, squeeze in the lemon juice and stir again. Season to taste. You can serve this immediately, hot, or in summer you can serve it chilled.

Yield: 6 servings, each with 10 grams of carbohydrate and 3 grams of fibre, for a total of 7 grams of usable carbs and 4 grams of protein. (Note: Much of the carbohydrate in artichokes is inulin, which remains largely undigested, so this carb count is actually misleadingly high.)

◯ Olive Soup

Olives are so good for you that you should be eating more of them! This makes a fine first course.

> 1 litre chicken stock
>
> 1/2 tsp guar or xanthan
>
> 100 g minced black olives
>   (you can buy tins of minced black olives)
>
> 225 ml double cream
>
> 75 ml dry sherry
>
> Salt
>
> Freshly ground black pepper

1. Put 125 ml of the chicken stock in the blender with the guar gum and blend for a few seconds. Pour into a saucepan and add the rest of the stock and the olives.

2. Heat until simmering, then whisk in the cream. Bring back to a simmer, stir in the sherry and season to taste.

Yield: 6 servings, each with 3 grams of carbohydrate and 1 gram of fibre, for a total of 2 grams of usable carbs and 2 grams of protein.

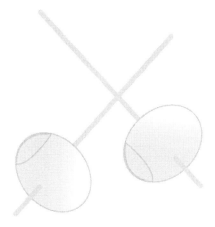

ꙮ Turkey Meatball Soup

This makes a light, quick and tasty supper all by itself.

225 g turkey mince

1 1/2 Tbsp oat bran

2 Tbsp minced fresh parsley

1/2 tsp salt

1/2 tsp poultry seasoning

1/8 tsp freshly ground black pepper

1 Tbsp olive oil

50 g grated carrot

300 g diced courgette

1 Tbsp finely chopped onion

1 clove garlic, crushed

1 litre chicken stock

1 tsp dried oregano

2 eggs, beaten

30 g grated Parmesan cheese

1. In a mixing bowl, combine the turkey mince with the oat bran, parsley, 1/2 tsp salt, poultry seasoning and pepper. Mix well and form into balls the size of marbles. Set aside.

2. In a large, heavy-bottomed saucepan, heat the olive oil over a medium-high heat. Add the carrot and let it sauté for 2 to 3 minutes. Then add the courgette, onion and garlic, and sauté the vegetables for another 5 to 7 minutes.

3. Add the chicken stock and oregano and bring the soup to a simmer for 15 minutes. Drop the turkey meatballs into the soup one by one and let it simmer for another 10 to 15 minutes. Taste the soup at this point and add more salt and pepper to taste, if desired.

4. Just before you're ready to serve the soup, stir it slowly with a fork as you pour the beaten eggs in quite slowly. Simmer another minute and ladle into bowls. Top each serving with 1 tablespoon of Parmesan and serve.

Yield: 4 servings, each with 7 grams of carbohydrate and 2 grams of fibre, for a total of 5 grams usable carbs and 21 grams of protein.

☉ Kim's Week-After-Christmas Soup

This is what my sister did with the carcass from her Christmas turkey. Our mother always made turkey and rice soup, but we low-carbers needed a new tradition and here it is.

>   1 turkey carcass
>   1 Tbsp salt
>   2 Tbsp vinegar
>   5 small turnips, cut into large-ish cubes
>   4 sticks celery, cut into 1-cm lengths
>   225 g mushrooms, sliced
>   1 large onion, chopped
>   2 courgettes, each about 15 cm long, diced into small chunks
>   350 g frozen sliced green beans
>   1 chicken stock cube or 1 tsp chicken stock crystals
>   2 Tbsp dried basil
>   Salt and freshly ground black pepper

1. In a large pot, break up the turkey carcass, leaving bits of meat clinging to it. Cover it with water, add the salt and vinegar, and simmer on low until the water is reduced to about 4 litres. Let cool.

2. Pour the whole thing through a strainer and return the stock to the pot. Pick the meat off the turkey bones. Discard the bones, cut up the meat and return it to the pot.

3. Add the turnips, celery, mushrooms, onion, courgette, beans, stock and basil, and simmer until the vegetables are soft. Salt and pepper to taste and serve.

Yield: 12 servings, each with 12 grams of carbohydrate and 4 grams of fibre, for a total of 8 grams of usable carbs. Your protein count will depend on how much meat was left on your turkey carcass, but assuming 225 g of diced turkey total, you'll get 15 grams of protein per serving.

↻ Portuguese Soup

If this were really authentic, it would have potatoes in it. But this decarbed version is delicious and it's a full meal in a bowl. Read the labels on the smoked sausage carefully – they range from 1 gram of carb per serving up to 5.

75 ml olive oil

80 g chopped onion

3 cloves garlic, crushed

350 g diced turnip

300 g diced cauliflower

450 g kale

650 g smoked sausage

400 g tinned chopped tomatoes

2 litres chicken stock

1/4 tsp Tabasco sauce

Salt and freshly ground black pepper

1. Put 75 ml of the olive oil in a large soup pot and sauté the onion, garlic, turnip and cauliflower over a medium heat.

2. While that's cooking, chop the kale into bite-sized pieces and add it to the pot. (You may need to cram it in at first, but don't worry – it cooks down quite a bit.) Let the vegetables sauté for another 10 minutes or so, stirring to turn the whole thing over every once and a while.

3. Slice the smoked sausage lengthways into quarters, then crossways into 1-cm pieces. Heat the remaining 2 tablespoons of oil in a heavy frying pan over a medium heat and brown the smoked sausage a little.

4. Add the browned sausage, tomatoes and 1 3/4 litres of the chicken stock to the kettle and use the remainder of the stock to rinse the tasty browned bits out of the frying pan and add that, too. Bring to a simmer and cook until the vegetables are soft (30 to 45 minutes). Stir in the Tabasco and salt and pepper to taste and serve.

Yield: 10 servings, each with 13 grams of carbohydrate and 2 grams of fibre, for a total of 11 grams of usable carbs and 23 grams of protein.

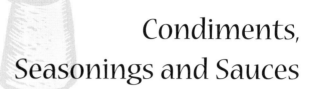

CHAPTER THIRTEEN

Condiments, Seasonings and Sauces

Once you start reading labels, you'll be shocked at how many of your favourite seasonings, sauces and especially condiments, are simply loaded with sugar, glucose, flour, cornflour and other things you'd rather keep to a minimum. Most brands of ketchup have 4 grams of carbohydrate per tablespoon, for heaven's sake, and barbecue sauce tends to run even higher! You can carve significant chunks of carbohydrates out of your diet by making your own sauces at home instead.

ꙮ Cheese Sauce

Try this over broccoli or cauliflower. It's wonderful!

    125 ml double cream
    75 g grated Cheddar cheese
    1/4 tsp dry mustard

1. In a heavy-bottomed saucepan over the lowest heat, warm the cream to just below a simmer.
2. Whisk in the cheese about 1 tablespoon at a time, only adding the next tablespoonful after the last one has melted. When all the cheese is melted in, whisk in the dry mustard and serve.

Yield: Enough to serve with 450 g of broccoli or cauliflower, or about 4 servings of sauce, each with 1 gram of carbohydrate, no fibre and 6 grams of protein.

ꙮ Stir-Fry Sauce

If you like Chinese food, make this up and keep it on hand. Then you can just throw any sort of meat and vegetables in your wok or frying pan and have a meal in minutes.

    125 ml soy sauce
    125 ml dry sherry
    2 cloves garlic, crushed
    2 Tbsp grated fresh ginger
    2 tsp Splenda

Combine the ingredients in a container with a tight-fitting lid and refrigerate until you're ready to use.

Yield: 225 ml. Each 2-tablespoon serving has 2 grams of carbohydrate, no fibre and no protein.

↺ Not-Very-Authentic Peanut Sauce

This is inauthentic because I used substitutes for such traditional ingredients as lemon grass and fish sauce. I wanted a recipe that tasted good but could be made without a trip to a speciality grocer's.

> 1 piece of fresh ginger about the size of a walnut, peeled and thinly sliced across the grain
>
> 100 g natural peanut butter, creamy
>
> 125 ml chicken stock
>
> 1 1/2 tsp lemon juice
>
> 1 1/2 tsp soy sauce
>
> 1/4 tsp Tabasco sauce
>
> 1 large or 2 small cloves garlic, crushed
>
> 1 1/2 tsp Splenda

Put all the ingredients in a blender and run it until everything is well combined and smooth. If you'd like it a little thinner, add another tablespoon of chicken stock.

Yield: About 500 ml, or 16 servings, each with 2 grams of carbohydrate, a trace of fibre and 2 grams of protein.

○ Hoisin Sauce

This Chinese sauce is usually made from fermented soya bean paste, which has tons of sugar in it. Peanut butter is inauthentic, but it tastes quite good nevertheless.

4 Tbsp soy sauce

2 Tbsp creamy natural peanut butter

2 Tbsp Splenda

2 tsp white vinegar

1 clove garlic, crushed

2 tsp toasted sesame oil

1/8 tsp Chinese Five Spice powder

Put all the ingredients in a blender and run it until everything is smooth and well combined. Store in a snap-top container.

Yield: Roughly 75 ml. Each 1-tablespoon serving contains 2 grams of carbohydrate, a trace of fibre and 2 grams of protein.

Of course, this sauce is essential for Mu Shu Pork (see page 358) or Mu Shu Anything, for that matter, but it's also good for dipping plain chicken wings in.

○ Taco Seasoning

Many purchased seasoning blends include sugar or cornflour – my food counter book says that several popular brands have 5 grams of carbs in 2 teaspoons! This is low-carb, very easy to put together, tastes great and works out less expensive than the premixed stuff.

2 Tbsp chilli powder

1 1/2 Tbsp cumin

1 1/2 Tbsp paprika

1 Tbsp onion powder

1 Tbsp garlic powder

1/8 to 1/4 tsp cayenne pepper (less makes a milder seasoning, more takes the spice up a notch)

Combine all the ingredients, blending well, and store in an airtight container. Use 2 tablespoons of this mixture to flavour 450 g of minced beef, turkey or chicken.

Yield: About 8 tablespoons, or 4 batches' worth. 2 tablespoons will add just under 2 grams of carbohydrate to a 100-g serving of taco meat.

◌ Chicken Seasoning

This is wonderful sprinkled over chicken before roasting.

3 Tbsp salt

1 tsp paprika

1 tsp onion powder

1 tsp garlic powder

1 tsp curry powder

1/2 tsp freshly ground black pepper

Combine all the ingredients well and store in a salt shaker or the shaker from an old container of herbs. Sprinkle over chicken before roasting; I use it to season at the table, as well.

Yield: 30 to 40 g. There are 7 grams of carb in this whole recipe and 1 gram of fibre, for a total of 6 grams of usable carbs, so the amount in the teaspoon or so you sprinkle over a piece of chicken is negligible.

☉ Cajun Seasoning

This New Orleans-style seasoning is good sprinkled over chicken, steak, pork, fish, or just about anything else you care to try it on.

    2 1/2 Tbsp paprika
    2 Tbsp salt
    2 Tbsp garlic powder
    1 Tbsp freshly ground black pepper
    1 Tbsp onion powder
    1 Tbsp cayenne pepper
    1 Tbsp dried oregano
    1 Tbsp dried thyme

Combine all ingredients thoroughly and store in an airtight container.

Yield: 50 g. In the entire batch there are 37 grams of carbohydrate and 9 grams of fibre, for a total of 28 grams of usable carbs. Considering how spicy this is, you're unlikely to use more than a teaspoon or two at a time and 1 teaspoon has just 1 gram of carbohydrate and a trace of fibre.

↻ Jerk Seasoning

Sprinkle this over chicken, pork chops or fish before cooking for an instant hit of hot, sweet and spicy flavour.

- 1 Tbsp onion flakes
- 2 tsp ground thyme
- 1 tsp ground allspice
- 1/4 tsp ground cinnamon
- 1 tsp freshly ground black pepper
- 1 tsp cayenne pepper
- 1 Tbsp onion powder
- 2 tsp salt
- 1/4 tsp ground nutmeg
- 2 Tbsp Splenda

Combine all the ingredients and store in an airtight container.

Yield: About 30 g. Each teaspoon contains 1 gram of carbohydrate, a trace of fibre and no protein.

◯ Dana's No-Sugar Ketchup

Supermarket ketchup has more sugar in it per 30 g than ice cream does! This great-tasting ketchup has all the flavour of your favourite brand, without the high carb count. The guar or xanthan isn't essential, but it makes your ketchup a little thicker and helps keep the water from separating out if you don't use it up quickly.

180 g tinned tomato purée

150 ml cider vinegar

75 ml water

30 g Splenda

2 Tbsp finely chopped onion

2 cloves garlic, crushed

1 tsp salt

1/8 tsp ground allspice

1/8 tsp ground cloves

1/8 tsp freshly ground black pepper

1/4 tsp guar or xanthan

Put all the ingredients in a blender and run the blender until the bits of onion disappear. (You'll have to scrape down the sides as you go, because this mixture is thick.) Store in the refrigerator, in a container with a tight-fitting lid.

Yield: 350 ml of ketchup. 1 tablespoon has 2.25 grams of carbohydrate, a trace of fibre and a trace of protein.

☉ Low-Carb Steak Sauce

75 ml Dana's No-Sugar Ketchup (see left)

1 Tbsp Worcestershire sauce

1 tsp lemon juice

Combine well and store in an airtight container in the fridge.

Yield: 5 servings of 1 tablespoon, each with 2.25 grams of carbohydrate, a trace of fibre and a trace of protein.

☉ Cocktail Sauce

Use this for dipping cold, boiled prawns in, of course. Commercial cocktail sauce, like so many other condiments, is full of sugar.

75 ml Dana's No-Sugar Ketchup (see left)

1 tsp prepared horseradish

2 or 3 drops Tabasco

1/2 tsp lemon juice

Just stir together and dip!

Yield: 75 ml, with 10 grams of carbohydrate, a trace of fibre and a trace of protein in the whole batch.

◯ Aioli

This is basically just very garlicky mayonnaise. It's good on all kinds of vegetables and on fish, too.

    4 cloves garlic, crushed very thoroughly
    1 egg
    1/4 tsp salt
    2 Tbsp lemon juice
    100 to 150 ml olive oil

Put the garlic, egg, salt and lemon juice in a blender. Run the blender for a second and then pour in the oil in a very thin stream, as you would when making mayonnaise. Turn off the blender when the sauce is thickened.

Yield: About 225 ml, or 8 servings of 2 tablespoons, each with 1 gram of carbohydrate, only a trace of fibre and 1 gram of protein.

◯ Wonderful Memphis-Style Dry Rub BBQ

The Mystery Chef sent me this recipe. Good on ribs, chops and chicken, and far lower-carb than barbecue sauce.

    1 Tbsp paprika
    2 tsp chilli powder
    3/4 tsp salt
    1/4 tsp dry mustard
    1/4 tsp garlic powder
    1/8 tsp freshly ground black pepper

Mix all the ingredients together and store the mixture in a salt shaker. Sprinkle on both sides of whatever meat you're cooking and grill.

Yield: Enough for 1 1/2 kg of ribs, or about 3 servings. If, indeed, 3 of you eat this entire recipe, you'll each get 2 grams of carbohydrate and 1 gram of fibre, for a total of 1 gram of usable carbs and no protein.

↻ Reduced-Carb Spicy Barbecue Sauce

1 clove garlic, crushed
1 small onion, finely chopped
50 g butter or oil
4 Tbsp Splenda
1 tsp salt
1 tsp dry mustard
1 tsp paprika
1 tsp chilli powder
1/2 tsp freshly ground black pepper
2 tsp black treacle
350 ml water
75 ml cider vinegar
1 Tbsp Worcestershire sauce
1 Tbsp prepared horseradish
180 g tinned tomato purée
1 Tbsp smoky barbecue sauce

1. In a saucepan, cook the garlic and onion in the butter for a few minutes.
2. Stir in the Splenda, salt, mustard, paprika, chilli powder and pepper. Add in the treacle, water, vinegar, Worcestershire sauce and horseradish, and stir to combine. Let the mixture simmer for 15 to 20 minutes.
3. Whisk in the tomato purée and smoky barbecue sauce, and let the sauce simmer another 5 to 10 minutes.
4. Let the mixture cool, transfer it to a jar with a tight-fitting lid and store in the refrigerator.

Yield: About 600 ml of sauce. Each 2-tablespoon serving has 3 grams of carbohydrate and 1 gram of fibre, for a total of 2 grams of usable carbs and no protein.

🍓 If you're wondering whether it's worth making your own barbecue sauce from scratch, think on this for a moment: Your average commercial barbecue sauce has between 10 and 15 grams of carbs per 2-tablespoon serving – and do you know anyone who ever stopped at 2 tablespoons of barbecue sauce?

ා Tequila Lime Marinade

75 ml lime juice (bottled is fine)

75 ml water

3 Tbsp tequila

1 Tbsp Splenda

1 Tbsp soy sauce

2 cloves garlic, crushed

Combine the ingredients and store in the refrigerator until ready to use.

Yield: Roughly 170 ml (enough for a dozen boneless, skinless chicken breasts or 1 kg of prawns). In the whole batch there are 13 grams of carbohydrate and 1 gram of fibre, for a total of 12 grams of usable carbs and no protein, but since you drain most of the marinade off, you won't get more than a gram or two of carbs total.

ා Teriyaki Sauce

Good on chicken, beef, fish – just about anything.

125 ml soy sauce

75 ml dry sherry

1 clove garlic, crushed

2 Tbsp Splenda

1 Tbsp grated fresh ginger

Combine all the ingredients and refrigerate until ready to use.

Yield: Just over 200 ml. Each 1-tablespoon serving will have about 3 grams of carbohydrate, a trace of fibre and a trace of protein.

◌ Jerk Marinade

Jerk is a Jamaican way of life. Make it with one pepper if you want it just nicely hot, or with two peppers if you want it traditional – also known as take-the-top-of-your-head-off hot.

> 1 or 2 Scotch Bonnet or habenero peppers, with or without seeds (the seeds are the hottest part)
>
> 1/2 small onion
>
> 3 Tbsp oil
>
> 1 Tbsp ground allspice
>
> 2 Tbsp grated fresh ginger
>
> 1 Tbsp soy sauce
>
> 1 tsp dried thyme
>
> 1 bay leaf, crumbled
>
> 1/4 tsp cinnamon
>
> 1 Tbsp Splenda
>
> 2 cloves garlic, crushed

Put all the ingredients in a food processor with the S-blade in place and process until it's fairly smooth. (You'll get a soft paste that looks like mud but smells like heaven!) Smear this over the meat of your choice and let it sit for a day before cooking. Always wash your hands after handling hot peppers!

Yield: Enough for about 4 servings of meat, each serving serving of Jerk Marinade adding 4 grams of carbohydrate and 1 gram of fibre, for a total of 3 grams of usable carbs and no protein.

🍓 If you just can't take the heat, you can chicken out and use a jalapeño or two instead of the habeneros or Scotch Bonnets and your jerk marinade will be quite mild, as these things go. But remember: there is no such thing as a true mild jerk sauce.

◌ Chinese Looing Sauce

This is a Chinese sauce for 'red cooking.' You stew things in it and it imparts a wonderful flavour to just about any sort of meat.

    500 ml soy sauce

    1 star anise

    125 ml dry sherry (the cheap stuff is fine)

    4 Tbsp Splenda

    1 Tbsp grated fresh ginger

    1 litre water

> Star anise is available in Asian markets and health food shops. It actually does look like a star and it's essential to the recipe. Don't try to substitute regular anise.

Combine the ingredients well and use the mixture to stew things in. (Specifically, see Looed Chicken on page 250 and Looed Pork on page 358.) After using Chinese Looing Sauce, you can strain it and refrigerate or freeze it to use again, if you like.

Yield: 1 1/2 litres of looing sauce, or plenty to submerge your food in. In the whole batch there are about 50 grams of usable carbohydrates, but only a very small amount of that is transferred to the foods you stew in it.

↻ Cranberry Sauce

Unbelievably easy and good with roast chicken or turkey – as though you needed to be told!

1/2 tsp plain gelatine (optional)

225 ml water

350 g fresh cranberries

125 g Splenda

If you're using the gelatine, dissolve it in 125 ml of the water, then add it to the cranberries and Splenda in a saucepan over a medium to high heat. Bring it to the boil and boil it hard until the cranberries pop. Keep it in a tightly covered jar in the fridge.

Yield: Roughly 500 ml. Each 2-tablespoon serving will have 4 grams of carbohydrate and 1 gram of fibre, for a total of 3 grams of usable carbs.

🍓 If you cannot find fresh cranberries, frozen will work just as well. Available all the year round from your supermarket!

☙ Cranberry Chutney

Think of this as cranberry sauce with a kick. It's good with any curried poultry, or even with plain old roast chicken.

    350 g cranberries
    225 ml water
    100 g Splenda
    2 cloves garlic, crushed
    1 Tbsp mixed spice
    1/2 tsp ground ginger
    1/8 tsp salt

Combine all the ingredients in a saucepan over a medium heat, bring it to the boil and boil until the cranberries pop (7 to 8 minutes).

Yield: Roughly 500 ml. Each 2-tablespoon serving will have just over 3 grams of carbohydrate and 1 gram of fibre, for a total of 2 grams of usable carbs and only a trace of protein.

🍓 This recipe improves if you let the boiled mixture sit for a while before serving. Try it with a little cinnamon, too.

↻ Hollandaise for Sissies

An easy, unintimidating sauce for asparagus, artichokes, broccoli, or whatever you like.

4 egg yolks
225 ml soured cream
1 Tbsp lemon juice
1/2 tsp salt
Dash of Tabasco

🍓 You'll need either a double boiler or a heat diffuser for this; it needs very gentle heat. If you're using a double boiler, you want the water in the bottom hot, but not boiling. If you're using a heat diffuser, use the lowest possible heat under the diffuser.

Put all the ingredients in a heavy-bottomed saucepan or the top of a double boiler. Whisk everything together well, let it heat through and serve it over vegetables.

Yield: 6 to 8 servings, each with about 2 grams of carbohydrate, a trace of fibre and 3 grams of protein.

↻ No-Fail Hollandaise

This recipe is courtesy of *Lowcarbezine!* reader Linda Carroll-King. Make sure you follow her directions to use room-temperature eggs – that's what makes this recipe no-fail.

100 g butter

4 eggs yolks at room temperature

1 Tbsp fresh lemon juice

White pepper

1. Heat the butter until it foams in a saucepan over a low heat; don't let it burn.
2. While the butter is heating, put the egg yolks, lemon juice and pepper to taste, in a blender.
3. When the butter is foaming, start the blender. Without giving the butter time to cool, slowly pour it into the blender. Whiz for several seconds and it's done.

Yield: This is about 125 ml, or 4 servings, each with 1 gram of carbohydrate, a trace of fibre and 3 grams of protein.

↻ Green Tomato Chutney

Most chutneys are full of sugar, so I invented my own – now I plant extra tomatoes in the summer to have enough to make this. It's wonderful with anything curried.

> 4 litres green tomatoes, cut into chunks
>
> 700 ml cider vinegar
>
> 1 whole ginger root, sliced into very thin rounds
>
> 5 or 6 cloves garlic, thinly sliced
>
> 1 Tbsp whole cloves
>
> 5 or 6 sticks whole cinnamon
>
> 150 g Splenda, or to taste
>
> 1 Tbsp black treacle

🍓 There are two things you need to know when buying and cooking with ginger. The first is that a whole ginger root is also sometimes called a 'hand' of ginger. The second is that you should always cut ginger across the grain, not along it, or you'll end up with woody ginger.

Combine all the ingredients in a large stainless steel or enamel pan – no iron, no aluminium. (This is an acidic mixture and if you use iron or aluminium you'll end up with your chutney chock full of iron, which will turn it blackish, or aluminium, which simply isn't good for you.) Simmer on low for 3 to 4 hours. Store in tightly closed containers in the refrigerator.

Yield: Roughly 2 litres. Each 2-tablespoon serving will have 5 grams of carbohydrate and 1 gram of fibre, for a total of 4 grams of usable carbs and no protein.

ꙩ Duck Sauce

This is good on Crab and Bacon Bundles. It's good with chicken, too. It does have the sugar that's in the peaches, of course, but not all the added sugar of commercial duck sauce. And it tastes better, too.

> 600 g sliced, peeled fresh peaches
>
> 125 ml water
>
> 2 Tbsp cider vinegar
>
> 2 Tbsp Splenda
>
> 1/4 tsp black treacle
>
> 1/8 tsp salt
>
> 1 tsp soy sauce
>
> 1 clove garlic, crushed

1. Put all the ingredients in a heavy-bottomed saucepan and bring them to a simmer. Cook, uncovered, until the peaches are soft (about 30 minutes).

2. Purée the duck sauce in a blender, if you like, or do what I do: simply mash the sauce with a potato masher or a fork. (I like the texture better this way.)

Yield: About 500 ml. Each 2-tablespoon serving has 3 grams of carbohydrate and 1 gram of fibre, for a total of 2 grams of usable carbs and no protein.

🍓 It's best to freeze this if you're not going to use it up right away.

⌒ Tootsie's Pesto

Tootsie is my friend Kay's mother and this is her recipe. Supermarket pesto is awfully expensive and not nearly so fresh and good! This makes a highly concentrated product; feel free to thin it a bit with olive oil before you use it.

50 g fresh basil leaves, washed and patted dry

4 good-size garlic cloves

100 g shelled walnuts or pine kernels

225 ml extra-virgin olive oil

150 g freshly grated Parmesan cheese

30 g freshly grated Romano cheese

Salt and freshly ground black pepper, to taste

1. Combine the basil, garlic and nuts, and chop in a food processor with the S-blade. Leave the motor running and add the olive oil in a slow, steady stream.

2. Shut off the food processor and add the Parmesan, Romano, a big pinch of salt and a liberal grinding of pepper. Process briefly to blend.

Yield: 225 ml. Each 1-tablespoon serving will have 1 gram of carbohydrate, a trace of fibre and 2 grams of protein.

🍓 Your can store your pesto by freezing it in an ice cube tray and then wrapping it in small pieces of clingfilm, or you can keep it in a plastic container with a snap-on lid in the fridge. Kay says she particularly likes this thinned a bit with olive oil and served on cooked green beans. Pesto is also good with chicken and seafood.

Cookies, Cakes and Other Sweets

I am in two minds about this chapter (a chapter which, by the way, contains recipes for treats as delicious as any sugary desserts you've ever made). On the one hand, I think it's a bad idea to get in the habit of eating these sugarless sweets with the same frequency with which you used to eat the sugary stuff. I feel strongly that weaning yourself away from wanting sweets all the time, from not considering a meal complete until you've had a dessert, is a very good and important thing.

On the other hand, I understand – boy, do I understand! – the lure of sweets. As a kid I quite literally stole to get sugar. And I know that, for some of you, these recipes will be the thing that lets you stick to your diet and break your sugar addiction altogether.

So this is what I suggest: if you're fighting severe sugar cravings or if you're subject to frequent temptation, keep one or two of these desserts on hand. They really do taste great and satisfy your taste buds. However, they will not cause the blood sugar rush – or crash – of the sugary stuff and therefore, with the help of these desserts, you should be able slowly to back away from sweets until they're just an occasional treat. And that, my friend, is where I would love for you to be.

☾ Butter Cookies

225 g butter

225 g cream cheese

30 g plus 1 Tbsp Splenda

1 egg

225 g sieved soya powder

1/2 tsp baking powder

1/2 tsp ground cinnamon

1. Use an electric mixer to cream the butter and cream cheese together until well blended and soft. Add 30 g Splenda, and cream until completely combined. Beat in the egg.

2. Sieve the soya powder, then sieve again with the baking powder (to combine the baking powder with the soya powder and to break up any lumps in the baking powder). Sieve the combined powders into the mixing bowl and mix to make a soft dough.

3. Chill the dough for several hours in a covered container or wrapped in foil; this will make it easier to handle.

4. When the dough is chilled, preheat the oven to 190ºC/Gas Mark 5. Make small balls of the dough and place them on an ungreased baking tray.

5. Mix 1 tablespoon of Splenda with the cinnamon on a small plate or saucer. Take a flat-bottomed drinking glass and butter the bottom. Then dip the buttered glass in the cinnamon and Splenda, and use it to press the cookies flat.

6. Bake for about 9 minutes, checking at 8 minutes, to make sure the bottoms aren't browning too fast. The cookies are done when the bottoms are just starting to brown.

🍓 You'll need to dip your 'pressing glass' in the cinnamon and Splenda for each cookie, but you won't have to rebutter the bottom each time. The butter just keeps the glass from sticking to the cookies and, of course, puts cinnamon and Splenda on each one!

Yield: About 6 dozen, each with 1 gram of carbohydrate, a trace of fibre and 1 gram of protein.

🍓 Don't butter the baking tray or spray it with nonstick cooking spray. Why not? These cookies are so rich, they practically float on the butter that cooks out of them. I had no trouble with them sticking – I had trouble with them sliding around the baking tray while they were baking! I call them The Incredible Migrating Cookies. Hopefully, your baking trays are flatter and your oven more level than mine.

↻ Chocolate Walnut Balls

These are great to make around Christmastime, when high-carb temptations abound.

100 g butter, at room temperature

50 g cream cheese

90 g Splenda

1 egg

1 tsp vanilla extract

350 g sieved soya powder

1/4 tsp salt

1 1/2 tsp baking powder

50 g unsweetened baking chocolate

50 g chopped walnuts

1. Preheat the oven to 190°C/Gas Mark 5.
2. With an electric mixer, cream the butter and cream cheese until soft and well combined. Add the Splenda and cream until well combined. Add the egg and the vanilla, and beat until well combined.
3. Sieve the soya powder, then resieve with the salt and baking powder. Add the powders to the butter mixture. (It's easier to beat it in if you add it one-half at a time.)
4. Melt the chocolate and beat that in, then add the nuts and beat them in well.

5. Butter or spray baking trays with nonstick cooking spray. Roll the dough into small balls and place them on the sheets. Bake for 8 to 10 minutes.

Yield: About 40 cookies, each with 2 grams of carbohydrate and 1 gram of fibre, for a total of 1 gram of usable carbs and 1 gram of protein.

⊙ Peanut Butter Cookies

I can't tell these from my mother's peanut butter cookies!

> 100 g butter, at room temperature
>
> 90 g Splenda
>
> 1 Tbsp blackstrap or dark treacle
>
> 1 egg
>
> 225 g natural peanut butter (creamy is best)
>
> 1/2 tsp salt
>
> 1/2 tsp baking soda
>
> 1/2 tsp vanilla
>
> 100 g soya powder
>
> 2 Tbsp oat bran

1. Preheat the oven to 190°C/Gas Mark 5.
2. Use an electric mixer to beat the butter until creamy. Add the Splenda, treacle and beat again until well combined.
3. Beat in the egg, peanut butter, salt, baking soda and vanilla. Beat in the soya powder and oat bran.
4. Butter or spray baking trays with nonstick cooking spray. Roll the dough into small balls and place them on the sheets. Use the back of a fork to press the balls of dough flat, leaving those traditional peanut butter cookie crisscross marks. Bake for 10 to 12 minutes.

Yield: About 4 1/2 dozen cookies, each with 2.3 grams of carbohydrate and 1 gram of fibre, for a total of 1.3 grams of usable carbs and 2 grams of protein.

↻ Hazelnut Shortbread

If you've always loved shortbread, meet the new low-carb replacement.

> 300 g hazelnuts
>
> 225 g butter, at room temperature
>
> 60 g Splenda
>
> 1 egg
>
> 1/2 tsp salt
>
> 1/4 tsp baking powder
>
> 100 g vanilla-flavoured whey protein powder
>
> 2 Tbsp water

1. Preheat the oven to 170ºC/Gas Mark 3.
2. Grind the hazelnuts to a fine meal with a food processor. Set aside.
3. Use an electric mixer to beat the butter until it's fluffy. Add the Splenda and beat well again. Beat in the egg, again combining well.
4. Sprinkle the salt and baking powder over the top of the mixture and add half of the ground hazelnuts. Beat them in, add the rest of the hazelnuts and beat again.
5. Beat in the vanilla-flavoured whey protein powder and then the water to make a soft, sticky dough.
6. Line a shallow baking tin (a Swiss roll tin is best – mine is 30 x 40 cm) with baking parchment and turn the dough out on to the parchment. Cover it with another piece of parchment and through the top sheet, press the dough out into an even layer covering the whole tin. (The pressed dough should be about 5 mm thick.)
7. Peel off the top sheet of parchment and score the dough into squares using a pizza cutter or a knife with a straight, thin blade. Bake for 25 to 30 minutes, or until golden.

> 🍓 You'll need to rescore the lines before removing the short-bread from the tin. Use a straight up-and-down motion and the shortbread will be less likely to break outside the score lines.

Yield: 4 dozen shortbreads, each with 1.5 grams of carbohydrate, a trace of fibre and 1 gram of protein.

ᕦ Almond Cookies

Crumbly and delicate, but delicious!

> 225 g butter, at room temperature
>
> 125 g Splenda
>
> 1 egg
>
> 225 g smooth almond butter
>
> 1/2 tsp salt
>
> 1/2 tsp baking soda
>
> 150 g vanilla-flavoured whey protein powder
>
> 2 Tbsp water
>
> 30 whole, shelled almonds

1. Preheat the oven to 190°C/Gas Mark 5.
2. Use an electric mixer to beat the butter until smooth and fluffy. Add the Splenda and beat again, scraping down the sides, until very well combined.
3. Beat in the egg, then add the almond butter, salt and baking soda.
4. Beat in the protein powder about 1/2 cup at a time.
5. Add the water and beat until everything is well combined.
6. Use a measuring tablespoon to scoop heaped tablespoons of dough on to greased baking trays (each cookie should be made of about 2 tablespoons of dough). Press an almond into the centre of each cookie. Bake for 10 to 12 minutes, or until the cookies just begin to brown around the edges.

Yield: 2 1/2 dozen nice big cookies, each with 3.5 grams of carbohydrate and 0.5 grams of fibre, for a total of 3 grams of usable carbs and 4 grams of protein.

⟳ Sesame Cookies

100 g butter

125 g Splenda

1 egg

225 g tahini (roasted sesame butter)

1/2 tsp salt

1/2 tsp baking soda

150 g vanilla-flavoured whey protein powder

30 g sesame seeds

1. Preheat the oven to 190°C/Gas Mark 5.
2. Use an electric mixer to beat the butter and Splenda together until smooth and fluffy. Beat in the egg, mixing well, and then the tahini, again mixing well.
3. Add the salt and baking soda, then beat in the protein powder 1/2 cup at a time. Beat in the sesame seeds last.
4. Spray a baking tray with nonstick cooking spray and drop the dough on to it in spoonfuls. Bake for 10 to 12 minutes, or until golden.

Yield: About 4 1/2 dozen cookies, each with 2 grams of carbohydrate, a trace of fibre and 6 grams of protein.

⟳ Mom's Chocolate Chip Cookies

With this recipe, I assume the title of Low-Carb Cookie God.

225 g butter, at room temperature

180 g Splenda

1 1/2 tsp black treacle

2 eggs

100 g ground almonds

100 g vanilla-flavoured whey protein powder

30 g oat bran

1 tsp baking soda
1 tsp salt
100 g chopped walnuts or pecans
350 g sugar-free chocolate chips

🍓 If you can't get sugar-free chocolate chips, you need to make some from sugar-free chocolate bars. Break 7 or 8 of the bars, which are around 30 g each, into three or four pieces each and place the pieces in a food processor with the S-blade in place. Pulse the food processor until your chocolate bars are in pieces about the same size as commercial chocolate morsels and set them aside until you're ready to use them.

Note: If you haven't ground your almonds yet, now would be a good time to do that, as well.

1. Preheat the oven to 190°C/Gas Mark 5.
2. Use an electric mixer to beat the butter, Splenda and treacle until creamy and well blended. Add the eggs, one at a time and beat well after each addition.
3. In a separate bowl, stir together the ground almonds, protein powder, oat bran, baking soda and salt. Add this mixture, about 1/2 cup at a time, to the Splenda mixture, beating well after each 1/2-cup addition, until it's all beaten in. Stir in the nuts and chocolate chips.
4. Spray a baking tray with nonstick cooking spray and drop the dough in rounded tablespoons on to it. These cookies will not spread and flatten as much as standard chocolate chip cookies, so if you want them flat, flatten them a bit now.
5. Bake for 10 minutes, or until golden. Cool on baking sheets for a couple minutes, then remove to wire racks to cool completely.

Yield: About 4 1/2 dozen cookies, each with 3 grams of carbohydrate, a trace of fibre and 5 grams of protein. (This carbohydrate count does not include the polyols used to sweeten the sugar-free chocolate, since it remains largely undigested and unabsorbed.)

☌ Coconut Shortbread

100 g butter, at room temperature

125 ml coconut oil

3 Tbsp Splenda

150 g vanilla-flavoured whey protein powder

75 g unsweetened desiccated coconut

2 Tbsp water

1. Preheat oven to 190°C/Gas Mark 5.
2. Using an electric mixer, beat together the butter, coconut oil and Splenda until light and creamy. Beat in the protein powder, coconut and water, in that order, scraping down the sides of the bowl several times to make sure everything is well blended.
3. Line a Swiss roll tin with baking parchment and turn the dough out on to it. Place another sheet of baking parchment on top and press the dough out into a thin, even sheet. Use a sharp knife, or better yet, a pizza cutter, to score the dough into small rectangles. Bake for 7 to 10 minutes, or until golden. Cool and break apart.

Yield: 4 dozen cookies, each with 1 gram of carbohydrate, a trace of fibre and 6 grams of protein.

↻ Pecan Sandies

Peggy Witherow sent me a recipe for Pecan Sandies that she wanted de-carbed and this is the result.

> 225 g butter, at room temperature
>
> 125 g Splenda
>
> 1 egg
>
> 150 g vanilla-flavoured whey protein powder
>
> 170 g chopped pecans
>
> 1/2 tsp salt

1. Preheat the oven to 170°C/Gas Mark 3.

2. Beat the butter and Splenda together until light and creamy. Beat in the egg, mixing well. Then beat in the protein powder, pecans and salt.

3. Spray a baking tray with nonstick cooking spray. Form the dough into balls about the size of a marble and flatten them slightly on the baking tray. Bake for 10 to 15 minutes, or until golden.

Yield: 4 1/2 dozen cookies, each with 2 grams of carbohydrate, a trace of fibre and 5 grams of protein.

↻ Oatmeal Cookies

225 ml coconut oil

225 g butter, at room temperature

180 g Splenda

1 tsp treacle

2 eggs

100 g ground almonds

100 g vanilla-flavoured whey protein powder

1/2 tsp salt

1 tsp baking soda

1 tsp cinnamon

100 g rolled oats

100 g chopped pecans

1. Preheat the oven to 180°C/Gas Mark 4.
2. With an electric mixer, beat together the coconut oil, butter and Splenda until well combined, creamy and fluffy.
3. Beat in the treacle and eggs, combining well, followed by the ground almonds, protein powder, salt and baking soda, scraping down the sides of the bowl a few times and making sure the ingredients are well combined.
4. Beat in the cinnamon, rolled oats and pecans.
5. Spray a baking tray with nonstick cooking spray and drop dough on to it by the scant tablespoonful, leaving plenty of room for spreading. Bake for 10 minutes, or until golden. Transfer the cookies carefully to wire racks to cool.

Yield: About 5 dozen outrageously good cookies, each with 3 grams of carbohydrate, a trace of fibre and 4 grams of protein.

↻ Cocoa-Peanut Logs

This very simple recipe is an adaptation of a recipe that was around back in the '60s.

> 4 sugar-free dark chocolate bars (about 30 g each)
>   or 170 g sugar-free chocolate chips
>
> 100 g natural peanut butter (salted is best)
>
> 400 g crisp soya cereal (Keto Crisp)

1. Over very low heat (preferably using a double boiler or a heat diffuser), melt the chocolate and the peanut butter. Blend well. Stir in the cereal until it's evenly coated.

2. Coat a 25 x 30-cm tin with nonstick cooking spray, or line it with foil. Press the cereal mixture into the tin and chill for at least a few hours. Cut into squares and store in the refrigerator until ready to serve.

Yield: About 3 dozen logs, each with 1.5 grams of carbohydrate, a trace of fibre and about 5 grams of protein. (This does not include the polyols in the chocolate. And remember, those polyols have to be eaten in moderation, or you'll be in gastric distress!)

☺ Peanut Butter Brownies

This was the first recipe I ever tried from Diana Lee's *Baking Low Carb* and I've been recommending her book ever since. The peanut butter topping sinks to the bottom and you get fudgy brownie on top and chewy peanut butter cookie on the bottom.

Brownie Layer

5 Tbsp butter

30 g unsweetened baking cocoa

2 eggs

75 ml double cream

75 ml water

1 tsp vanilla extract

30 g Splenda

1 tsp liquid saccharine

75 g vanilla-flavoured whey protein powder

2 Tbsp oat flour

1 Tbsp baking powder

Peanut Butter Topping

75 ml natural peanut butter

3 Tbsp butter

2 Tbsp Splenda

1 egg

2 Tbsp vanilla-flavoured whey protein powder

1. Preheat the oven to 180°C/Gas Mark 4.

2. Melt the butter and stir in the cocoa. Add the eggs, cream, water, vanilla, Splenda and saccharine, and mix well.

3. Add the protein powder, oat flour and baking powder, and mix just until well moistened.

4. Spray a 20 x 20-cm baking dish with nonstick cooking spray and pour the batter into it.

5. Mix the peanut butter, butter, Splenda, egg and protein powder together and spoon the mixture on top of the brownie batter. Bake for 15 minutes – do not overbake.

Yield: 16 brownies, each with 5 grams of carbohydrate and 1 gram of fibre, for a total of 4 grams of usable carbs and 12 grams of protein.

↻ Fudge Toffee

Jen Eloff of sweety.com, says her husband Ian is mad for this toffee. Another winner from *Splendid Low-Carbing*.

> 250 g Splenda
> 100 g whole milk powder (available in health food stores)
> 100 g natural whey protein powder
> 100 g unsalted butter, melted
> 75 ml whipping cream
> 2 Tbsp water
> 50 g unsweetened baking chocolate, melted

1. In a large bowl, combine the Splenda, milk powder and protein powder.
2. In a small bowl, combine the butter, cream and water. Stir this into the dry ingredients. Stir in the melted chocolate until well combined.
3. Press the mixture into a 23 x 23-cm baking dish. Freeze for approximately 30 minutes, then refrigerate. Cut into squares and serve.

Yield: Makes 36 squares, each with 3 grams of carbohydrate, a trace of fibre and 3 grams of protein.

↻ Sugar-Free Chocolate Mousse To Die For!

This is the very first low-carb dessert I came up with and it still amazes people.

> 4-serving size pack of chocolate sugar-free instant pudding mix
> 300 g soft tofu
> 1 heaped Tbsp unsweetened cocoa powder
> 1/4 to 1/2 tsp instant coffee crystals
> (more, if you like mocha flavouring)
> 350 ml double cream, chilled

1. Use an electric mixer to beat the pudding mix, tofu, cocoa powder and coffee crystals until very smooth.
2. In a separate bowl, whip the cream until just about stiff.
3. Turn the mixer to its lowest setting, blend in the pudding mixture and turn off the mixer – quickly. (If you over-beat, you'll end up with chocolate butter.)

Yield: Made with 225 ml of double cream, you'll get 6 servings, each with 8 grams of carbohydrate and 1 gram of fibre, for a total of 7 grams of usable carbs and 5 grams of protein. Made with 350 ml of double cream, your yield increases to at least 7 servings, each with 7.5 grams of carbohydrate and just under 1 gram of fibre, for a total of about 6.5 grams of usable carbs and 4 grams of protein. (I like this made with the smaller amount of cream, for a sturdier texture, but I know people who like it with the larger amount, for a fluffier texture. It's your choice.)

Sugar-Free Vanilla Mousse to Die For! Here's one for those non-chocoholics out there: just use sugar-free vanilla instant pudding mix and a teaspoon of vanilla extract and omit the cocoa powder and the coffee crystals.

Yield: Made with 225 ml of cream, you'll get 6 servings, each with 7 grams of carbohydrate, a trace of fibre and 4 grams of protein. Made with 350 ml of cream, you'll get 7 servings, each with 6.5 grams of carbohydrate, a trace of fibre and 4 grams of protein.

◯ Strawberry Cups

This is a good make-ahead dinner-party dessert and it's a really beautiful colour.

225 ml water

4-serving size pack of sugar-free lemon gelatine

300 g frozen unsweetened strawberries, partly thawed

225 ml double cream

1/2 tsp vanilla extract

1 tsp Splenda (if desired)

1. Bring the water to the boil. Put the gelatine and boiling water in a blender and whirl for 10 to 15 seconds to dissolve the gelatine. Add the strawberries and whirl again, just long enough to blend in the berries.

2. Put the blender container in the refrigerator for 10 minutes, or just until the mixture starts to thicken a bit.

3. Add 200 ml of the double cream and run the blender just long enough to mix it all in (10 to 15 seconds). Pour into 5 or 6 pretty dessert cups and chill. Whip the remaining cream with the vanilla and a teaspoon of Splenda (if using), to garnish.

Yield: About 5 servings, each with 6 grams of carbohydrate and 1 gram of fibre, for a total of 5 grams of usable carbs and 3 grams of protein.

☽ Mixed Berry Cups

For you raspberry and blackberry lovers, here's a quick and tasty dessert.

> 4-serving size pack of sugar-free raspberry gelatine
> 225 ml boiling water
> 2 tsp lemon juice
> Grated peel of 1/2 orange
> 100 g frozen blackberries, partly thawed
> 225 ml double cream
> 1/2 tsp vanilla extract
> 1 tsp Splenda (optional)

1. Put the gelatine, water, lemon juice and orange peel in a blender and whirl for 10 to 15 seconds to dissolve the gelatin. Add the blackberries and blend again, just long enough to mix in the berries.

2. Put the blender container in the refrigerator for 10 minutes, or just until the mixture starts to thicken a bit. Add 200 ml double cream and run the blender just long enough to mix it all in (10 to 15 seconds). Pour into 5 or 6 pretty dessert cups and chill.

3. Whip the remaining cream with vanilla and a teaspoon of Splenda (if using), to garnish.

Yield: 5 servings, each with 5 grams of carbohydrate and 1 gram of fibre, for a total of 4 grams of usable carbs and 2 grams of protein.

☉ Hazelnut Crust

This is a great substitute for a digestive biscuit-crumb crust with any cheesecake. And I think it tastes even better than the original.

225 g hazelnuts

50 g vanilla-flavoured whey protein powder

4 Tbsp butter, melted

1. Preheat the oven to 180°C/Gas Mark 4.

2. Put the hazelnuts in a food processor with the S-blade in place. Pulse the processor until the hazelnuts are ground to a medium-fine texture. Add the protein powder and butter and run to combine.

3. Spray a pie plate or springform tin, depending on which your recipe specifies, with nonstick cooking spray and press this mixture firmly and evenly into the pan. Don't try to build your crust too high up the sides, but if you're using a springform tin, be sure to cover the seam around the bottom and press the crust into place firmly over it.

4. Place your crust in a preheated oven on the bottom rack and bake for 12 to 15 minutes, or until lightly browned and slightly pulling away from the sides of the pan. Remove the crust from the oven and let it cool while you make the filling.

Yield: Assuming 12 slices of cheesecake, this crust will add to each slice 4 grams of carbohydrate and 1 gram of fibre, for a total of 3 grams of usable carbs and 10 grams of protein.

Almond Crust: Here's another great nut crust for you to try. Just substitute 200 g almonds for the hazelnuts in Hazelnut Crust and decrease the vanilla-flavoured whey protein powder to 30 g. Follow the directions to make the crust and bake for 10 to 12 minutes, or until lightly golden. Cool.

Yield: Assuming 12 slices of cheesecake, this crust will add to each slice 4 grams of carbohydrate and 2 grams of fibre, for a total of 2 grams of usable carbs and 7 grams of protein.

◯ Chocolate Cheesecake

You'll be surprised how good a cheesecake you can make from cottage cheese! It's high in protein, too.

> 500 g cottage cheese
>
> 2 eggs
>
> 125 ml soured cream
>
> 50 g unsweetened baking chocolate, melted
>
> 30 g Splenda
>
> 1 Hazelnut Crust or Almond Crust (see page 453),
>   prebaked in a large, deep pie plate

1. Preheat the oven to 190°C/Gas Mark 5.
2. Put the cottage cheese, eggs and soured cream in your blender. Run the blender, scraping down the sides now and then, until this mixture is very smooth. Add the melted chocolate and Splenda and blend again.
3. Pour into the prebaked crust. Place the cake on the top rack of the oven and place a flat dish of water on the bottom rack. Bake for 40 to 45 minutes.
4. Cool, then chill well before serving. Serve with whipped cream.

Yield: 12 servings, each with 7 grams of carbohydrate and 2 grams of fibre, for a total of 5 grams of usable carbs and 16 grams of protein. (Analysis includes the crust.)

᭑ Cheesecake to Go with Fruit

This lemon-vanilla cheesecake is wonderful with strawberries, blueberries, cherries – any fruit you care to use. It also makes a nice breakfast.

> 500 g cottage cheese
>
> 2 eggs
>
> 125 ml soured cream
>
> 30 g vanilla flavoured whey protein powder
>
> 30 g Splenda
>
> Grated peel and juice of 1 fresh lemon
>
> 1 tsp vanilla extract
>
> 1 Hazelnut Crust or Almond Crust (see page 453), prebaked in a large, deep pie plate

1. Preheat the oven to 190°C/Gas Mark 5.

2. Put the cottage cheese, eggs, soured cream, protein powder, Splenda, lemon peel and juice and vanilla extract in a blender and blend until very smooth.

3. Pour into the prebaked crust. Place the cake on the top rack of the oven and place a flat dish of water on the bottom rack. Bake for 30 to 40 minutes. Cool, then chill well before serving.

Yield: 12 servings, each with 8 grams of carbohydrate and 2 grams of fibre, for a total of 6 grams of usable carbs and 21 grams of protein. (Analysis includes crust.)

🍓 Serve this cheesecake with the fruit of your choice. I like to serve it with thawed frozen, unsweetened strawberries, blueberries or peaches, mashed coarsely with a fork and sweetened slightly with Splenda. If you use 170 g of strawberries with 2 tablespoons of Splenda for the whole cake, you'll add 2 grams of carbohydrate per slice, plus a trace of fibre and a trace of protein. Use 170 g cherries – you can get these tinned, with no added sugar – and sweeten them with 30 g Splenda and you'll add 3 grams per slice. I'm lucky enough to have a cherry tree, and cherry cheesecake is one of the joys of early summer for me!

☉ Sunshine Cheesecake

This has a lovely, creamy texture and a bright, sunshine-y orange flavour.

225 g cottage cheese

225 g cream cheese, beaten to soften

225 ml soured cream

4 eggs

Grated peel of 1 orange

1 Tbsp orange extract

90 g Splenda, or to taste

2 Tbsp lemon juice

Tiny pinch salt

1 Hazelnut Crust or Almond Crust (see page 453), prebaked in a springform tin

1. Put the cottage cheese, cream cheese, soured cream, eggs, orange peel, orange extract, Splenda, lemon juice and salt in a blender and run the blender until everything is well-blended and a bit fluffy.
2. Pour into the prebaked crust. Place the cake on the top rack of the oven and place a flat dish of water on the bottom rack. Bake for 50 minutes. The cheesecake will still jiggle slightly in the centre when you take it out.
3. Cool, then chill well before serving.

Yield: 12 servings, each with 8 grams of carbohydrate and 2 grams of fibre, for a total of 6 grams of usable carbs and 17 grams of protein. (Analysis includes crust.)

🍓 This is wonderful with sugar-free chocolate syrup. Many grocery stores carry it; it's worth your while to take a look.

↻ Blackbottomed Mockahlua Cheesecake

You'll have to make yourself some Mockahlua before you can make this. What better incentive could you have?

Blackbottom Layer

3 sugar-free dark chocolate bars (about 30 g each)

75 ml double cream

1 Almond Crust (see page 453), prebaked in a springform tin

Mockahlua Filling

700 g cream cheese, softened

100 g Splenda

200 ml soured cream

1 Tbsp vanilla extract

4 eggs

105 ml Mockahlua (see page 481)

1. Preheat the oven to 170ºC/Gas Mark 3.
2. Over the lowest possible heat, melt the chocolate bars (preferably in a heat diffuser or a double boiler, to keep the chocolate from burning). When the chocolate is melted, stir in the cream, blending well. Pour over the crust and spread evenly.
3. In large bowl, use an electric mixer to beat the cream cheese until smooth, scraping down the sides of the bowl often. Beat in the Splenda and soured cream and mix well. Beat in the vanilla and eggs, one by one, beating until very smooth and creamy. Beat in the Mockahlua last and mix well.
4. Pour into the chocolate-coated crust. Place the cake in the oven and on the rack below it or on the floor of the oven place a flat dish of water. Bake for 1 hour.
5. Cool in the pan on a wire rack. Chill well before serving.

Yield: 12 servings, each with 10 grams of carbohydrate and 2 grams of fibre, for a total of 8 grams of usable carbs and 18 grams of protein. (Analysis includes crust, but omits the polyols in the sugar-free chocolate.)

↻ Butter-Pecan Cheesecake

All you butterscotch fans are going to love this one.

Pecan Cookie Crust

110 g butter, softened

60 g Splenda

75 g vanilla-flavoured whey protein powder

75 g chopped pecans

1/2 tsp salt

Butterscotch Filling

700 g cream cheese, beaten to soften

100 g Splenda

200 ml soured cream

2 tsp butter flavouring

1 Tbsp vanilla extract

1 Tbsp black treacle

4 eggs

1. Preheat the oven to 170ºC/Gas Mark 3.
2. Beat the butter and Splenda together until light and creamy. Then beat in the vanilla whey, pecans and salt. Spray a springform tin with non-stick cooking spray and press the crust evenly and firmly into the bottom of the pan, plus just far enough up the sides to cover the seam at the bottom.
3. Bake for 12 to 15 minutes, until lightly golden. Set aside to cool while you make the filling.
4. In a large bowl, use an electric mixer to beat the cream cheese until smooth, scraping down the sides of the bowl often. Next beat in the Splenda and the soured cream and mix well. Beat in the butter flavouring, vanilla and treacle; add the eggs one by one, beating until very smooth and creamy.
5. Pour the mixture into the crust. Place the cake in the oven and on the oven rack below it or on the floor of the oven place a flat dish of water. Bake for 1 hour.

6. Cool in the pan on a wire rack. Chill well before serving.

🍓 For a nice touch, decorate this with some pecan halves.

Yield: 12 servings, each with 9 grams of carbohydrate and 1 gram of fibre, for a total of 8 grams of usable carbs and 18 grams of protein. (Analysis includes crust.)

♋ Pumpkin Cheesecake

Vicki Cash gives people in America this elegant alternative to pumpkin pie for Thanksgiving dessert. It's from her *Low Carb Success Calendar* and it's not to be missed.

> 50 g, coarsely chopped
> 500 g cream cheese, softened
> 1/2 to 100 g Splenda sweetener
> 2 tsp vanilla extract
> 350 g pure tinned pumpkin
> 125 ml soured cream
> 4 eggs
> 1 1/2 tsp cinnamon
> 1 tsp ginger
> 1/2 tsp nutmeg
> 1/4 tsp ground cloves
> 1/4 tsp salt

1. Preheat the oven to 150°C/Gas Mark 2.
2. Butter the bottom and sides of a 25-cm springform cheesecake tin. Sprinkle the bottom of the tin with chopped pecans, distributing evenly.
3. In a large mixing bowl, use an electric mixer to beat the cream cheese, Splenda and vanilla until fluffy, stopping occasionally to scrape the sides of the bowl and beaters.

4. Add the pumpkin and soured cream, mixing thoroughly on medium speed. Add the eggs one at a time, mixing thoroughly between each one. Mix in the cinnamon, ginger, nutmeg, cloves and salt.

5. Pour the batter over the nuts in the tin. Bake for 60 to 70 minutes, or until a knife placed in centre comes out clean. Cool for 20 minutes before removing from the tin and chill for at least 2 hours before serving.

Yield: 12 servings, each with 7 grams of carbohydrate and 1 gram of fibre, for a total of 6 grams of usable carbs and 6 grams of protein.

☉ Grasshopper Cheesecake

If you're a mint-chocolate chip ice cream fan, this is your cheesecake! Chocolate extract can be a little hard to find, but it's worth it for this. If you can only find 'flavouring', not extract (you'll know because flavourings are in teeny little bottles), keep in mind that these are far more concentrated and taste as you go.

1 Almond Crust or Hazelnut Crust (see page 453),
  prebaked in a springform tin

Chocolate Layer
3 sugar-free dark chocolate bars (about 30 g each)
75 ml double cream

Grasshopper Filling
700 g cream cheese, softened
100 g Splenda
200 ml soured cream
1 tsp peppermint extract
1 1/2 Tbsp chocolate extract
1 or 2 drops green food colouring (optional, but pretty)
4 eggs

1. Preheat oven to 170°C/Gas Mark 3. In the top of a double boiler over hot water (or in a heavy-bottomed saucepan over the lowest possible heat), melt the chocolate and whisk in the cream until smooth. Spread this mixture evenly over the crust and set aside.

2. In a large bowl, use an electric mixer to beat the cream cheese until smooth, scraping down the sides of the bowl often. Beat in the Splenda and the soured cream and mix well. Beat in the peppermint and chocolate extracts, food colouring (if using) and eggs, one by one, beating until very smooth and creamy.

3. Pour the mixture into the chocolate-coated crust. Place the cake in the oven and on the oven rack below it or on the floor of the oven place a flat dish of water. Bake for 1 hour.

4. Cool in the tin on a wire rack. Chill well before serving.

Yield: 12 servings, each with 9 grams of carbohydrate and 2 grams of fibre, for a total of 7 grams of usable carbs and 18 grams of protein. (Analysis includes crust, but omits the polyols in the sugar-free chocolate.)

◯ Kathy's Peanut Butter Protein Bars

From reader Kathy Miller. These would make a filling snack, or even breakfast or lunch.

> 50 g butter
>
> 100 g natural peanut butter (preferably chunky), at room temperature
>
> 100 g cream cheese, softened
>
> 175 g cups vanilla-flavoured whey protein powder
>
> 1 Tbsp vanilla
>
> 2 Tbsp Splenda
>
> 50 g chopped peanuts

1. Melt the butter (a microwave works well for this) and add the peanut butter and softened cream cheese to it. Mix together with a spoon (no need to get out a blender or mixer) and then add the protein powder, vanilla, Splenda and peanuts; stir well. (It will be very crumbly.)
2. Taste and see if it is sweet enough. If not, add a little more Splenda.
3. Press the mixture firmly into a 20 x 20-cm pan. Slice into 12 pieces and put the whole pan in the freezer. Remove when the bars are firm.

Yield: 12 bars, each with 9 grams of carbohydrate and 1 gram of fibre, for a total of 8 grams of usable carbs and 31 grams of protein.

> 🍓 For storage, it's a good idea to package these in individual freezer bags in the freezer.

◯ Great Balls of Protein!

You may recognise this updated version of an old health food standby.

> 450-g jar natural peanut butter, oil and all
>
> 225 g vanilla-flavoured whey protein powder
>
> Splenda, saccharine or whatever sweetener you prefer (optional)

Sesame seeds (optional)

Unsweetened desiccated coconut (optional)

Sugar-free chocolate bars (optional)

Cocoa powder (optional)

🍓 This is easiest to make if you have a powerful stand mixer or a heavy-duty food processor. If you don't, don't try to use a smaller appliance – you'll only burn it out and destroy it! Rather than dooming your old mixer, just roll up your sleeves, scrub your hands and dive in.

1. Thoroughly combine the peanut butter with the protein powder. (I find that working in about 30 g of the protein powder at a time is about right.) This should make a stiff, somewhat crumbly dough.

2. Work the sweetener of your choice (if using) into the dough.

🍓 It's best to sprinkle any sweetener evenly before combining it with a mixture this thick.

3. Roll into balls about 2.5 cm in diameter.

4. It's nice to coat these with something. If you like sesame seeds, you can toast them by shaking them in a dry, heavy frying pan over medium heat until they start popping and jumping around the pan and then roll the balls in them while they're still warm. You could roll them in coconut, if you prefer; most supermarkets sell it unsweetened and shredded. Again, you can toast it lightly in a dry frying pan and add a little Splenda. Or you could melt sugar-free chocolate bars and dip your Balls of Protein in chocolate – although it would probably be simpler to chop them up and mix them in. Another option is to roll them in unsweetened cocoa.

Yield: About 50 balls, each with 3 grams of carbohydrate, a trace of fibre and 10 grams of protein. (Analysis does not include coatings for balls.)

☞ Whipped Topping

The pudding adds a very nice texture to this topping and it helps the whipped cream 'stand up', as well as adding a slightly sweet vanilla flavour to the cream, of course.

> 225 ml double cream, well chilled
>
> 1 Tbsp vanilla sugar-free instant pudding powder

Whip the cream and pudding mix together until the cream is stiff.

Yield: About 500 ml, or 16 servings of 2 tablespoons, each with only a trace of carbohydrate, no fibre and a trace of protein.

🍓 This is incredible with berries, as a simple but elegant dessert. It's also terrific on Irish Coffee!

☞ Lemon Sherbet

Low-carb, low-fat, low-calorie – and delicious!

> 4-serving size pack of sugar-free lemon gelatine
>
> 500 ml boiling water
>
> 500 ml plain yoghurt
>
> 2 tsp lemon extract
>
> 3 Tbsp Splenda
>
> 30 g vanilla-flavoured whey protein powder

1. Put the gelatine powder in the blender and add the water. Blend for 20 seconds, or just long enough to dissolve the gelatin.

2. Add the other ingredients and blend well. Put the blender container in the refrigerator and let it chill for 10 to 15 minutes. Take it out and blend it again for about 10 seconds, chill it for another 10 to 15 minutes and then give it another quick blend it when it's done chilling.

3. Pour the sherbet mixture into a home ice cream freezer and freeze according to the directions for your freezer.

Yield: 8 servings of 125 ml – but just try to eat only 125 ml! Just try! Each serving has 2.5 grams of carbohydrate (if you use the figure of

4 grams of carbs in 225 ml of plain yoghurt); even if you go with the count on the label, this only has 4 grams of carbohydrate per serving, no fibre and 9 grams of protein.

ᕗ Creamy Strawberry Ice Lollies

From sweety.com's Jennifer Eloff and her terrific cookbook *Splendid Low-Carbing*, these popsicles are bound to liven up your summer.

>   350 ml plain yoghurt
>   225 ml double cream
>   75 g Splenda
>   150 g frozen, unsweetened strawberries
>   1/4 tsp strawberry Kool-Aid powder or cordial

In a blender, blend the yoghurt, cream, Splenda, strawberries and Kool-Aid powder until smooth. Pour into ice lolly moulds and freeze.

Yield: 13 ice lollies, each with 3 grams of carbohydrate, a trace of fibre and 1 gram of protein.

Orange Ice Lollies: Make just like Creamy Strawberry Ice Lollies, only substitute 2 tablespoons of frozen orange juice concentrate for the strawberries and instead of the Kool-Aid powder or cordial, add 2 teaspoons lemon juice and 1/4 teaspoon orange extract.

Yield: 13 ice lollies, each with 4 grams of carbohydrate, a trace of fibre and 1 gram of protein.

Coconut Banana Creamy Ice Lollies: In a blender, blend the following until smooth: 400 ml tinned unsweetened coconut milk, 225 ml plain yoghurt, 125 g Splenda, 150 ml double cream, 1 medium banana (sliced) and 1/2 tsp banana or vanilla extract. Pour into ice lolly moulds and freeze.

Yield: 16 ice lollies, each with 5 grams of carbohydrate and 1 gram of fibre, for a total of 4 grams of usable carbs and 1 gram of protein.

☉ Flavoured Whip

Reader David Drake Hunter sends this easy dessert recipe.

500 ml double cream, chilled

1 or 2 tsp sugar-free fruit-flavoured drink mix powder (your choice of flavour)

Pour the cream into a bowl, add the drink mix crystals to taste and beat into whipped cream.

Yield: About 8 servings, each with only a trace of carbohydrate, fibre and protein.

☉ Maria's Flan

My childhood friend Maria found me on the Internet a couple of years ago and we got together. Her mother is Colombian, so Maria had grown up eating flan, a traditional Latin–American dessert. Here's the version we came up with together.

Syrup

2 Tbsp Splenda

1 tsp black treacle

2 Tbsp water

Custard

225 ml double cream

225 ml milk and cream, mixed

6 eggs

1 tsp vanilla extract

Pinch of nutmeg

Pinch of salt

75 g Splenda

1. Preheat the oven to 180°C/Gas Mark 4.

2. Combine the Splenda, treacle and water, stirring until the lumps are gone.

3. Spray an ovenproof glass pie plate with nonstick cooking spray and pour the mixture into it, spreading it over the bottom. Microwave for 2 minutes on Medium power.

   🍓 You could substitute the sugar-free syrup of your choice for this syrup; just use 2 to 3 Tbsp.

4. Whisk together well the double cream, milk-cream mixture, eggs, vanilla, nutmeg, salt and Splenda, and pour the mixture over the syrup in the pie plate.

5. Place the pie plate carefully in a large, flat baking dish and pour water around it, not quite up to the brim of the pie plate. Put the baking dish with the pie plate in its water bath in the oven. Bake for 45 minutes, or until a knife inserted in the centre comes out clean.

6. Cool and cut the flan into wedges. Traditionally, each piece is inverted on a plate, with the syrup on top, to serve.

Yield: 8 generous servings, each with 5 grams of carbohydrate, no fibre and 6 grams of protein.

⟲ Mocha Custard

225 ml boiling water

30 g unsweetened baking chocolate

1 rounded tsp instant coffee crystals

225 ml double cream

3 eggs

30 g Splenda

A pinch of salt

1. Preheat the oven to 150°C/Gas Mark 2.
2. Put the boiling water in your blender container and drop in the chocolate. Leave it to stand for 5 minutes or so.
3. Add the coffee crystals, double cream, eggs, Splenda and salt, and blend for a minute or so.
4. Spray a 1-litre casserole with nonstick cooking spray and pour the mixture into it. (If you prefer, pour into individual custard cups.)
5. Place in a larger dish filled with hot water, so the casserole or custard cups are in the water bath and place the entire thing in the over. Bake for 1 hour and 20 minutes.
6. Cool, then chill well before serving. (The chilling makes a big difference to the texture.)

Yield: 4 generous servings, each with 6 grams of carbohydrate and 1 gram of fibre, for a total of 5 grams of usable carbs and 6 grams of protein.

☾ Lemon-Vanilla Custard

Don't save this just for dessert – it makes a lovely breakfast, too.

225 ml double cream
225 ml milk and cream, mixed
3 eggs
30 g Splenda
1 tsp lemon extract
1/2 tsp vanilla extract
2 Tbsp vanilla-flavoured whey protein powder
Pinch of salt
Grated peel of 1/2 lemon

1. Preheat the oven to 150°C/Gas Mark 2.
2. Put all the ingredients in a blender and blend well.
3. Spray a 1-litre casserole with nonstick cooking spray and pour the mixture into it. (If you prefer, use individual custard cups.) Place in a larger dish filled with hot water, so the casserole or custard cups are in the water bath and place the entire thing in the oven. Bake for 2 hours. Cool and chill well.

Yield: 4 generous servings, each with 8 grams of carbohydrate, a trace of fibre and 13 grams of protein.

ꙩ Peanut Butter Silk Pie

Incredible, decadent, outrageous, utterly scrumptious. A real special-occasion dessert and a sure-fire crowd pleaser.

Crust
200 g shelled raw hazelnuts
50 g butter, melted
50 g vanilla-flavoured whey protein powder

Chocolate Layer
4 sugar-free dark chocolate bars (about 30 g each)
5 Tbsp double cream
1/4 tsp instant coffee crystals

Peanut Butter Silk Layer
225 g cream cheese, softened
125 g Splenda
225 g creamy natural peanut butter
1 Tbsp butter, melted
1 tsp vanilla extract
225 ml double cream

1. Preheat the oven to 170°C/Gas Mark 3.
2. Use the S-blade in a food processor to grind the hazelnuts to a meal. Add the butter and protein powder and run until well combined.
3. Spray a large pie plate with nonstick cooking spray and press the hazelnut mixture firmly into bottom of the pie plate (it won't build up the side very far).
4. Bake for 10 to 12 minutes, or until lightly browned. Remove from the oven to cool.
5. Melt the chocolate over the lowest possible heat, as chocolate burns very easily. (If you have a double boiler or a heat diffuser, this would be a good time to use it!) Whisk in the cream and coffee crystals and continue stirring until the crystals disappear. Spread this mixture evenly over the bottom of the hazelnut crust.

6. Use an electric mixer to beat the cream cheese, Splenda, peanut butter, butter and vanilla together until creamy.

7. In a separate bowl, whip the double cream until stiff. Turn the mixer to the lowest setting and beat the whipped cream into the peanut butter mixture one-third at a time.

8. Spread the peanut butter filling gently over the chocolate layer and chill. (This is best made a day in advance, to allow plenty of time for chilling.)

Yield: 10 generous servings, each with 12 grams of carbohydrate and 2 grams of fibre, for a total of 10 grams of usable carbs and 20 grams of protein.

☽ Pumpkin Pie with Pecan Praline Crust

I'm very proud of this recipe. In the USA, it would be served at Thanksgiving Dinner and no one would guess it's made without sugar.

Crust

250 g shelled raw pecans

1/4 tsp salt

2 1/2 Tbsp Splenda

1 1/2 tsp black treacle

4 Tbsp butter, melted

2 Tbsp water

Pumpkin Pie Filling

400 g tinned pumpkin

350 ml double cream

3 eggs

100 g Splenda

1/2 tsp salt

2 tsp black treacle

1 Tbsp mixed spice

1/2 tsp ground ginger

1. Preheat the oven to 180°C/Gas Mark 4.

2. Put the pecans and salt in a food processor with the S-blade in place. Pulse until the pecans are chopped to a medium consistency.

3. Add the Splenda, treacle and butter, and pulse again until well blended. Add the water and pulse again, until well combined. At this point, you'll have a soft, sticky mass.

4. Spray a 25-cm pie plate with nonstick cooking spray, or butter it well. Turn the pecan mixture into it and press firmly in place, all over the bottom and up the sides by 4 cm or so. Try to get it an even thickness, with no holes and if you wish, run a finger or a knife around the top edge, to get an even, nice-looking line.

5. Bake for about 18 minutes. Cool.

6. Increase the oven temperature to 220°C/Gas Mark 7.

7. Combine the pumpkin, double cream, eggs, Splenda, salt, treacle, ground ginger and spice in a bowl and whisk together well. Pour into the prebaked and cooled pie shell. Bake for 15 minutes, lower the oven temperature to 180°C/Gas Mark 4 and bake for an additional 45 minutes. Cool and serve with whipped cream.

Yield: 8 servings, each with 14 grams of carbohydrate and 4 grams of fibre, for a total of 10 grams of usable carbs and 6 grams of protein.

Wondering how many carbs you're really saving by making your pumpkin pie from scratch? A lot – especially when you consider that a slice of commercial frozen pumpkin pie has 37 grams of usable carbs, or well over three times as much!

☺ Helen's Chocolate Bread Pudding

Helen was my dad's mother and this was our family's traditional Christmas dessert the whole time I was growing up. People have threatened to marry into the family to get the secret recipe, but since this is the decarbed version, it's not a secret! It is still high-carb enough that you'll want to save it for a special occasion, though.

> 500 ml milk and cream, mixed
>
> 225 ml double cream
>
> 225 ml water
>
> 6 slices 'light' white bread
> (5 grams of usable carbs per slice or less)
>
> 75 g unsweetened baking chocolate
>
> 75 g Splenda
>
> 2 eggs, beaten
>
> 1 tsp vanilla extract
>
> Pinch salt

1. Preheat the oven to 190°C/Gas Mark 5.
2. Combine the milk-cream mixture, double cream and water, and scald; bring it just up to a simmer.
3. While it's heating, spray a large casserole with nonstick cooking spray, tear the bread into small bits and put them in the dish. Pour the hot milk and cream mixture over the bread and let it stand for 10 minutes.
4. Melt the chocolate and add it to the bread mixture; it's good to use a little of the hot cream to rinse out the pan you melted the chocolate in, so you get all of it. Stir well. Now stir in the Splenda, eggs, vanilla and salt, mixing very well. Bake for 1 hour, or until firm. Serve with Not-So-Hard Sauce (see overleaf).

Yield: 8 servings, each with 12 grams of carbohydrate and just over 1 gram of fibre, for a total of 11 grams of usable carbs and 7 grams of protein.

↻ Not-So-Hard Sauce

Traditional hard sauce is made with sugar, butter and egg, plus vanilla and rum or brandy, and when it's refrigerated it gets quite hard – hence the name. However, with Splenda instead of sugar, my hard sauce just didn't work – it fell apart in little globs. I added cream cheese and it all came together, but it doesn't get quite so hard when refrigerated, which is why this is Not-So-Hard Sauce. It still tastes great, though!

> 125 g Splenda
>
> 5 Tbsp butter, softened
>
> 1/8 tsp salt
>
> 1 tsp vanilla extract
>
> 1 egg
>
> 30 g cream cheese, softened
>
> Nutmeg

1. Use an electric mixer to beat the Splenda and butter together until well blended. Beat in the salt, vanilla extract and egg. At this point, you'll be sure you've made a dreadful mistake.

2. Beat in the cream cheese and watch the sauce smooth out! Mix very well, until light and fluffy. Pile your Not-So-Hard Sauce into a pretty serving dish, sprinkle it lightly with nutmeg and refrigerate until well-chilled.

Yield: About 225 ml, or a 2-tablespoon serving of sauce for each serving of Helen's Chocolate Bread Pudding. Each serving will have 3 grams of carbohydrate, no fibre and 1 gram of protein.

ꝏ Coeur à la Crème

This is a classic French dessert, traditionally made in a heart-shaped mould. Coeur à la Crème moulds are hard to come by, but you can buy an average 500-g heart-shaped mould and make three or four holes in it with a nail, which is what I did. Serve with fresh strawberries or Strawberry Sauce (see overleaf) for a truly beautiful Valentine's Day dessert.

>   500 g cream cheese, softened
>   2 Tbsp Splenda
>   3 Tbsp double cream
>   2 Tbsp soured cream
>   1/4 tsp salt

🍓 Warning: This is not a quick dessert to whip up before your sweetheart comes over. You need to start making this at least 24 hours in advance, to give it plenty of time to chill.

1. Use an electric mixer to beat the cream cheese until it's very creamy. Beat in the Splenda, double cream, soured cream and salt, mixing very well.

2. Line your mould with a double layer of dampened muslin and pack the cheese mixture into it, pressing it in well. Place the mould on a plate to catch any moisture that drains out and chill for at least 24 hours.

Yield: 8 servings, each with 2 grams of carbohydrate, no fibre and 5 grams of protein.

⟲ Strawberry Sauce

Traditionally, Coeur à la Crème is served with fresh strawberries, but I make this for Valentine's Day and I'm generally not impressed with the quality of the fresh strawberries I can get in February. I'd rather use frozen.

> 450 g frozen, unsweetened strawberries, thawed
>
> 1 Tbsp lemon juice
>
> 2 or 3 Tbsp Splenda

Simply pour your strawberries and any liquid in the package into a bowl and stir in the lemon juice and Splenda. Mash your strawberries a little with a fork, if you'd like; I like mine fairly chunky.

Yield: 8 servings, each with 6 grams of carbohydrate and 1 gram of fibre, for a total of 5 grams of usable carbs and only a trace of protein.

⟲ Courgette-Carrot Cake

> About 180 g hazelnuts
>
> 2 eggs
>
> 125 ml oil
>
> 125 ml yoghurt
>
> 50 g vanilla-flavoured whey protein powder
>
> 1 tsp baking soda
>
> 1/2 tsp salt
>
> 2/3 cup Splenda
>
> 1 1/2 tsp cinnamon
>
> 1/4 tsp nutmeg
>
> 30 g grated courgette
>
> 30 g grated carrot

1. Preheat the oven to 180ºC/Gas Mark 4.

2. In a food processor with the S-blade in place, use the pulse control to grind the hazelnuts to a mealy consistency. (You want 150 g of ground hazelnuts when you're done and for some inexplicable reason they seem to actually grow a little rather than shrink a little when you grind them.) Set the ground hazelnuts aside.

3. In a large mixing bowl, whisk the eggs until well blended. Add the oil, yoghurt, ground hazelnuts, protein powder, baking soda, salt, Splenda, cinnamon and nutmeg, mixing well after each addition. (It's especially important that the baking soda be well distributed through the mixture.) Add the courgette and carrots last, mixing well.

4. Thoroughly coat a ring mould or bundt tin with nonstick cooking spray and turn the batter into it.

   If you sprayed your mould or tin ahead of time, give it another shot just before adding the batter. And don't expect the batter to fill the pan to the rim; it fills my bundt tin about halfway.

5. Bake for 45 minutes and turn out gently on to a wire rack to cool.

Yield: 8 generous servings, each with 8 grams of carbohydrate and 2 grams of fibre, for a total of 6 grams of usable carbs and 16 grams of protein.

   This doesn't need a darned thing – it's simply delicious exactly the way it is. If you wish to gild the lily, however, you could top it with whipped topping, pumpkin cream or cream cheese frosting. This cake, by the way, makes a fabulous breakfast and since it's loaded with protein and good fats, it should keep you going all morning.

⟲ Adam's Chocolate Birthday Cake

I made a low-carb feast for my friend Adam's birthday and this was the cake. It's not a layer cake, it's a snack-type cake: dense, moist and fudgy – a lot like brownies. It's easy, too, because it needs no frosting, tasting great just as it is.

110 g finely ground hazelnuts

50 g vanilla-flavoured whey protein powder

3 Tbsp unsweetened cocoa powder

1 tsp baking soda

125 g Splenda

1/2 tsp salt

5 Tbsp oil (peanut, sunflower, as you prefer)

1 Tbsp cider vinegar

225 ml cold water

1. Preheat the oven to 180°C/Gas Mark 4.
2. In a bowl, combine the hazelnuts, protein powder, cocoa, baking soda, Splenda and salt, and stir them together quite well. (Make sure there are no lumps of baking soda!)
3. Spray a 25 x 25-cm baking dish with nonstick cooking spray and turn the batter into it. Make two holes in this batter. Pour the oil into one, the vinegar into the other and the water over the whole thing. Mix with a spoon or fork until everything's well combined. Bake for 30 minutes.

Yield: 9 servings, each with 7 grams of carbohydrate and 1 gram of fibre, for a total of 6 grams of usable carbs and 12 grams of protein.

ᔕ Gingerbread

I've always loved gingerbread and this is as good as any high-carb gingerbread I've ever had! Don't worry about that courgette; it completely disappears, leaving only moistness behind.

> 100 g ground almonds
>
> 50 g vanilla-flavoured whey protein powder
>
> 1 tsp baking soda
>
> 1/2 tsp salt
>
> 2 1/2 tsp ground ginger
>
> 1/2 tsp ground cinnamon
>
> 60 g Splenda
>
> 125 ml plain yoghurt
>
> 75 ml oil
>
> 1 tsp black treacle
>
> 1 egg
>
> 2 Tbsp water
>
> .50 g shredded courgette

1. Preheat the oven to 180ºC/Gas Mark 4.
2. In a mixing bowl, combine the almonds, protein powder, baking soda, salt, ginger, cinnamon and Splenda, and mix them well.
3. In a separate bowl or measuring jug, whisk together the yoghurt, oil, treacle, egg and water. Pour into the dry ingredients and whisk just until everything's well combined and there are no dry spots. Add the courgette and whisk briefly to distribute evenly.
4. Spray a 20 x 20-cm baking dish with nonstick cooking spray and turn the batter into it. Bake for 30 minutes, or until a cocktail stick inserted in the middle comes out clean.

Yield: 9 servings, each with 9 grams of carbohydrate, a trace of fibre and 17 grams of protein.

🍓 Try serving this with Whipped Topping (see page 464).

◌ Cream Cheese Frosting

This is my sister's recipe. It's good on the Courgette-Carrot Cake or the Gingerbread.

> 200 ml double cream, chilled
> 225 g cream cheese, softened
> 60 g Splenda
> 1 tsp vanilla

1. Whip the double cream until it's stiff.
2. In a separate bowl, beat the cream cheese until very smooth, then beat in the Splenda and vanilla. Turn the mixer to its lowest speed and blend in the whipped cream, then turn off the mixer, quick!

Yield: 9 servings, each with 3 grams of carbohydrate, no fibre and 2 grams of protein.

◌ Gingered Melon

Light and elegant – and people following a low-fat diet can eat it, too.

> 1/2 ripe cantaloupe melon
> 1/2 ripe honeydew melon
> 75 ml lime juice
> 2 Tbsp Splenda
> 1 tsp grated fresh ginger

1. Peel the melons and cut into bite-sized chunks or, if you have a melon baller, cut balls from them. Place in a serving dish.
2. Combine the lime juice, Splenda and ginger. Pour over the melons, toss and serve.

Yield: 8 servings, each with 12 grams of carbohydrate and 1 gram of fibre, for a total of 11 grams of usable carbs and 1 gram of protein.

↻ Strawberries in Wine

Simple and simply delicious.

225 g fresh strawberries
125 ml burgundy wine
1 Tbsp Splenda
Cinnamon stick

1. Hull the strawberries and slice or cut them into quarters.
2. Mix the wine and the Splenda and pour the mixture over the berries. Add the cinnamon stick and refrigerate, stirring from time to time, for at least 12 hours (but 2 days wouldn't hurt!)

Yield: 4 servings, each with 8 grams of carbohydrate and 3 grams of fibre, for a total of 5 grams of usable carbs and 1 gram of protein.

↻ Mockahlua

My sister, a longtime Kahlua fan, says this is addictive. And my husband demanded to know, 'How did you do that?' You can make this with decaf, if caffeine bothers you.

550 ml water
370 g Splenda
3 Tbsp instant coffee crystals
1 tsp vanilla
1 bottle (75 cl) 100-proof vodka (inexpensive is fine)

1. In a large pitcher or measuring jug, combine the water, Splenda, coffee crystals and vanilla. Stir until the coffee and Splenda are completely dissolved.
2. Pour the mixture through a funnel into a 1.5- or 2-litre bottle. (A clean 1.5-litre wine bottle works fine, so long as you've saved the cork.) Pour in the vodka. Cork and shake well.

Yield: 32 servings of 40 ml – a standard 'shot.' Each will have 2 grams of carbohydrate, no fibre and the merest trace of protein.

Mochahlua: Try this one if you like a little chocolate with your coffee. Just cut the water back to 350 ml and substitute a 400-ml bottle of sugar-free chocolate coffee flavouring syrup for the Splenda and vanilla. This has only a trace of carbohydrate per shot, because the liquid Splenda used to sweeten the chocolate coffee flavouring syrup doesn't have the malto-dextrin used to bulk the granular Splenda.

Mockahlua and Cream: This makes a nice 'little something' to serve at the end of a dinner party, in lieu of a heavier dessert. For each serving you'll need a shot of Mockahlua (or Mochalua) and 2 shots of double cream. Simply mix and sip!

Yield: Each serving has 4 grams of carbohydrate, no fibre and 2 grams of protein.

☺ Kay's Hot Rum Toddy

A delicious winter libation – for adults only! The rum is carb-free, but it will slow down your metabolism, so go easy.

> 280 g Splenda
>
> 2 tsp black treacle
>
> 1 tsp ground nutmeg
>
> 1 tsp ground cinnamon
>
> 1 tsp ground cloves
>
> 1 tsp ground cardamom
>
> 1 bottle (750 ml) top-quality dark rum

1. Put the Splenda, treacle, nutmeg, cinnamon, cloves and cardamom in a food processor with the S-blade in place. Process until it's smooth and creamy, scraping down the sides of the processor once or twice to make sure everything combines evenly.

2. Scoop this 'batter' mixture into a snap-top container and keep it in the fridge. (The batter will keep well and that means you make only a serving or two at a time, if you like.)

3. To serve the toddy, warm a coffee mug by filling it with boiling water and pouring it out. Then fill it again, halfway, with more boiling water. Add 1 or 2 tablespoons of the batter and stir until it dissolves into the water (a small whisk works well for this). Add two shots of dark rum, stir and sip.

Yield: About 12 servings. Each 2-tablespoon serving of batter will have 5 grams of carbohydrate, a trace of fibre and a trace of protein.

> 🍓 Kay says that one theory of hot-toddy making is that it is impossible to use too much batter and you should keep stirring more in until you are bored with stirring. Another theory of hot toddy making is that it is impossible to use too much rum and that you should keep stirring in more until your friends panic. Use your best judgement.

↶ Irish Coffee

If you're having this after dinner, you may want to use decaf instead of caffeinated coffee.

> 50 ml Irish whiskey
> 170 ml hot coffee
> 1 to 2 tsp Splenda
> 1 Tbsp Whipped Topping (see page 464)

Put the whiskey into a stemmed Irish coffee glass or a mug. Fill with coffee. Stir in 1 or 2 teaspoons of Splenda and top with whipped cream.

Yield: 1 serving, with 2 grams of carbohydrate, no fibre and only a trace of protein.

☿ Cocoa

The lowest carbohydrate hot chocolate mix on the market is higher in carbs than this one.

225 ml double cream
225 ml water
2 Tbsp unsweetened cocoa powder
1 1/2 or 2 Tbsp Splenda
2 Tbsp vanilla-flavoured whey protein powder
Tiny pinch salt

Over the lowest possible heat (it doesn't hurt to use a heat diffuser or a double-boiler) combine the cream and water. When they're starting to get warm, add the cocoa, Splenda, protein powder and salt; whisk until well combined. Bring just barely to a simmer and pour into cups.

Yield: 2 servings, each with 10 grams of carbohydrate and 2 grams of fibre, for a total of 8 grams of usable carbs and 15 grams of protein.

🍓 The amount of protein in this cocoa means that a cup of this doesn't make a bad breakfast. And for grown-ups, this is very nice with a shot of Mockahlua or Mochalua in it – but not in the morning!

☿ Creamy Vanilla Coffee

Reader Honey Ashton sent me this sweet little treat and says it's also good iced.

1 hot cup decaffeinated coffee
2 Tbsp low-carb vanilla shake meal-replacement powder
1 or 2 tsp sugar-free vanilla coffee-flavouring syrup.
Cinnamon (optional)

Combine the coffee, vanilla shake powder and coffee-flavouring syrup. Garnish with cinnamon (if using).

Yield: 1 serving, with no more than 2 grams of carbohydrate, no fibre and no protein.

◯ Chai

My darling friend Nicole is a devotee of this spiced Indian tea. She suggested I come up with a low-carb version for this book and here it is. Make up a batch and your whole house will smell wonderful.

> 1 Tbsp fennel seed or anise seed
>
> 6 green cardamom pods
>
> 12 whole cloves
>
> 1 cinnamon stick
>
> 5 mm of fresh root ginger, thinly sliced
>
> 1/4 tsp whole black peppercorns
>
> 2 bay leaves
>
> 1 1/2 litres water
>
> 2 Tbsp loose Darjeeling tea
>
> 30 g Splenda
>
> 1/8 Tbsp black treacle
>
> 125 ml double cream mixed with 125 ml water,
> or 225 ml milk and cream, mixed

1. Combine the fennel, cardamom, cloves, cinnamon, ginger, peppercorns, bay and water. Bring to a simmer and leave to simmer for 5 minutes.

2. Add the tea, turn off the heat, cover and let the mixture steep for 10 minutes.

3. Strain and stir in the Splenda, treacle and cream.

> 🍓 You can refrigerate this for a day or two and reheat it in the microwave whenever you want a cup.

Yield: 8 servings of 1 cup each. Made with double cream, each serving will have about 7 grams of carbohydrate, no fibre (you've strained it out) and 2 grams of protein. Made with milk and cream mixed, it'll have 8 grams of carbs, no fibre and 2 grams of protein.

↻ Eggiweggnog

This is for those of you who are unafraid of raw eggs.
My husband would gladly have this for breakfast every day!

> 3 eggs
> 125 ml double cream
> 125 ml milk and cream, mixed
> 2 Tbsp Splenda
> 1 tsp vanilla extract
> Pinch of salt
> Pinch of nutmeg

Put the eggs, double cream, milk-cream mixture, Splenda, vanilla
and salt in a blender and run it for 30 seconds or so. Pour into glasses,
sprinkle a little nutmeg on top and drink up.

Yield: 2 servings, each with 9 grams of carbohydrate, no fibre and
11 grams of protein.

◌ Cooked Eggnog

This is for people who need to think first before eating raw egg – and it's mighty tasty, too. It just takes more work.

500 ml milk and cream, mixed

225 ml double cream

30 g Splenda

1 tsp vanilla extract

1/4 tsp salt

6 eggs

225 ml water

Nutmeg

1. In a big glass measuring jug, combine the milk-cream mixture and cream. Microwave it at Medium-High power for 3 to 4 minutes, or until it's very warm through, but not boiling. (This is simply a time-saver and is not essential; if you prefer, you can simply heat it over a low heat in the saucepan you'll use to finish the recipe.)

2. After microwaving, pour the cream mixture into a heavy-bottomed saucepan and whisk in the Splenda, vanilla, salt and eggs. Turn the heat down to lowest heat (if you have a heat diffuser or a double boiler, this would be a good time to use it) and stand there and stir your eggnog constantly until it's thick enough to coat a metal spoon with a thin film. This will, I'm sorry to say, take at least 5 minutes and maybe as much as 20.

3. Stir in the water and chill. Sprinkle a little nutmeg on each serving and feel free to add a little alcohol, if you like!

Yield: About 6 servings of 225 ml, each with 5 grams of carbohydrate, a trace of fibre and 9 grams of protein.

Acknowledgements

There were a great number of people whose collective efforts have made this cookbook possible in what seemed like an impossibly short time:

First, I'd like to thank my husband, Eric Schmitz, who has been my unfailing right hand all through this project, grocery shopping, recipe testing, eating my failures without complaint and accepting the strain on the food budget. He also helped me run the nutritional calculations for these recipes, which is about the only reason this book was done by its deadline. I quite literally couldn't have done it without him.

Three cookbook authors have kindly allowed me to reprint recipes from their cookbooks. They're great books and great recipes and you should buy them all. Those cookbooks and their authors are:

Baking Low Carb and Bread and Breakfast: Baking Low Carb II, both by my pal Diana Lee. The best place to get Di's books is through Amazon.com, but you could try to order them through your local bookstore. These are the only books I know that are solely devoted to low-carb baking. Recipes reprinted with permission from *Baking Low Carb*, 1999, Diana Lee. Recipes reprinted with permission from *Bread and Breakfast: Baking Low Carb II, 2001*, Diana Lee.

Splendid Low-Carbing, by Jennifer Eloff. Jen is the Splenda Queen and since she lives in Canada, where Splenda's been available for many years, Jen's had far more experience with it than I. Jennifer sells her book herself through her website, **www.sweety.com**, and she has other books on cooking with Splenda, as well. Recipes reprinted with permission from *Splendid Low-Carbing*, 2001, Jennifer Eloff.

Lo-Carb Cooking, by Debra Rowland, is the source, among other things, for recipes for 'cornbread' and cheese popovers – and there are many more great-sounding recipes in her book that I didn't have room for. Deb sells *Lo-Carb Cooking* herself; you can reach her at **d_rowland3@hotmail.com**. Recipes reprinted with permission from *Lo-Carb Cooking*, 2001, Debra Rowland.

Also contributing greatly to this book is Vicki Cash, who allowed me to use the recipes from her *2002 Low Carb Success Calendar*. If Vicki puts out a calendar again, I strongly suggest you snap it up! Recipes reprinted with permission from *The 2002 Low Carb Success Calendar*, 2001, Just Ducky Productions.

My *Lowcarbezine!* readers responded to my requests with piles of great low-carb recipes for this book. The ones whose recipes have been used are named with their recipes. I thank them, but I also thank those people who sent recipes I didn't use. Quite often it was because we already had a similar recipe or because the carb count was judged to be just a bit too high; it was very rarely because we just didn't like a recipe. So whether your recipe is here or not, thank you, thank you, from the bottom of my heart. And who knows? We may use your recipe in another book! I also thank all of you who have come up with ideas for recipes you wanted me to develop. My *Lowcarbezine!* readers are one of the genuine joys of my life.

I was far too busy coming up with recipes of my own to test all of the recipes coming in from readers, so I recruited a crack troop of recipe testers. Again, I couldn't have done it without them. My recipe testers were Kim Carpender, Deborah Crites, Jane Duquette, Julie McIntosh, Ray Todd Stevens, Carol Vandiver, Maria Vander Vloedt and Kay Winefordner – not to mention their families and friends. Thank you, one and all.

Finally, I'd like to thank my mother, Jane Carpender, for letting me help her cook from the time I was tiny. Because of her, I knew how to measure accurately, separate an egg, bake cakes, make gravy, knead bread, rice potatoes and perform dozens of other cooking tasks by the time I was seven or eight years old. If I know my way around a kitchen, it's because of my mother. Thanks, Mum! All you parents out there, cook with your kids. Not only is it wonderful quality time together and a great defence against junk food, but it also teaches kids skills that will serve them well for the rest of their lives.

Index

Y

Yankee Pot Roast, 349–350
Yeast, 40, 124
Yoghurt
    carbohydrate count, 40–41
    recipe for, 121
Yorkshire Pudding, 347

Z

Zesty Seafood Soup, 400